M000276519

ENCOUNTERS: Chinese Language and Culture

Use the Access Code below to register for the
Encounters: Chinese Language and Culture Website.

1. Go to: www.encounterschinese.com
2. Click "Register" and follow the instructions
3. Use this code

12qf0cq0ss

Yale UNIVERSITY PRESS
New Haven and London

yalebooks.com/languages

ENCOUNTERS
Chinese Language and Culture
Student Book 1

ENCOUNTERS
Chinese Language and Culture

Student Book 1

汉语和中国文化

▶ **Cynthia Y. Ning**
University of Hawai'i at Mānoa

▶ **John S. Montanaro**
Yale University

Instructor's Annotations by **Amy Shen**
Middlebury-Monterey Language Academy

Audio Program Created by **Julian K. Wheatley**

Yale UNIVERSITY PRESS
New Haven and London

华语教学出版社
SINOLINGUA

Published with assistance from the Office of the President, Yale University.

Copyright © 2012 by Yale University and China International Publishing Group.
All rights reserved.
This book may not be reproduced, in whole or in part, including illustrations, in any form (beyond that copying permitted by Sections 107 and 108 of the U.S. Copyright Law and except by reviewers for the public press), without written permission from the publishers.

Director of Digital Publishing: David Schiffman

Project Director: Mary Jane Peluso
Editorial Assistant: Elise Panza
Project Manager: Karen Hohner
Copy Editor: Jamie Greene
Managing Editor: Jenya Weinreb
Designer and Compositor: Wanda España/Wee Design Group
Illustrator: Huifeng Lü
Cover Designer: Sonia Shannon
Art Managers: Karen Hohner with assistance from Linda Rodolico
Production Controller: Maureen Noonan
Marketing Managers: Sarah Clark and Niamh Cunningham

Printed in the United States of America.

ISBN: 978-0-300-16162-5 (student edition)
ISBN: 978-0-300-16166-3 (annotated instructor's edition)
Library of Congress Control Number: 2009934896

A catalogue record for this book is available from the British Library.

This paper meets the requirements of ANSI/NISO Z39.48-1992 (Permanence of Paper).

10 9 8 7 6 5 4 3 2

We dedicate ***Encounters*** to the memory of John DeFrancis, who began his seven-decade career as the first Ph.D. student in Chinese Studies at Yale University and who then published numerous books and articles on the subject of China and the Chinese language. He was a gentle man who lived a full, good life and gave so much to so many.

Contents

Unit Three: "Don't leave before I arrive" **69**
不見不散 *Bújiànbúsàn*
Making an appointment

Unit Five: "Family and friends"

親朋好友 *Qīnpénghǎoyǒu*
Talking about family and friends

Unit Seven: "Meeting our needs"

各有所求 *Gèyǒusuǒqiú*

Discussing personal needs

Unit Nine: "You get what you pay for" 215

一分價錢 一分貨 *Yì fēn jiàqian yì fēn huò*
Shopping and bargaining

Preface

Welcome to **Encounters: Chinese Language and Culture**! The publication of this book brings a long-held dream to reality: it inaugurates a groundbreaking language teaching program and sets a new standard in the field of language teaching.

Acutely attentive to the needs of today's students and teachers, the program encourages learning through approaches that are practical, communicative, culturally rich, and delightfully engaging.

Encounters is designed for English-speaking individuals ready to embark on the adventure of learning Mandarin Chinese. Lively and immediate, the program immerses the learner in Chinese language and culture right from the start. **Encounters** employs a range of techniques to encourage rapid and confident student progress. Those who are learning the Chinese language—as well as their teachers—will find a new level of inspiration at each stage of their **Encounters** experience.

A fully integrated array of learning materials focuses on communication and authentic language used in real-life contexts. Central among these materials is a dramatic video series, filmed entirely on location throughout China. The **Encounters** textbook features abundant exercises and learning activities linked to the video episodes and other media.

Informed by the latest language learning research and enriched by the creativity of a remarkable team of language and media experts who participated in its development, **Encounters** represents a new generation of language programs. It masterfully guides learners along a well-prepared path toward intercultural communication and understanding, a path that also leads to fuller participation in the modern global community.

We hope that the **Encounters** program will assist you on an enjoyable and successful learning journey. We wish you well as you encounter the fascinating language, people, and culture of China!

—Cynthia Y. Ning, *University of Hawai'i at Mānoa*
—John S. Montanaro, *Yale University*

Academic Committee

YALE UNIVERSITY PRESS

Richard C. Levin
理查德雷文
President, Yale University
耶鲁大学校长

Linda K. Lorimer
罗琳达
Secretary and Vice President,
　Yale University
耶鲁大学副校长兼校务卿

Dorothy Robinson
多乐茜 罗宾逊
Vice President and General
　Counsel, Yale University
耶鲁大学副校长兼法律总顾问

John Donatich
约翰 多纳蒂奇
Director, Yale University Press
耶鲁大学出版社社长

Mary Jane Peluso
玛丽珍 珀卢索
Project Director
项目主任
Publisher of World Languages,
　Yale University Press
耶鲁大学出版社世界语言部
　出版人

Cynthia Y. Ning
任友梅
Author
语言教学部分撰稿人
Associate Director,
　University of Hawai'i
　Center for Chinese Studies
夏威夷大学中国研究中心
　副主任
U.S. Director, Confucius Institute
　at the University of Hawai'i
孔子学院 院长
Executive Director,
　Chinese Language Teachers
　Association, 2000–2009
中文教师学会 执行主任

John S. Montanaro
孟德儒
Author
语言教学部分撰稿人
Senior Lector in Chinese,
　Yale University
耶鲁大学 资深中文讲师

David Murray
大卫 莫瑞
Executive Producer and
　Creative Director
总制片、总导演

CHINA INTERNATIONAL PUBLISHING GROUP

Cai Mingzhao
蔡名照
Former President, China
　International Publishing Group
中国国际出版集团 前任总裁

Zhou Mingwei
周明伟
President, China International
　Publishing Group
中国国际出版集团 总裁

Huang Youyi
黄友义
Vice President and Editor-in-
　Chief, China International
　Publishing Group
中国国际出版集团 副总裁、
　总编辑

Wang Gangyi
王刚毅
Deputy Editor-in-Chief, China
　International Publishing Group
中国国际出版集团 副总编辑

Wang Junxiao
王君校
Senior Project Officer
高级项目主管
President, Sinolingua
华语教学出版社 社长

Han Hui
韩晖
Project Director
项目主任
Editor-in-Chief, Sinolingua
华语教学出版社 总编辑

Guo Hui
郭辉
Assistant Project Director
项目主任助理
Associate Editor-in-Chief,
　Sinolingua
华语教学出版社 副总编辑

Zhou Kuijie
周奎杰
Culture Consultant
文化顾问
Former Editor-in-Chief,
　New World Press
原新世界出版社总编辑

Geng Zhi
耿直
Language Advisor
语言顾问

Zhao Rongguo
赵荣国
Producer
制片

Liu Jiefeng
刘杰峰
Producer
制片

Lu Jianming
陆俭明
Professor, Peking University
北京大学中文系 教授

Cui Xiliang
崔希亮
President, Beijing Language and
　Culture University
北京语言大学校长

Acknowledgments

Encounters was initiated in the fall of 2006 by President Richard C. Levin of Yale University and Mr. Cai Mingzhao, then President of China International Publishing Group. A number of people have been and continue to be involved in this extraordinary program. We thank everyone who has touched *Encounters* in some way.

Cyndy Ning dedicates her work to her husband, Allan Ngai Lim Yee, who died suddenly in 2009, and to her daughter, Robyn Ning Yee. John Montanaro thanks his wife, Patricia, his daughter, Pamela, and his son, John Scott, as well as his "fabulous five" grandchildren, Andrew, Jacob, Alyssa, Madison, and Meghan.

The authors and the publisher thank Sheree Carter-Galvan, Pamela Chambers, Rosita Chang, Annelise Finegan, Katherine Gilbert, Chunman Gissing, Nora Guo, Eric Gustafson, Hazel Hasegawa, Hugo Krispyn, Frederick Lau, Helen Lee, Rongzhen Li, Yuhong Li, Fan Liu, Alexis Mills, Pauline Ning, Robert Ning, Sam Ning, Noreen O'Connor-Abel, Amy Shen, Jialin Sun, David Topolewski, Stephen Tschudi, Daniel Tschudi, Qinghong Wang, Yingjing Wang, Julian Wheatley, Kristine Wogstad, Myrtle Wong, Kuang-tien Yao, Robyn Yee, Martin Yu, Meiping Zhu, and Chuanlu Zhu.

We also deeply appreciate the work of all our reviewers at various stages and of different components of the *Encounters* project:

Gloria Bien, Colgate University
Peter Bonanno, Suffield Academy
Lixin Cai, Concordia University
Bei (Ben) Chen, University of North Texas
Chiu-Hung Chen, University of Miami
Leeann Chen, Embry-Riddle Aeronautical University
Xiaoqiang Cheng, Indiana University South Bend
De Chao (Ralph) Chiao, Columbus Alternative High School
Ruby Shu Costea, Montgomery College
Erica Dieselman, Hingham High School
Amy Dooling, Connecticut College
Wen-Hua Du, University of Wisconsin–Milwaukee
Scott Galer, Brigham Young University–Idaho
Bernard Geoxavier, Belmont Hill School
Sharon Guan, DePaul University
Jeffrey J. Hayden, Kalamazoo College
Jing Ping He, Marvin Ridge High School, Union County Public School
Wei Hong, Purdue University
Chi-Chiang Huang, Hobart and William Smith Colleges
Hsu Chu-Ju Huang, Millburn High School

Jen-Syan Hwang, Central High School (St. Paul)
Yanmei Jia, Perry County Central High School
Li Jin, DePaul University
Haishan Lai, University of Richmond
Qiang Li, University of Iowa
Weijie Li, Kapiolani Community College
Wendan Li, University of North Carolina at Chapel Hill
Yu Li, Emory University
Huey Hannah Lin, West Virginia University
Annie W. Liu, North Central College
Jack Liu, California State University
Lin Liu, Snowden International School
Shuyu Liu, Laney College
Michelle Low, University of Northern Colorado
Christopher Lupke, Washington State University
Lixia Ma, Phillips Academy
Duosi Meng, University of Illinois at Chicago
Liuxi Meng, Kennesaw State University
Lili Pan, Lexington High School
Ying Peng, Loyola University
Terry Qian, Loyola Marymount University
Adam Ross, Lakeside School

Cynthia Shen, University of Florida
LanLan Sheng, Newton South High School
Miao-Fen Tseng, University of Virginia
Tracy Tsou, Concord-Carlisle High School
Jing Wang, Indiana University–Purdue University Indianapolis (IUPUI)
Xiaojun Wang, Western Michigan University
Helen Wu, University of Toronto Scarborough
Yongan Wu, University of North Florida
Janet Xing, Western Washington University
Wen Xing, Trinity University
Weirong Yan, Missouri State University
Yinong Yang, Buckingham Browne & Nichols
Xiaohua Yu, Piedmont High School
Fangyuan Yuan, University of Pennsylvania/U.S. Naval Academy
Jing Zhai, Marquette University
Weidong Zhang, Winona State University
Yan Zhang, University of Wyoming
Zheng-sheng Zhang, San Diego State University
LanHui Zhang-Ryder, Northern Illinois University
Yongping Zhu, University of Wisconsin, Madison

Introduction

▶ Overview

The comprehensive *Encounters* program:
- Employs a functional, task-based approach.
- Presents authentic language and culture through engaging dramatic video episodes.
- Focuses on communication in the spoken language.
- Includes reading material in both traditional and simplified characters.
- Links cultural video interviews to language functions.
- Presents clearly focused grammar instruction and practice.
- Adheres to ACTFL Proficiency Guidelines.
- Assists teachers with a fully annotated instructor's edition, materials to excite students' interest, and a wide selection of useful tools in various media.

▶ Program Components

The *Encounters* program comprises:
- A beautifully produced *video series*, filmed entirely on location in China and featuring a dramatic story line and segments devoted to Chinese culture and history.
- A full-color *student textbook*, completely integrated with the video series and other *Encounters* components. The introductory unit presents the basics of Mandarin Chinese: the four tones, pronunciation, pinyin spelling, numbers, radicals, and traditional and simplified characters.
- An *annotated instructor's edition* of the textbook, packed with teaching tips, extra classroom activities, and suggestions for using the program in the classroom.
- A *character writing workbook* showing each character's evolution, etymology, and usage. Stroke diagrams guide students in forming the characters; strategies for remembering characters are also provided.
- An *audio program* to assist students with listening comprehension, pronunciation, vocabulary, and model conversations.
- A *website* that offers students and teachers streaming video and audio content, and other resources for speaking, reading, and writing Chinese.

The Dramatic Story Line

A hip artist, an adventurous Australian traveler, a thoughtful Chinese scholar, a worried American father, a young teacher from the United States, and another teacher from China: these are just some of the international characters whose stories unfold in the *Encounters* video series.

This compelling story transports viewers to the real cities, villages, homes, schools, markets, streets, and cultural sites of this vast nation. In these various places, the nine main characters find that their lives intersect in unexpected ways. They make discoveries about themselves and others, they converse with strangers and friends, and along the way they provide viewers with remarkable insights into the language and culture of China.

The Cast of Characters

APRIL, 24, of Chinese origin. She is quiet but resilient and strong. Born in the United States to a Chinese immigrant family, she grew up in San Diego. April accompanies her husband, Alejandro, to China.

ALEJANDRO, 29, Mexican American, married to April. He is passionate and has a very big personality. A photographer assigned to document the changes happening in contemporary China, he believes in the value of his work.

LYNN, 25, an American from Los Angeles. She leaves her home and, through a series of detours, eventually travels to Yangshuo to teach English. She tries hard to fit in and be accepted by the community, clearing away misunderstandings along the way.

TANG YUAN, 24, Chinese, a folk artist in Yangshuo. He loves art and has achieved some local success. He is kind, warm-hearted, and very respectful of his parents, but he can also behave rebelliously.

CHEN FENG, 27, Chinese, a businessman in Beijing, originally from a small village in southern China. He is idealistic, confident, and extremely ambitious. Though he is a bit of a workaholic, he also enjoys taking risks. At the beginning of his career, he works hard and expects the same from everyone else (although he is the hardest on himself). He and Li Wen are a couple.

LI WEN, 27, Chinese, teaches English in Yangshuo. She is gentle and very understanding. She and Chen Feng have been together for some time; however, because of the distance between them, things haven't always been easy. After serious discussions, they decide that Li Wen should quit her job in Yangshuo and move to Beijing because it's best for their relationship.

MAO ZHIPENG (also known as Xiao Mao), 28, Chinese, a college friend of Chen Feng's and a partner in the firm that Chen Feng directs. He is keenly observant of the business market, and his personality balances Chen Feng's risk-taking nature. He is from Beijing, and as such, he can't shake some of the common attitudes associated with people from the capital city—namely, a sense of privilege and entitlement. Lured by high-paying employment and the related prestige at a bigger company, he struggles between loyalty to a friend and the tug of reality.

PROF. YANG, 58, Chinese, professor at Chen Feng's university. He loves Tai Chi and Chinese chess and is very skilled at calligraphy. He is tender and caring, often acts as a father figure to Chen Feng, and gives advice by drawing metaphors from life. He is a good friend and a great teacher.

MICK, Australian, a traveling cyclist. He is funny, adventurous, and gregarious, but not much is known about his age, profession, or background. He has been all over the world, but he is troubled from time to time by his aimless wanderings.

In addition to the dramatic narrative that propels the action in each *Encounters* episode, cultural segments explore and illuminate aspects of life in China. Real people from various walks of life discuss their perspectives on such topics as Chinese perceptions of foreign visitors, courteous bargaining in street markets, major Chinese festivals, and different forms of appropriate greetings.

Because *Encounters* is a fully integrated program, the material presented in each episode is linked to corresponding chapters and activities in the textbook, to audio activities, and to an array of online offerings, including practice exercises and related cultural information.

▶ A Unit Tour

The ***Encounters*** textbook presents a carefully structured and cumulative approach to learning Mandarin Chinese. Students progress from listening and speaking activities to the more challenging skills of reading and writing Chinese characters. The emphasis is on communicative skills, as the primary goal of the ***Encounters*** program is to foster proficiency in everyday Chinese.

Each unit offers an inviting combination of in-class, individual, pair, and group activities. Humor, music, and a lighthearted attitude encourage learners to approach the study of Chinese with enthusiasm and confidence. "FYI" boxes provide dozens of study and learning tips, and appealing illustrations keep interest levels high. By weaving cultural information throughout the text—rather than relegating it only to end-of-chapter notes—***Encounters*** reinforces the notion that language is inseparable from culture.

Colorful icons illustrate, at a glance, the variety of learning opportunities and activities available in each chapter.

watch episode

watch video

listen

unit rap

Unit titles are presented in English, pinyin, and Chinese characters. Traditional characters are used to evoke decorative calligraphy, which is often presented only in the traditional form, even in China.

The introductory page for each textbook unit features a photograph from the corresponding video episode. Skills taught and practiced in the unit are related to the events that students observe in the episode.

A list of skills to be covered in the unit clarifies learning goals and helps students stay organized.

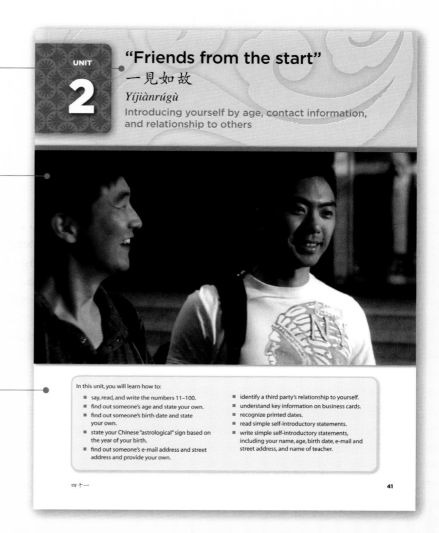

UNIT

2

"Friends from the start"
一見如故
Yíjiànrúgù
Introducing yourself by age, contact information, and relationship to others

In this unit, you will learn how to:

- say, read, and write the numbers 11–100.
- find out someone's age and state your own.
- find out someone's birth date and state your own.
- state your Chinese "astrological" sign based on the year of your birth.
- find out someone's e-mail address and street address and provide your own.

- identify a third party's relationship to yourself.
- understand key information on business cards.
- recognize printed dates.
- read simple self-introductory statements.
- write simple self-introductory statements, including your name, age, birth date, e-mail and street address, and name of teacher.

四十一   41

Various listening and learning activities are enriched by their connections to the ongoing video and by their insights into Chinese culture.

FYI boxes, liberally scattered throughout the book, provide relevant cultural information that will both fascinate students and deepen their understanding of the Chinese language and the culture and people of China.

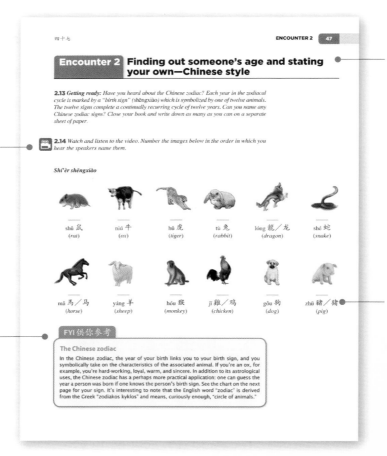

Each unit contains several interesting and enlightening "Encounters," presenting material that covers common real-life situations.

Both traditional and simplified characters are used throughout the materials. Only 20 percent of characters have two forms, and students will encounter both forms in areas where Chinese is spoken. Students can easily learn to recognize both but need to write only in the form that is meaningful or useful to them.

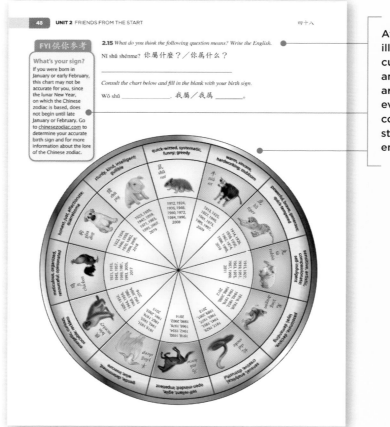

Attractive illustrations, intriguing cultural commentary, and exercises that are directly tied to events in the video combine to spark student interest and encourage learning.

Suggestions for practice conversations appear throughout each unit. Students build confidence and practical conversational skills through these entertaining oral exercises.

2.16 Mingling: *Walk around the room and find out your classmates' signs. Consult the chart and, using their answers, try to figure out whether they are the same age as, older than, or younger than you.*

2.17 Homework: *Outside of class, determine the birth signs of three people. Draw a picture or bring a photograph of each person, and note approximately how old each one is (for example, "in her 40s"). Use this information to report your findings to the class.*

Encounter 3 Finding out someone's birth date and stating your own

▶ **Months of the year**

2.18 *If January is* yīyuè *or* 一月*, write the names of the remaining eleven months in either pinyin or characters (or both) in the blanks below.*

February   _____
March   _____
April   _____
May   _____
June   _____
July   _____
August   _____
September   _____
October   _____
November   _____
December   _____

2.19 Pair work: *With a partner, take turns saying each month of the year. After you go through the sequence once, repeat so you each have an opportunity to say every month. Repeat this process until you are both comfortable with the sequence. Finally, test each other on the Chinese names of the months by dictating random months for your partner to translate.*

2.26 Watch and listen to the video segment. Then fill in the blanks below.

a. What are the two numbers you hear in this exchange? _____ and _____

b. What do you think *nián* 年 means? _____

c. What do you think the following means? Write the English.

Nǐ shì něi nián shēng de? 你是哪年生的？_____

d. Fill in the blanks with your own year of birth.

Wǒ shì _____ nián shēng de.   我是_____年生的。

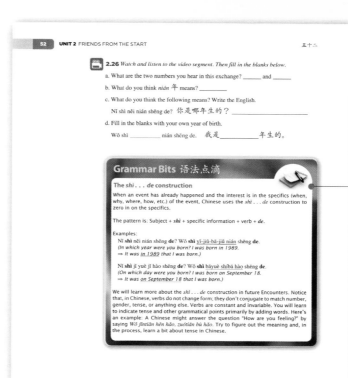

Grammar Bits 语法点滴

The shi . . . de construction

When an event has already happened and the interest is in the specifics (when, why, where, how, etc.) of the event, Chinese uses the *shi . . . de* construction to zero in on the specifics.

The pattern is: Subject + **shi** + specific information + verb + **de**.

Examples:
Nǐ **shì** něi nián shēng **de**? Wǒ **shì** yī-jiǔ-bā-jiǔ nián shēng **de**.
(In which year were you born? I was born in 1989.
⇒ *It was in 1989 that I was born.)*

Nǐ **shì** jǐ yuè jǐ hào shēng **de**? Wǒ **shì** bāyuè shíbā hào shēng **de**.
(On which day were you born? I was born on September 18.
⇒ *It was on September 18 that I was born.)*

We will learn more about the *shi . . . de* construction in future Encounters. Notice that, in Chinese, verbs do not change form; they don't conjugate to match number, gender, tense, or anything else. Verbs are constant and invariable. You will learn to indicate tense and other grammatical points primarily by adding words. Here's an example: A Chinese might answer the question "How are you feeling?" by saying *Wǒ jīntiān hěn hǎo, zuótiān bù hǎo.* Try to figure out the meaning and, in the process, learn a bit about tense in Chinese.

Numerous Grammar Bits boxes shed light on grammar issues as they arise. These short lessons, highlighted in separate boxes, provide students with a manageable amount of information and an important review tool.

With a strong emphasis on practicality, lessons deal with up-to-date issues and communication in today's world. This Encounter, constructed around the topic of e-mail, asks students to listen, speak, and write about e-mail. An FYI box enriches the lesson with a discussion of translation, transliteration, and how English and Chinese terms sometimes intermingle in our high-tech, interconnected world.

A rap written specifically for each unit sets key expressions and vocabulary in a fun musical setting. Go to the *Encounters* website at www.EncountersChinese.com.

As a first step to "intensive reading," dialogues based on familiar content are set out in both traditional and simplified characters. Decoding these dialogues helps students gain basic literacy skills in Chinese.

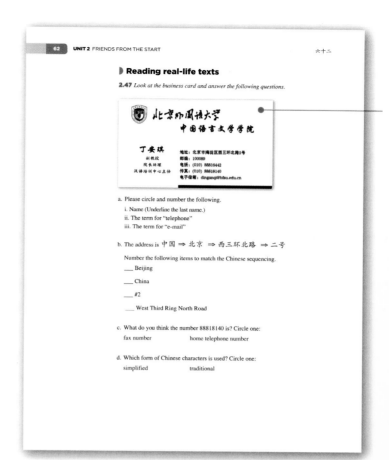

62   UNIT 2 FRIENDS FROM THE START   六十二

▶ Reading real-life texts

2.47 *Look at the business card and answer the following questions.*

a. Please circle and number the following.
   i. Name (Underline the last name.)
   ii. The term for "telephone"
   iii. The term for "e-mail"

b. The address is 中国 ⇒ 北京 ⇒ 西三环北路 ⇒ 二号

   Number the following items to match the Chinese sequencing.
   ____ Beijing
   ____ China
   ____ #2
   ____ West Third Ring North Road

c. What do you think the number 88818140 is? Circle one:
   fax number   home telephone number

d. Which form of Chinese characters is used? Circle one:
   simplified   traditional

六十五   ENCOUNTER 6   65

a. Please circle and number the following:
   i. Date in Chinese
   ii. Day of the week

b. What is the day of the week? Write in English: _____

c. There is an ad for an insurance company. Please circle and number the following:
   i. The address in New York
   ii. The address in China

d. Which form of Chinese characters is used? Circle one:
   simplified   traditional

▶ Learning to write characters

2.51 *For stroke order and other useful information about each of the following characters from this unit, go to the Character Writing Text. Choose traditional or simplified characters and practice writing them until you can reproduce them on demand.*

您，多，大，小，幾／几，歲／岁，了，的，地，址，
年，月，日，號／号，生，那，哪，兒／儿，這／这，位

▶ Writing a note

2.52 *Write a brief self-introduction in your choice of traditional or simplified Chinese characters. Include information about your name, age, birth date, e-mail address, street address, and the name of your teacher.*

Cultural Bits 文化点滴

Self-introduction

View the video segment "Self-introduction" and then discuss the following questions with your classmates.

- What might you want to tell a new informal Chinese acquaintance about yourself upon meeting him or her for the first time?
- What are the benefits of being "overly polite"?
- What is the role of the "social title"?
- Why do Chinese people ask each other *Nǐ shǔ shénme*? How many of the twelve animals can you name? Do you know yours?

By incorporating materials found in real life—business cards and newspapers, for example—lessons provide practical information enabling students to perform everyday tasks in Chinese.

Each unit includes a list of Chinese characters for writing mastery.

Cultural Bits boxes, which connect to the cultural segments of the video, provide a jumping-off point for explorations of Chinese society. Thought-provoking questions encourage students to investigate how Chinese culture is different from or similar to their own.

A complete Recap section appears at the conclusion of every unit. These pages include a summary of grammar topics, a vocabulary list, and a checklist of tasks that students are expected to have mastered in the unit. The Recap encourages students to review their progress, identify gaps in their learning, and congratulate themselves on their accomplishments.

We invite you to explore this exciting new language program and encourage you to visit *www.EncountersChinese.com*.

"You'll pick it up fast"

一學就會

Yì xué jiù huì

Introduction to Chinese

In this Introduction, you will:

- practice the four tones of Mandarin Chinese as you learn the numbers 1–10.
- learn about tonal shifts (sandhi) and the special case of *yī* (the number one).
- become familiar with the pronunciation of Chinese and the pinyin system of spelling Chinese syllables.
- practice linking pinyin spelling with the sounds of Chinese by working with two poems from the Tang dynasty.
- learn about numbers and radicals.
- learn about traditional and simplified characters.

You have already met some of the characters in *Encounters* in the Introduction on pages xxi–xxii. Watch the Introductory Episode of the dramatic series to find out more about who these characters are and where they live. You will get to know them well as you continue through units 1–10.

Now, let's learn about the Chinese language.

Encounter 1   Tones and numbers

 0.1 *Watch the animation about the four tones on the video.*

 0.2 *Listen to these numbers and circle the ones you hear.*

0 = líng	1 = yī	2 = èr	3 = sān	4 = sì	5 = wǔ
6 = liù	7 = qī	8 = bā	9 = jiǔ	10 = shí	

The numbers 1, 3, 7, and 8 are pronounced in the FIRST of the four full tones of Mandarin, as in the "Help!" of the animation. This is the high, level tone, as when you are not sure and say "Ummm" in a high pitch. Can you hum the first tone?

 0.3 *Listen to these numbers and circle the ones you hear.*

0 = líng	1 = yī	2 = èr	3 = sān	4 = sì	5 = wǔ
6 = liù	7 = qī	8 = bā	9 = jiǔ	10 = shí	

The numbers 0 and 10 are pronounced in the SECOND of the four full tones of Mandarin, as in the "What?" of the animation. This is the rising tone, like the rising pitch of an English question, such as "Yes?" Can you hum the second tone?

 0.4 *Listen to these numbers and circle the ones you hear.*

0 = líng	1 = yī	2 = èr	3 = sān	4 = sì	5 = wǔ
6 = liù	7 = qī	8 = bā	9 = jiǔ	10 = shí	

The numbers 5 and 9 are pronounced in the THIRD of the four full tones of Mandarin, as in the "'kay" of the animation. This is the dipping tone, like the first syllable of "uh-huh." Can you hum the third tone?

 0.5 *Listen to these numbers and circle the ones you hear.*

0 = líng	1 = yī	2 = èr	3 = sān	4 = sì	5 = wǔ
6 = liù	7 = qī	8 = bā	9 = jiǔ	10 = shí	

The numbers 2, 4, and 6 are pronounced in the FOURTH of the four full tones of Mandarin, as in "Fine!" of the animation. This is the falling tone, like the emphatic pitch on "Yes!" Can you hum the fourth tone?

0.6 *Listen to these numbers and make the appropriate arm motions based on the tone.*

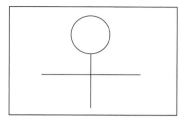

First tone:
Arms straight out to the side, level

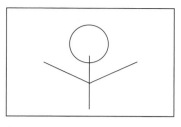

Second tone:
Arms raised at 45° angle

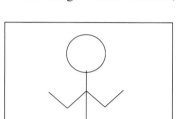

Third tone:
Arms crooked at elbows in a "V"

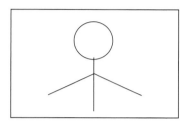

Fourth tone:
Arms lowered at 45° angle

0.7 *Draw the appropriate tone marks (for example: ā, á, ǎ, or à) over each of the boldfaced letters. Note that the tone mark is always placed above a vowel, never above a consonant.*

l**i**ng	y**i**	**e**r	s**a**n	s**i**	w**u**	li**u**	q**i**	b**a**	ji**u**	sh**i**
sh**i**	ji**u**	b**a**	q**i**	li**u**	w**u**	s**i**	s**a**n	**e**r	y**i**	l**i**ng
w**u**	q**i**	ji**u**	s**a**n	y**i**	b**a**	li**u**	s**i**	**e**r	l**i**ng	sh**i**
s**a**n	q**i**	l**i**ng	s**i**	y**i**	w**u**	sh**i**	li**u**	**e**r	b**a**	ji**u**

FYI 供你参考

The neutral tone

Besides the four full tones, there's yet another—the neutral tone—so called because it is said lightly, without stress, and is much shorter in length than any of the four full tones. It has no tone mark. Some words that have only a grammatical function routinely have a neutral tone, as do many suffixes. In some (though not all) two-syllable words, the second syllable has a neutral tone. Even though a neutral tone is unstressed, it is not completely without pitch; this it takes from the preceding full-tone syllable. Here are eight of the numbers followed by the measure word *ge*—the numbers "one" and "two" have been excluded. More about these numbers and *ge* will follow in this and later units; for the moment, just note that *ge* is pronounced in the neutral tone.

| sān ge | sì ge | wǔ ge | liù ge |
| qī ge | bā ge | jiǔ ge | shí ge |

FYI 供你参考

Tonal shifts (sandhi) on _yī_ (the number one)

In connected speech, tones are rarely given their full value. Tones in juxtaposition can influence each other and change their value. This is called sandhi. A few words regularly change their tone in certain environments. An example is _yī_ (the number one).

- It stays first tone when it stands alone, as during counting.
- It becomes second tone when followed by a fourth tone: _yī_ + _bàn_ ⇒ _yíbàn_ (half).
- It becomes fourth tone when followed by a first, second, or third tone: _yī_ + _tiān_ ⇒ _yìtiān_ (a day); _yī_ + _nián_ ⇒ _yìnián_ (a year); _yī_ + _miǎo_ ⇒ _yìmiǎo_ (a second).
- In the middle of a phrase, _yī_ is usually neutral: _xiǎngyixiǎng_ (think a moment). As we go on, we will see examples of this and other tonal shifts.

▶ More on numbers

0.8 _Write the telephone numbers below as you hear them._

a. Buckingham Palace, London: _____

b. Opera House, Sydney: _____

c. Louvre Museum, Paris: _____

d. "Bird's Nest" Stadium, Beijing: _____

e. Taj Mahal, Agra: _____

f. White House, Washington, D.C.: _____

0.9 _Write your own telephone number, including area code, in pinyin with tone marks._

___ ___ ___ – ___ ___ ___ – ___ ___ ___ ___

FYI 供你参考

Pinyin

Pinyin is a system of spelling out the sounds of Mandarin Chinese using the letters of the English alphabet, along with the umlauted _ü_. It is an aid to accurate pronunciation used by Chinese and foreigners alike. Developed in China in the1950s, pinyin is now used all over the world, including Taiwan. Although not developed specifically for speakers of English, it is a fairly easy system to learn. Always keep in mind, however, that the sounds of the language must be mastered through the ear, not the eye.

0.10 _Pair work: Watch and listen to the video segment. Practice "finger-counting" yourself. Then work with a partner. One person calls out a number randomly from 1 through 10, and the other makes the corresponding hand signal. Then reverse: One person makes a hand signal and the other person calls out the corresponding number._

Encounter 2   Chinese syllables

All Chinese syllables are composed of three parts.

The initial consonant: There are 21 initial consonants in Chinese (plus *y* and *w*). They are called initials because, unlike consonants in English, they appear only at the beginning of a syllable. Note that syllables in pinyin can begin with one or two consonants, but each letter or consonant combination represents only one sound.

The final vowel: Each syllable ends with a vowel, or with a final *n* or *ng*. Note that two vowels can be combined to form one sound (diphthong).

The tone: As you have already learned, there are four full tones in Mandarin, plus a neutral tone.

> **FYI 供你参考**
>
> **About Chinese sounds**
>
> Chinese has the ability to express meaning with as much vividness and clarity as any other language, but it does so with a fairly limited stock of approximately 400 unique sounds or, more precisely, syllables. When you studied English, one of your first tasks was to learn the alphabet. This knowledge helped form the basis of a useful supply of sounds and words. In studying Chinese, you will need to learn the syllables of Chinese. The foundation of all Chinese words is its set of single-syllable sounds, the 400 or so monosyllables. Thus Chinese is often thought of as a monosyllabic language, in part because each Chinese character is a single syllable. However, Chinese words are most commonly constructed with two syllables. In fact, more than 80 percent of Chinese words are composed of at least two syllables. Three- and four-syllable words exist but are far less common.

The following charts present the vowels and consonants of Chinese. Note that all the sounds in the charts are one syllable, not two. Remember: Derive the sounds from what you hear, not from what you see. Keep in mind that the pinyin alphabet is only a memory aid, a device to help learners recall the actual sound. Chinese children use pinyin in their textbooks more or less as you are going to do. Listen carefully to the sounds of Chinese syllables and refer to these charts often, especially in the beginning weeks of study. Acquiring decent pronunciation is one of your most important tasks.

▶ The initial consonants + *y* and *w*

0.11 *Look at the chart on page 6. Listen to the initial consonants, in boldface, which are combined with a final vowel (not in boldface) in order to make them pronounceable. Pronounce the hint as you would in English. The first hint (awe) provides a guide to the pronunciation of the Chinese final vowel* o. *Note that all the sounds in this chart are pronounced in the first tone, just the way Chinese children practice them in school. In fact, Chinese children often commit the chart to memory.*

The Initial Consonants				Hint
bo	po	mo	fo	(awe) > bwaw > pwaw > mwaw > fwaw
de	te	ne	le	(uh) > duh > tuh > nuh > luh
ge	ke	he		(uh) > guh > kuh > huh
ji	qi	xi		(ee) > jee > chee > syee
zi	ci	si		(zz) > dz > tsz > sz
zhi	chi	shi	ri	(rr) > jr > chr > shr > rrr

There are two additional letters—*y* and *w*—used in pinyin when none of the above consonants begin a word.

w (pronounced /w/ as in English "**win**" and "**war**"). Chinese example: *wei* (way), *wu* (woo)

y (pronounced /y/ as in English "**yes**" and "**you**"). Chinese examples: *ying* (rhymes with "sing"), *you* (rhymes with "low")

▶ The final vowels + *n* and *ng*

 0.12 *Listen to the final vowels, in boldface below, which are here combined with selected initial consonants. Note that the final vowels can be either a single vowel or a combination of vowels, sometimes with* n *or* ng.

	+ a	+ e	+ i	+ o	+ u	+ n	+ ng
a (b**a**)			bai	bao		ban	bang
e (n**e**)			nei			nen	neng
i (j**i**)	jia	jie			jiu	jin	jing
i + a (j**ia**)			jiao			jian	jiang
							jiong
o					dou		dong
u (zh**u**)	zhua		zhui	zhuo		zhun	
u + a (zh**ua**)			zhuai			zhuan	zhuang
ü (j**ü**)		jüe				jün	
		lüe					
						jüan	

Encounter 3 Poems from the Tang dynasty (618–907 CE)

In normal speech, speakers of Chinese (as of any other language) tend to run words together and slur their pronunciation (often because others can understand them anyway, and they wish to save time and effort). In common conversations, a beginning learner usually cannot tell which tones specific words have. In Tang poetry, however, tones are highly valued. When reciting poetry, native speakers tend to enunciate each syllable; tones and rhymes serve to accentuate the beauty of the lyricism. The following exercises introduce you to two of the best known of the Tang poems for the foreign learner: *Jìng yè sī* 靜夜思 "Thoughts on a Quiet Night," by poet *Lǐ Bái* (also pronounced *Lǐ Bó*) 李白 (701–762 CE), and *Dēng Guànquèlóu* 登鶴雀樓 "Climbing Stork Tower," by *Wáng Zhīhuàn* 王之渙 (668–742 CE). By working through these poems, you will begin to get a sense for the sounds of Chinese and how pinyin represents these sounds. If you feel up to it, go ahead and memorize one or both of the poems. When you recite a poem, you will delight many a native speaker of Chinese!

▶ "Thoughts on a Quiet Night"

 0.13 *Watch and listen to Chinese school children reciting "Thoughts on a Quiet Night." As you listen, write the correct tone marks over each of the syllables below.*

(Line 1) Chuang qian ming yue guang.
(Line 2) Yi shi di shang shuang.
(Line 3) Ju tou wang ming yue.
(Line 4) Di tou si gu xiang.

"Waiting for Guests by Lamplight," National Palace Museum, Taipei, Taiwan

Now complete the following note about Tang poetry.

This example is typical of one kind of Tang poem. It is made up of _____ lines, including _____ characters in each line, for a total of _____ characters. Lines _____, _____, and _____ rhyme, and each of the rhyming words in this poem is in the _____ tone.

🎧 **0.14** *Listen again.* <u>*Don't look at the previous exercise.*</u> *Write the initial consonant for each of the characters in the poem.*

(Line 1) ____uáng ____ián ____íng ____uè ____uāng.

(Line 2) ____í ____ì ____ì ____àng ____uāng.

(Line 3) ____ǔ ____óu ____àng ____íng ____uè.

(Line 4) ____ī ____óu ____ī ____ù ____iāng.

🎧 **0.15** *Listen again. We've flipped the next exercise upside down, so you're not tempted to peek. Write the appropriate letter in each of the blanks.*

(Line 4) Dī tó__ sī gù x_ā__ __ __.

(Line 3) Jǔ tó__ __ wà__ __ mí__ __ y_è.

(Line 2) Yí shì dì shā__ __ sh_ā__ __.

(Line 1) Ch_ā__ __ q_ā__ __ mí__ __ y_è g_ā__ __.

🎧 **0.16** *Listen again. The following passage is a word-by-word English translation of the poem. For the fun of it, write the tone of the Chinese word above each corresponding English word.*

(Line 1) Bed front bright moon brilliant.

(Line 2) Suspect be ground upon frost.

(Line 3) Lift head gaze bright moon.

(Line 4) Lower head think ancestral home.

🎧 **0.17** *Listen again. The following passage is a translation into more natural (but not lyrical) English. Below each English line, write out a transcription in pinyin (complete with tones!) of that line.*

(Line 1) Before my bed, the moonlight is bright.

_____

(Line 2) I take it for frost on the ground.

_____

(Line 3) Lifting my head, I gaze at the bright moon.

_____

(Line 4) Lowering my head, I think of my old home.

_____

0.18 *Listen again. The following is the poem in traditional Chinese characters. Circle the word for "moon" as you come across it.*

床前明月光，
疑是地上霜。
舉頭望明月，
低頭思故鄉。

0.19 *Listen for the last time. The following is the poem in simplified Chinese characters. Circle each character whose simplified form is different from the traditional.*

床前明月光，
疑是地上霜。
举头望明月，
低头思故乡。

0.20 *How many characters did you circle in the previous exercise? Answer: _____.
What percentage of the characters used in this text have been simplified?
Answer: _____ percent.*

This percentage roughly holds true for many texts you will encounter as you study Chinese (but not for very short ones, like signs). The issue of traditional vs. simplified characters (along with their history) will be further explored and explained in Unit 1.

▶ "Climbing Stork Tower"

0.21 *Now watch and listen to a recitation of the poem "Climbing Stork Tower" by the poet Wáng Zhīhuàn. As you listen, write the correct tone marks over each of the syllables below.*

(Line 1) Bai ri yi shan jin.

(Line 2) Huang He ru hai liu.

(Line 3) Yu qiong qian li mu.

(Line 4) Geng shang yi ceng lou.

Now complete the following note:

This poem, like the previous one, is made up of _____ lines, including _____

characters in each line, for a total of _____ characters. Lines _____ and _____

rhyme, and each of the rhyming words in this poem is in the _____ tone.

0.22 *Listen again. The following passage is a word-by-word English translation of the poem. For the fun of it, write the tone of the Chinese word above each corresponding English word.*

(Line 1) White sun lean mountain end.

(Line 2) Yellow River enter sea flow.

(Line 3) Wish exhaust thousand mile gaze.

(Line 4) More ascend one story floor.

 0.23 *Listen again. The following passage is a translation into more natural (but not lyrical) English. Below each line, write out a transcription in pinyin (complete with tones!) of that line.*

(Line 1) The white sun sets in the mountains.

_____

(Line 2) The Yellow River flows to the seas.

_____

(Line 3) To gaze another thousand miles.

_____

(Line 4) Climb up to yet another story.

_____

 0.24 *Listen again. The following is the poem in traditional Chinese characters. Circle the words for "sun," "mountain," and "one" as you come across them.*

白日依山盡，
黃河入海流。
欲窮千里目，
更上一層樓。

 0.25 *Listen for the last time. The following is the poem in simplified Chinese characters. Circle each character whose simplified form is different from the traditional.*

白日依山尽，
黄河入海流。
欲穷千里目，
更上一层楼。

0.26 *How many characters did you circle in the previous exercise? Answer: _____.
What percentage of the characters used in this text have been simplified? Answer:
_____ percent. Compare your answer here with the one you obtained for exercise 0.21.*

You are now ready to memorize one or more of the poems, if you'd like. Memorization
is an important part of the Chinese educational system, and is generally mandatory for
students in school.

Encounter 4   Introduction to Chinese characters

0.27 *The earliest records of Chinese characters on oracle bone inscriptions include
versions that are more pictographic than modern Chinese characters. Match these
"pictographic" characters with their English equivalents.*

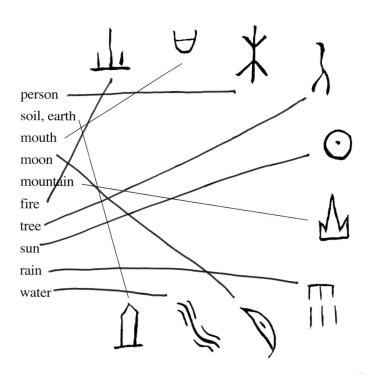

person
soil, earth
mouth
moon
mountain
fire
tree
sun
rain
water

0.28 *Now, based on the matches you made in the previous exercise, can you figure
out what these modern characters mean?*

火 口 木 人 日 山 土 水 月 雨

0.29 *Label each character in the previous exercise with one of the following identifications.*

rén *(human, person)*   tǔ *(soil, earth)*   shuǐ *(water)*   yǔ *(rain)*   mù *(tree, wood)*

shān *(mountain)*   kǒu *(mouth)*   rì *(sun)*   huǒ *(fire)*   yuè *(moon)*

▶ Recognizing radicals

In addition to standing on their own, the ten characters above also serve as radicals, or "meaning components," of many other Chinese characters. Radicals can be thought of as building blocks that provide a broad link to the meaning of multicomponent characters. Notice how the first character below means "mountain range" and its radical component is, naturally, "mountain." Radicals can serve you well as memory aids; there are nearly 200 of them, but you should concentrate on learning the 50 most common ones.

0.30 *Circle the radicals you recognize in the characters below.*

嶺	旦	雲	吹	峰
mountain range	dawn, day	clouds	to blow	peak, summit
映	雪	吞	峽	晚
shine, reflect	snow	to swallow	canyon, gorge	evening, night
雷	喝	朔	地	址
thunder	to drink	new moon	earth, land	site, location
林	朧	墳	枯	松
forest	rising moon	grave, tomb	withered	pine tree

0.31 *Some radicals can be somewhat altered when combined with another character component. Match the full forms on the left with the combination form on the right.*

火   亻
人   灬
水   氵

0.32 *Circle the radicals in the following characters.*

lantern, light   scorch   hot   an immortal

splash, splatter   wave, ripple   a servant   you

0.33 *Try to identify the radicals in the following characters.*

楚	吻	坤	晶	位	侣
崩	岳	有	森	唱	棟
洋	炒	暗	海	塊	吃
露	煙	基	僑	需	崎
期	梧	溪	朗	煮	只

▶ Recognizing numbers

0.34 *Read the following characters aloud.*

〇 0	一 1	二 2	三 3	四 4	五 5
六 6	七 7	八 8	九 9	十 10	

0.35 *Write the Arabic numerals for each of the following telephone numbers.*

八〇八・九五六・二六九二   808·956·2692

九一六・二二九・〇三七〇   916·229·0370

七一八・九六六・六一五五   718·966·6155

五一二・三〇二・二四〇〇   512·302·2400

0.36 *The Chinese character* 元 (yuán) *is the primary denomination in Chinese currency, equivalent in usage (but not in value) to a "dollar" in U.S. currency. What is the cost indicated by the following price tags?*

十元   10   六元   6   九元   9

▶ **Reading real-life texts**

0.37 *This is a sign for an establishment in Beijing called "The Vulcan Bar." Label each of the three large characters on the sign with one of the following: person, mountain, fire.*

What do you think a "mountain of fire" means? Write the English term: ___volcano___

0.38 *This is a sign for a famous spicy Sichuan dish. The character* 煮 *(zhǔ) means "boiled." Circle the radical for this character on the sign.*

What does the radical mean? ___cook (fire)___

What is the main ingredient of this dish? ___fish___

In what has this ingredient been boiled? ___water___

Suggest a good English name for this dish: _____

0.39 *This is a sign in a college cafeteria.* 區／区 *(qū) means "area."*

How much does each dish in this area cost? Write the English: _____

🎵 **Unit Rap**

Go to the **Encounters** website at www.EncountersChinese.com and listen to the song to re-view the numbers introduced in this unit. Listen again and sing along!

Encounter 5 | Writing

▶ Learning to write characters

0.40 For stroke order and other useful information about each of the following characters from this unit, go to the Character Writing Workbook. Practice writing them until you can reproduce them on demand.

一, 二, 三, 四, 五, 六, 七, 八, 九, 十

火, 口, 木, 人, 山, 水

0.41 Write your telephone number (including area code) in Chinese characters.

六 七 八 – 五 0 二 – 六 四 二 四

Cultural Bits 文化点滴

What is culture?

View the video segment "What is culture?" and then discuss the following questions with your classmates.

- Give a few examples of ways in which cultural understanding is crucial for certain bits of language, such as the expression *Chi le ma*?
- What is the difference between "large C" culture and "small c" culture? Give some examples of each.
- What images do you associate with Chinese culture?
- What are the four major inventions that China is known for?
- What are some elements that can contribute to culture shock, and how can they be avoided?

Recap

▶ Vocabulary

Numbers

líng zero	**sān** three	**liù** six	**jiǔ** nine
yī one	**sì** four	**qī** seven	**shí** ten
èr two	**wǔ** five	**bā** eight	

▶ Checklist of "can do" statements

After completing this unit, you should be able to perform each of the following tasks:

Structure of Chinese

☑ Make an accurate statement in English describing Chinese tones.

☑ At least some of the time, identify the tone of a Chinese syllable by indicating a number (if done orally) or a tone mark (if written).

☑ At least some of the time, identify the initial sound of a Chinese syllable by selecting the corresponding pinyin letter(s).

☑ At least some of the time, identify the final sound of a Chinese syllable by selecting the corresponding pinyin letter(s).

Listening and speaking

☑ Recognize and say the numbers 1–10 in various orders.

Reading and writing

☑ Recognize and write the characters for the numbers 1–10.

☐ Recognize ten common characters that are also radicals and write six of them.

☑ Identify ten common radicals in characters.

☑ Recognize the Chinese character for *yuán*.

"We're all one family"

四海一家

Sìhǎiyìjiā

Introducing yourself by nationality and background

In this unit, you will learn how to:

- greet someone.
- introduce yourself.
- say good-bye.
- understand formal and informal speech.
- say where you come from.

- ask for and give telephone numbers.
- express your thanks.
- apologize to someone.
- ask for repetition and clarification.
- understand traditional versus simplified characters.

Encounter 1   Greeting people and introducing yourself

▶ Greeting people

 1.1 *View Episode 1 of the dramatic series. Don't worry if you don't fully understand everything that is being said; just listen and enjoy!*

1.2 *What might you say in English when you greet someone? Make a list below.*

_____

_____

 1.3 *Watch and listen to the video segment. Then check the greetings you hear.*

- ☐ Nǐ hǎo!
- ☐ Hǎo ma?
- ☐ Nín hǎo!
- ☐ Xiǎo Wáng!
- ☐ Zěnmeyàng?
- ☐ Hǎo, hǎo.
- ☐ Hěn hǎo.

Compare your answers with those of your classmates and teacher.

 1.4 *Watch and listen to the video segment. Can you understand the meanings of the individual expressions below? Match the appropriate terms.*

a. Nǐ hǎo!	1. *Hello.* (formal; polite)
b. Nín hǎo!	2. *Hello.* (informal)
c. Hǎo ma?	3. *How about you?*
d. Hǎo.	4. *Fine.*
e. Nǐ ne?	5. *How are you? / Are you well?* (informal)
f. Wǒ yě hěn hǎo.	6. *I'm fine too.*

Compare your answers with those of your classmates and teacher.

FYI 供你参考

Greetings in Chinese

In Chinese culture, as in Western cultures, there are generally two types of word-based greetings—those that are exchanged with little or no further conversation, such as "Hi!" and "Hello!" (*Nǐ hǎo!* in Chinese), and those that follow a question-and-answer pattern, such as "How are you?" and "How have you been?" (*Nǐ hǎo ma?* in Chinese). Both are considered friendly and informal. As a beginning student of Chinese, you can safely use *Nǐ hǎo* as a common, informal greeting regardless of either the time of day or person addressed. As you will learn in this unit, the response to *Nǐ hǎo* is usually a *Nǐ hǎo* in return.

However, in Chinese culture (as in all cultures), context determines which greeting you will use and when. When you greet a person of a higher status, such as your teacher, you should use the more formal and polite *Nín hǎo* or *Nín hǎo ma?* *Nín* is roughly equivalent to the French "vous" or the Spanish "usted." It is also a good idea to use the polite form when greeting someone at a formal business or social occasion or someone who is significantly senior to you. Remember: when in doubt, use *nín*. It shows courtesy and respect—two highly valued characteristics in Chinese culture—and it presents you as a cultured and sophisticated individual.

In addition to *Nín (Nǐ) hǎo!* or *Nín (Nǐ) hǎo ma?*, another conventional greeting is simply to say the person's last name, followed by a respectful title, such as "Mr.," "Ms.," or "Professor." For example, *Yáng Xiānsheng* (Mr. Yang); *Zhāng Nǚshì* (Ms. Zhang); and *Lǐ Lǎoshī* (Professor Li, literally: Teacher Li). You can also combine last name, title, and a respectful greeting, such as in this formula: *Zhāng Lǎoshī, nín hǎo!* (with a slight nod of the head).

1.5 Mingling: *Turn to a nearby classmate and greet him or her in Chinese. Then repeat the exchange with a different classmate. If you know your classmate's name (Chinese or English), say it before the greeting. If you are interacting with your teacher, remember to use the polite form and/or a respectful title (e.g., Lǐ Lǎoshī, nín hǎo).*

FYI 供你参考

Other common greetings

Here are some other common ways to greet friends:

> Zǎo! *(early morning, until around 9:00 or 10:00 A.M.)*
>
> Zǎoshang hǎo! *(similar to zǎo with the same time restrictions, but much more formal)*

Keep in mind that *nǐ hǎo* can be used at any time of day. If you already know the person you are greeting, you don't actually need to say anything. You could just smile, nod, and say the person's name or name and title.

▶ Introducing yourself

 1.6 *Watch and listen to the video segment. What do you think they are saying to each other? Fill in the blanks in English.*

Lynn: Nǐ hǎo! Wǒ jiào Lynn.
        Hello. _____ Lynn.

Lǐ Wén: Nǐ hǎo! Wǒ jiào Lǐ Wén.
        Hello. _____ Li Wen.

Chén Fēng: Nín hǎo, Zhōu Lǎoshī.
        Wǒ jiào Chén Fēng.
        Hello, Professor Zhou.
        _____ Chen Feng.

Máo Zhìpéng: Wǒ jiào Máo
        Zhìpéng.

        _____

        Mao Zhipeng.

1.7 *Write your name in Chinese (pinyin with tones) or English to complete the sentence below. Use your first name or your full name, as you prefer. Practice saying the two sentences below quickly and smoothly, five to ten times.*

Nǐ hǎo! Wǒ jiào _____.

FYI 供你参考

Introductions

Have you noticed that Chinese people tend to introduce themselves using full names, whereas Westerners often do so with just first names? Take a moment to consider what this might indicate about Chinese and Western values related to one's identity. How do you generally like to introduce yourself?

In Chinese culture, it is more important to identify the group you belong to first—for example, your family, your workplace—before moving on to other details when introducing yourself. In Chinese, the last name comes first and is generally included as part of the introduction.

 1.8 *Watch and listen to the video segment. Fill in the blanks with pinyin.*

a.
Lynn: Nǐ hǎo. Wǒ jiào Lynn. Hěn gāoxìng
        rènshi nǐ.

Lǐ Wén: Nǐ hǎo. Wǒ jiào Lǐ Wén. Rènshi nǐ
        wǒ yě hěn _____.

b.

Nín hǎo, Zhōu Lǎoshī. Wǒ jiào Chén Fēng.
Hěn gāoxìng rènshi _____.

c.

Zhào Yǒnggāng: Hěn gāoxìng rènshi nǐmen.

Alejandro: _____

           _____.

d. What do you think is the meaning of *Hěn gāoxìng rènshi nǐ*? Write the English below:

_____

1.9 *Mingling:* Turn to two or three classmates and say your name in Chinese, using the sentences you have just practiced. Use your English name if you do not have a Chinese name. Listen carefully to their responses and take notes.

▶ Grammar: Personal pronouns

1.10 *As a class, name these famous people. Then complete each blank below with an appropriate English name. Note that* tā *means "he/she" and* míngzi *means "name."*

Tā jiào shénme? OR Tā jiào shénme míngzi?

     a.   b.   c.   d.

a. Tā jiào _____.   c. Tā jiào _____.

b. Tā jiào _____.   d. Tā jiào _____.

1.11 *Match the Chinese personal pronouns on the left with the appropriate English on the right. The suffix* -men *forms plural pronouns when it is added to singular pronouns.*

a. wǒ   1. *he/she*

b. nǐ   2. *I*

c. tā   3. *you* (singular)

d. wǒmen   4. *you* (plural)

e. nǐmen   5. *they*

f. tāmen   6. *we*

Encounter 2   Leave-taking and more introductions

▌ Saying good-bye

 1.12 *Watch and listen to the video segment. What do you think they are saying to each other? Fill in the blanks in English.*

Lǐ Wén: Lynn, zàijiàn!

_____

Lynn: Lǐ Wén, zàijiàn!

_____

1.13 *Mingling:* Say good-bye to your classmates, using their English or Chinese names.

> ### FYI 供你参考
>
> **Saying good-bye**
>
> Most cultures and languages have several ways to say good-bye. The most common way in Chinese is *zàijiàn* (*again + see = see you again/soon*).
>
> Try to develop the habit of saying good-bye to your friends by saying their name (and title, if you know it) before *zàijiàn;* it's more polite and authentic. For example: *Mǎlì* (Mary), *zàijiàn.* OR *Yáng Lǎoshī, zàijiàn.* Do remember to say good-bye; don't just walk out of class when it ends without saying good-bye to your teacher.
>
> Just as with greetings, there are also many conventional ways to say good-bye in Chinese culture. Try some of the following examples in an appropriate context. Pay particular attention to how English has influenced Chinese in one of the examples below.
>
> > Míngtiān jiàn (*tomorrow + see*): See you tomorrow.
> >
> > Yìhuǐr jiàn (*little while + see*): See you in a little while/in a few moments.
> >
> > Báibái: sound loan from English "bye-bye" that is often added to another form; thus, *Zàijiàn, báibái!*
>
> When saying good-bye to your teacher, remember that it's best to use his or her last name plus the term for "teacher" (*lǎoshī*); thus, *Wáng Lǎoshī, zàijiàn!*

▶ Grammar: The verbs *shì, jiào, xìng*

1.14 *Watch and listen to the video segment. Then fill in the blanks below.*

a. Chén Fēng, zhèi wèi _____ Yáng Jiàoshòu.
   Chen Feng, this is Professor Yang.

b. Wǒ _____ Mèng, _____ Mèng Dérú.
   My last name is Meng; my name is Meng Deru.

c. _____ Zhāng, _____ Zhāng Fúxīng.
   My last name is Zhang; my name is Zhang Fuxing.

1.15 *Match the Chinese on the left with the appropriate English on the right.*

a. shì   1. *be called, have the first name X*
b. jiào   2. *have the last name X*
c. xìng   3. *be*

1.16 *Complete the following self-introduction by a man named Manuel García. He is saying, "My last name is García; my name is Manuel García."*

Wǒ _____
García, _____
   Manuel García.

1.17 *Write the same self-introduction for yourself in pinyin, using your English or Chinese name. Try to write the pinyin with tone marks.*

Repeat this self-introduction aloud until you are comfortable with the words and can say the sentences quickly and accurately.

1.18 *Mingling:* *With a partner, practice saying hello, introducing yourself, and saying good-bye. After you both have had an opportunity to share, move to a new partner and repeat the process. Continue to circulate around the room to interact with new partners.*

Grammar Bits 语法点滴

Stative verbs

In Chinese, words that describe the subject—that say how it is or is not—are called "stative verbs" (some people call them "adjectives").

> hǎo *(be good, fine, OK)*
> gāoxìng *(be happy, delighted, glad)*

Stative verbs (SV) can be preceded by adverbs, such as *hěn* (a light sense of "very"). It is a good idea to always precede a stative verb used by itself with *hěn* (except in greetings).

> Wǒ hěn hǎo. *(I'm fine)*
> Wǒ hěn gāoxìng. (I'm happy.)

Equative verbs

Chinese also has "equative verbs" that are like an "equal" sign (thus: subject = noun). You already know three:

> **jiào** *(be called/named)*   **xìng** *(be surnamed, have the last name X)*
> Wǒ jiào Mike.   Wǒ xìng Wáng.
> Tā jiào Mark, Mark Phelps.   Lǎoshī xìng Chén.
> Nǐ jiào shénme míngzi?

Jiào may introduce either the full name (surname + given name) or just the given name, but NEVER just the surname; that's the function of *xìng*.

> **shì** *(be)*
> Wǒ shì lǎoshī.
> Tā shì Gāo Lǎoshī.

Note that although there is a tone mark on the linking verb *shì*, it is usually not stressed in connected speech: *shì* is pronounced in a neutral tone.

Also note that Chinese verbs do not change form to match the subject. In English, the verb "to be" must be conjugated to form "I **am**," "you **are**," "he/she **is**," etc.; in Chinese, the verb *shì* remains *shì*, regardless of the subject.

Remember that *shì* is NOT used to link subjects or pronouns with stative verbs (adjectives). The English "I am well/fine/OK" does NOT become ~~Wǒ shì hǎo~~ in Chinese, but instead becomes *Wǒ hěn hǎo*.

Grammar: Negation

 1.19 *Watch and listen to the video segment, and then answer the following questions.*

a. How much did the bicyclist think the bottle of water cost? _____ kuài (¥)

b. How much was it really? _____ kuài (¥)

c. Based on what you hear, what does *bù* mean? *bù* = _____

 1.20 *Watch and listen to the video again. Write the missing tones on the following sentences.*

a. Bù dong, bù dong. (*I don't understand.*)

b. Bú shi shui, shi shui. (*It's not "sleep"; it's "water."*)

c. Yí kuai wu, bú shi wu kuai. (*It's ¥1.5, not ¥5.*)

1.21 *Indicate with a* ∧ *where* bù *belongs in each of the following sentences. Note: Grammatically,* bù *should precede the verb.*

a. Wǒ shì Mary Smith.

b. Wǒ jiào Mary.

c. Wǒ xìng Smith.

d. Wǒ shì Měiguórén. (*I am American.*)

e. Wǒ shì Zhōngguórén. (*I am Chinese.*)

1.22 *Write a complete sentence in pinyin about one thing you are NOT.*

_____

FYI 供你参考

More on tone sandhi: The negative adverb *bù*

Tone sandhi, you'll remember, occurs when certain words change tones in certain environments. *Yī* (number one) is an example that you learned about in the introductory unit. *Bù* is another. Before the fourth tone, *bù* changes to the second tone: *bú*.

> Bú xìng Zhōu. (*[I'm] not surnamed Zhou.*)
> Bú shì wǒ. (*It's not me.*)

Recognizing when these words change tones will become automatic with practice.

Practice: How would you pronounce *bù* if you added it to each of these words?

| gāo (*tall*) | máng (*busy*) | hǎo (*good*) | lèi (*tired*) |
| jiāo (*teach*) | xué (*learn*) | xiě (*write*) | bèi (*memorize*) |

▶ Formal and informal speech

 1.23 *Watch and listen to the video segment. Match the Chinese sentences with their correct English equivalents. Note:* Qǐngwèn *means "May I ask . . ." and always precedes the inquiry.*

a. Tā xìng shénme?

b. Wǒ xìng Fàn.

c. Qǐngwèn, nín guìxìng?

1. *My last name is Fan.*

2. *May I ask your (honorable) last name?*

3. *What's his last name?*

1.24 *Based on what you have learned so far, fill in the following blanks with the correct pinyin.*

a. you (formal): _____

b. you (informal): _____

c. Hello (informal): ___*Nǐ hǎo*___.

d. Hello (formal): _____.

e. What's your last name (formal): ___*Nín guìxìng*___?

f. What's his last name (informal): _____?

FYI 供你参考

Levels of formality

Although *Nǐ xìng shénme?* is grammatically correct and often used in casual conversation, many Chinese would consider it too informal and abrupt if used when first meeting someone. When directly addressing someone older or of a higher social status than yourself (for example, your teacher or a client), it is more culturally appropriate to use *Nín guìxìng?* The response will generally then include *Miǎn guì*, meaning "Please dispense with the word *honorable*." Therefore, *Miǎn guìxìng Fàn* means "My last name is Fan, please dispense with the word *honorable*." The expression *Tā xìng shénme?* is always accepted when referring to a third party.

1.25 *Mingling: Circulate around the room, greeting classmates and asking their last names. Use informal speech with your classmates and formal speech with your teacher.*

Encounter 3 Talking about where you come from

1.26 *Watch and listen to the video segment. Then read the following fragments and circle the choice that correctly completes each sentence.*

a. Lynn is _____.
    • Chinese   • American

b. Lynn is from _____.
    • Los Angeles   • New York

c. Li Wen is from _____.
    • Guilin   • Shanghai

1.27 *Match the corresponding Chinese and English below.*

a. *I am American.*

b. *I'm from Shanghai.*

c. *Where are you from?*

1. Wǒ shì Shànghǎirén.

2. Nǐ shì nǎli rén?

3. Wǒ shì Měiguórén.

1.28 *Based on the exchange you watched in the video segment above, answer the following questions.*

a. What do you think *Měiguó nǎr* means? _____

b. What is the meaning of *nǎr* by itself? _____

1.29 *Read the exchange below and write the corresponding English equivalents where they are missing.*

A: Wǒ shì Měiguórén. *(I am an American.)*

    Wǒ jiā zài Měiguó. *(My home is in America.)*

B: Měiguó nǎr? (_____)

A: Wǒ jiā zài Niǔyuē *(New York)*; wǒ shì Niǔyuērén.

    (_____)

1.30 *Complete the following conversation with your own information. If you are not Chinese or American, you can visit a website like* www.zhongguolu.com/phrasebook/countries.html *to learn the name of your country in pinyin. Write that name in the first blank below. This is how you would say, "I am a person from _____." On the second blank, write the name of your state, province, or city in English. This is how you would say, "My home is in _____."*

A: Nǐ shì nǎr de rén?

B: Wǒ shì _____rén. *(name of country)*

A: Nǐ jiā zài nǎr?

B: Wǒ jiā zài _____. *(name of state, province, or city)*

Practice the above conversation with a partner until you are comfortable and can pronounce the sentences smoothly and accurately.

1.31 *Mingling: Turn to a partner and have the following guided dialogue. First, greet your partner by name, and then:*

A: Ask where he/she is from.
B: Respond with the name of a country.
A: Ask where in this country he/she is from.
B: Respond with the name of a state/province/city in Chinese or English.

Reverse roles and practice the dialogue again.

Grammar Bits 语法点滴

The particle *ma*

There are many ways to form questions in Chinese. One of the simplest is to add the question particle *ma* at the end of a statement. You don't need to change the word order, but your intonation should rise slightly at the end, as in English.

Tā shì Měiguórén. ⟶ Tā shì Měiguórén ma?

▶ Recognizing tones

1.32 *Watch and listen to the video segment. Mark the correct tone (for example: ā, á, ǎ, or à) over each of the boldfaced letters.*

Dajia **h**ao. *(Hi, everybody.)*
Ni hao. *(Hi.)*

Wo jiao **Ma**o Zh**i**peng. *(My name is Mao Zhipeng.)*
Wo jia zai Be**i**jing. *(I live in Beijing.)*
Wo shi Be**i**jingren. *(I am a Beijinger.)*

Ta jiao Chen Feng. *(His name is Chen Feng.)*
Ta b**u** zai zhel**i**. *(He's not here.)*
Ta zai Be**i**jing. *(He's in Beijing.)*

Zhang Xiaozhang, n**i**n h**a**o. *(Hi, Principal Zhang.)*
Ni hao, **Li** Wen. *(Hi, Li Wen.)*
Zhang Xiaozhang, n**i**n m**a**ng ma? *(Principal Zhang, are you busy?)*
Bu mang, b**u** mang. **Yo**u shi ma? *(Not busy, not busy. What's up?)*

▶ Grammar: Question words *nǎr, shénme, shéi*

1.33 *Review the second exchange from the previous activity and write the appropriate English equivalent in the blank below.*

Q: Tā shì shéi?
A: Tā shì Máo Zhìpéng. Tā shì Běijīngrén.
shéi = _____

1.34 *Match the appropriate Chinese and English question words.*

a. nǎr   1. *who*
b. shénme   2. *where*
c. shéi   3. *what*

Encounter 4   Asking for and giving phone numbers

1.35 *Watch and listen to the video segment. Then fill in the blanks below.*

a. What's your telephone number? Fill in the blank: *Nǐ de diànhuà hàomǎ shì* _____?

b. Write the pinyin for the term that means "telephone **number**": *diànhuà* _____

c. Write the pinyin for the word that marks possession: _____
   (Hint: nǐ de diànhuà hàomǎ = *your telephone number*)

d. Write the pinyin for "My telephone number is":
   _____

e. Write the pinyin for the term that indicates "and yours?": _____
   (Hint: Listen to what Lynn says after she tells Li Wen her telephone number.)

f. Write the English meaning of *shǒujī*: _____

1.36 *Complete the following sentences about yourself. Use the statements below for Mary Smith as a guide.*

I am Mary Smith. I am American. My home is in Boston. My home phone (or cell phone) number is 617-635-4500.

Wǒ jiào _____.

Wǒ shì _____.
   (*Write the pinyin of your country* + rén.)

Wǒ jiā zài _____.
   (*Write the name of your state or city in English.*)

Wǒ de _____ shì _____.
   (*Write your home or cell phone number.*)

1.37 *Watch and listen to the video segment. What is each person asking? Fill in each blank with the corresponding word or phrase from the box.*

> cell phone number / where someone lives / nationality
> name / home phone number

a. Nǐ jiào shénme míngzi?   d. Nǐ jiālǐ de diànhuà hàomǎ shì duōshao?

_____   _____

b. Nǐ shì nǎli rén?   e. Nǐ de shǒujī hàomǎ shì duōshao?

_____   _____

c. Nǐ jiā zhù nǎr?

_____

1.38 *Mingling: Turn to a classmate and ask the questions above. Note his or her responses below.*

Name: _____   Home phone number: _____

Nationality: _____   Cell phone number: _____

Hometown: _____

Grammar Bits 语法点滴

Review of question words

Question words are, obviously, words that ask for information or denote interrogative sentences. If you use a question word, then your sentence does not need the particle *ma*. Carefully note the position of Chinese question words. How is it different from English? The examples below illustrate various uses of *shénme*, *shéi*, *nǎr*, *něi*, and *duōshao*. In all of these examples, the answer to the question replaces the question word. Can you provide an answer to each question about the fictitious people below?

Tā jiào shénme? *(What is her name?)*
Tā jiào Wáng shénme? *(He is called Wang what?)* [Answer with Wang's FULL name.]
Tā xìng shénme? *(What is her [sur]name?)*
Tā shì shéi? *(Who is he/she?)*
Shéi shì Wáng Lǎoshī? *(Who is Professor Wang?)* [You would point him out.]
Nǐ zài nǎr? *(Where are you?)*
Zhāng Lǎoshī shì nǎr de rén? *(Where is Professor Zhang from?)*
Nǐ shì něi guó rén? *(What's your nationality?)*
Tā de diànhuà hàomǎ shì duōshao? *(What is his/her telephone number?)*

Encounter 5　Expressing thanks, apologizing, and asking for clarification

▶ Thanking and apologizing

1.39 *Watch and listen to the video segment. Then match each Chinese expression with the appropriate English equivalent.*

a. Qǐng.
b. Xièxie.
c. Duìbuqǐ.
d. Búyòng xiè.
e. Méi guānxi. ——————————
f. Bú kèqi. ——————————

1. *You're welcome.*
2. *I'm sorry.*
3. *Please go ahead.*
4. *Thank you.*
5. *That's all right. / No problem.*
6. *No need to be so polite. (You're welcome.)*

1.40 *Mingling:* Turn to a partner and practice saying "thank you" (followed by "you're welcome") and "I'm sorry" (followed by "that's all right"). Continue until you both feel confident with the exchanges.

1.41 *Pair work:* Complete the "red/white" activity with a partner, following these directions.

a. Hold a red chip in one hand and a white chip in the other. Do not let your partner know which chip is in each hand.
b. Invite your partner (say *Qǐng . . .*) to choose one of your hands. Reveal the selected chip and share it with your partner.
c. If your partner selects the red chip, he or she should say *Xièxie,* since you have shared something good (red is a lucky color in Chinese culture). You should respond with *Búyòngxiè.*
d. If your partner selects the white chip, you should say *Duìbuqǐ* since you have shared something sad (white is linked to mourning in Chinese culture). He or she should respond with *Méi guānxi.*
e. Reverse roles, and then continue with a different partner.

▶ Asking for clarification

1.42 *Watch and listen to the video segment. The following sentences are useful to keep in mind if you have trouble understanding what someone says. Read them carefully and then match the corresponding English and Chinese phrases.*

a. *Sorry. I don't understand.*
b. *Please say it again.*
c. *Please speak slower.*
d. *I understand now. Thank you.*

1. Qǐng shuō màn yìdiǎnr.
2. Qǐng zài shuō yíbiàn.
3. Wǒ dǒng le, xièxie.
4. Duìbuqǐ, wǒ bù dǒng.

1.43 *Fill in the blanks using the correct pinyin equivalents.*

a. understand: _____   d. slow: _____

b. speak or say: _____   e. slower: _____

c. say it again: _____

1.44 *Write answers to the following questions in pinyin.*

What would you say if . . .

a. someone spoke to you in Chinese using words you don't yet know?

_____

b. someone mumbled or did not speak clearly?

_____

c. someone spoke too quickly for you to understand?

_____

d. you finally understand what someone has been trying to tell you?

_____

▶ Putting it all together

1.45 *Mingling: Circulate around the room, interview six people, and complete the chart below. Remember to ask for clarification, if necessary, and use polite language if you interview your teacher. Begin each exchange with a greeting and finish by saying good-bye. Remember to also express thanks and apologies, when necessary, at the appropriate time.*

Name	Nationality	Hometown	Home phone #	Cell phone #

1.46 *Conversation: If possible, have a conversation with a native Chinese speaker. Provide the following information about yourself: name, nationality, telephone number. Ask for the same information from the other person. Remember to greet, thank, apologize, ask for clarification as necessary, and say good-bye. Share and discuss this dialogue with your teacher and classmates.*

🎵 Unit Rap

Go to the **Encounters** *website at* www.EncountersChinese.com *and listen to the song to review key expressions from Unit 1. Listen again and sing along!*

Encounter 6   Reading and writing

▶ Recognizing traditional vs. simplified characters

1.47 *Read the following terms aloud.*

我 (*I, me*)   你 (*you*)   他 (*he*)

我們 (*we*)   你們 (*you [plural]*)   他們 (*they*)

你好! (*Hello!*)   你好嗎? (*How are you?*)   請 (*please, please go ahead*)

謝謝! (*Thank you!*) 謝謝你! (*Thank you!*)   對不起 (*I'm sorry.*)

謝謝您! (*Thank you! [polite]*)   再見! (*Good-bye!*)

FYI 供你参考

Development of simplified characters

The characters in the previous activity are written in a form usually called "traditional" characters. Their forms are identical to the forms that have been used in China for centuries. In 1956, and again in 1964, the government of the People's Republic of China (PRC) published lists of "simplified" characters. Some of the traditionally used characters were simplified by reducing the number of total strokes needed to write them. For example, the character 見, traditionally written with seven strokes, was simplified to 见, written with four strokes. Only about a quarter to one-third of all characters in use were simplified; the rest were not. The hope was that if the characters were easier to write, they would be easier to learn. Taiwan, Hong Kong, and many overseas Chinese communities, however, continue to use only the traditional forms. The research community is divided on whether simplified or traditional characters are easier to learn, but in all Chinese-speaking communities, whether they use simplified or traditional forms, in the past decades the literacy rate has gone from one of the lowest in the world to one of the highest—currently just over 90 percent.

A "divided language" situation currently exists for the written Chinese language, unfortunately complicating your learning efforts. Will there be a unification of China's written language in the future? Stay tuned!

1.48 *In each group, match the traditional characters in the left column with their simplified equivalents in the right column. Keep in mind that only about a quarter to one-third of all characters have been simplified.*

a. 我	1. 你好吗	l. 再見	12. 叫
b. 你	2. 你请	m. 是	13. 再见
c. 他	3. 谢谢您	n. 姓	14. 么
d. 他們	4. 谢谢	o. 叫	15. 字
e. 你好	5. 谢谢你	p. 甚	16. 姓
f. 你好嗎	6. 我	q. 麼	17. 对
g. 請	7. 他们	r. 名	18. 起
h. 你請	8. 他	s. 字	19. 不
i. 謝謝	9. 你	t. 對	20. 名
j. 謝謝你	10. 请	u. 不	21. 是
k. 謝謝您	11. 你好	v. 起	22. 什

Recognizing radicals

1.49 *Review the radicals in the introductory unit, pages 11–14. Look for any occurrences of those radicals in both lists above. Try to link the meaning of the radical with the meaning of the character. Keep in mind that when radicals are part of multicomponent characters, their forms often change. Notice how some radicals have been simplified and are now written with fewer strokes. Share your conclusions with your classmates.*

Reading real-life texts

1.50 *This sign is on the campus of the university that Chen Feng, Li Wen, and Xiao Mao once attended. It says, "[Making our environment] green, beautiful, and clean / depends on you, on me, and on him (others)." Circle and label the terms "me," "you," "him."*

1.51 *On the same campus is this plaque.* 的 *is a particle that marks possession. Circle the term for "we." "We" + de = "our."*

1.52 *This handwritten sign on the desk of a receptionist says, "I'll be right back. Please wait just a bit! Thank you!" Circle the terms "please" and "thank you." Note that the second* xiè *in* xièxie *is here represented with a mark meaning "ditto, repeat the previous character."*

1.53 *This is a handwritten note that someone has passed to you in class. If you wanted to be friendly and polite, what would you write back? For now, write in English.*

你好！我叫王小明。請問，
你姓甚麼？叫甚麼名字？
謝謝你告訴我。

_____

_____

_____

▶ Learning to write characters

1.54 *For stroke order and other useful information about each of the following characters from this unit, go to the* **Character Writing Workbook.** *Choose traditional or simplified characters and practice writing them until you can reproduce them on demand.*

我，你，他，們／们，好，嗎／吗，是，姓，叫，甚／什，
麼／么，名，字，請／请，謝／谢，再，見／见，對／对，
不，起

▶ Writing a note

1.55 *Write a brief note to a classmate, telling him or her your name and asking for your classmate's name. Use characters as much as possible; substitute with pinyin or English as necessary. Use courtesy terms (for example, "thank you") whenever possible.*

Cultural Bits 文化点滴

Introductions, greetings, and good-byes

View the video segment "Introductions, greetings, and good-byes" and then discuss the following questions with your classmates.

- What role do introductions by friends play in getting to know people in Chinese society?
- What elements determine your status in regard to someone else? List some.
- What are some greetings other than *Nǐ hǎo* that Chinese often use with each other?
- What are some ways you can take leave of a person?
- What is the significance of the leave-taking statement *Wǒ bú sòng le, a?*

Recap

▶ Grammar

Stative verbs

Stative verbs, which describe the subject, can be preceded by adverbs such as *hěn* or negated with *bù*. Do not use *shì* with stative verbs.

hǎo (*be good, be fine, be OK*)
> Wǒ hěn hǎo. (NOT: ~~Wǒ shì hǎo.~~)
> Tāmen bù hǎo.

gāoxìng (*be happy, be delighted, be glad*)
> hěn gāoxìng
> bù gāoxìng
> Tā bù gāoxìng.

Equative verbs

Equative verbs link the subject with a noun that states what it is.

jiào (*be called*)
> Wǒ jiào Alejandro.

xìng (*have the surname*)
> Wǒ xìng Lǐ, jiào Lǐ Wén.

shì (*be*)
> Wǒ shì Zhōngguórén, bú shì Měiguórén.

Question words

Question words ask for information or denote interrogative sentences. The particle *ma* is not needed when a question word is used.

shéi (*who?*)
> Tā shì shéi? Tā jiào Lǐ Wén.

shénme (*what?*)
> Nǐ jiào shénme? Wǒ jiào Wáng Lì.

nǎr (*where?*)
> Nǐ jiā zài nǎr? Wǒ jiā zài Běijīng.

duōshao (*what number?*)
> Nǐ diànhuà duōshao hào?

Plurals

The suffix *-men* is added to the pronouns *wǒ*, *nǐ*, and *tā* to create the plural forms *wǒmen*, *nǐmen*, and *tāmen*.

Particles *ma* and *ne*

The particle *ma* is used at the end of a statement to form a question.
> Tā shì Měiguórén. ⇒ Tā shì Měiguórén ma?

The particle *ne* after X means "And what about X?"
> Wǒ hěn hǎo. Nǐ ne?
> Lǐ Wén shì Guìlínrén. Chén Xiàozhǎng ne?

Adverbs

Adverbs should precede verbs in a sentence.

The word *hěn* means "very," but when it precedes a stative verb, it often has little meaning.
> Wǒ hěn hǎo.

The word *yě* means "also." It can precede a verb or another adverb.
> Wǒ yě shì Měiguórén.
> Wǒ yě bú xìng Yáng.
> Wǒ yě hǎo.
> Wǒ yě hěn hǎo.

Possessive marker *de*

The word *de*, used after an appropriate noun or pronoun, marks possession.
> Nǐ de diànhuà hàomǎ shì duōshao?
> Jiālǐ de diànhuà hàomǎ shì duōshao?

Negation with *bù*

The word *bù* is used immediately before a verb or adverb to create a negative statement. It cannot be used to modify nouns.
> Wǒ bú shì Shànghǎirén.
> (NOT: ~~Wǒ bù Shànghǎirén.~~)

▶ Vocabulary

Beginning in Unit 2, vocabulary lists will include Chinese characters as well as English and pinyin. For now, concentrate on learning the sounds and meanings of the words.

Numbers

líng zero
yī one
èr two
sān three
sì four
wǔ five
liù six
qī seven
bā eight
jiǔ nine
shí ten

Pronouns

nǐ you
nǐmen you (plural)
nín you (formal)
tā he, she, it
tāmen they, them
wǒ I, me
wǒmen we, us

Place names

Běijīng Beijing
Déguó Germany
Guìlín Guilin
Jiāzhōu California
Luòshānjī Los Angeles
Měiguó United States
Niǔyuē New York
Shànghǎi Shanghai
Sūzhōu Suzhou
Zhōngguó China

Nouns/noun phrases

Déguórén German (person)
diànhuà hàomǎ telephone number
jiā home
jiālǐ de diànhuà hàomǎ home telephone number
Měiguórén American (person)
míngzi full name, first name
Niǔyuērén New Yorker
shǒujī hàomǎ cell phone number
Zhōngguórén Chinese (person)

Titles

lǎoshī teacher
xiàozhǎng principal

Stative verbs

duì be right
gāo be tall
gāoxìng be happy
hǎo be good
lèi be tired
máng be busy

Equative verbs

jiào be called, have the first name X
shì be
xìng be surnamed, have the last name X

Adverbs

hěn very
yě also, too

Question particles/words/phrases

duōshao what (number)
ma (question particle)
nǎr where
ne and what about X?
shéi who
shénme what
zěnmeyàng How's it going?

Greetings

hài Hi!
hǎo ma How are you?
nǐ hǎo Hello, good day.
nǐ zǎo Good morning to you.
nín hǎo Hello. (formal)
zǎo Good morning.
zǎoshang hǎo Good morning.

Good-byes

báibái bye-bye
míngtiān jiàn See you tomorrow.
yìhuǐr jiàn See you in a little while.
zàijiàn Good-bye.

Thanks and response

búyòng xiè You're welcome.
xièxie Thank you.

Apology and response

duìbuqǐ I'm sorry.
méi guānxi That's all right. / No problem.

Invitation/request

qǐng Please go ahead of me.
qǐngwèn May I ask . . .

Idiomatic or combinational usages

guìxìng surnamed
nǐ shì nǎr de rén / nǎli rén Where are you from?
nǐ shì něi guó rén What country are you from?
nín guìxìng What's your name? (formal)
qǐng shuō màn yìdiǎnr Please speak a little slower.
qǐng zài shuō yībiàn Please say it again.
wǒ bù dǒng I don't understand.
wǒ dǒng le I understand.
wǒ jiā zài Běijīng My home is in Beijing.

▶ Checklist of "can do" statements

After completing this unit, you should be able to perform each of the following tasks:

Listening and speaking

☐ Greet a friend by name.

☐ Greet your teacher by name and title.

☐ Say good-bye to your friend.

☐ Say good-bye to your teacher.

☐ Greet a new friend and provide your name.

☐ Ask the name of a new friend.

☐ Say where you are from.

☐ Ask a new friend where he or she is from.

☐ Give someone your telephone number.

☐ Ask for your friend's telephone number.

☐ Thank a friend.

☐ Thank your teacher.

☐ Respond to a thank-you from a friend.

☐ Apologize to someone.

☐ Respond to someone's apology.

☐ Say you do not understand.

☐ Ask someone to repeat a statement.

Reading and writing

☐ Recognize and write some common characters related to introductions.

☐ Read and write common phrases related to introductions.

☐ Read and write common courtesy phrases.

Understanding culture

☐ Name three cities in China.

☐ Name three Chinese surnames.

☐ Make an accurate statement in English describing Chinese tones.

☐ Make an accurate statement in English regarding the use of formal and informal terms for "you" in Chinese.

☐ Make an accurate statement about greeting formulas, both Chinese and Western.

"Friends from the start"

一見如故

Yíjiànrúgù

Introducing yourself by age, contact information, and relationship to others

In this unit, you will learn how to:

- say, read, and write the numbers 11–100.
- find out someone's age and state your own.
- find out someone's birth date and state your own.
- state your Chinese "astrological" sign based on the year of your birth.
- find out someone's e-mail address and street address and provide your own.

- identify a third party's relationship to yourself.
- understand key information on business cards.
- recognize printed dates.
- read simple self-introductory statements.
- write simple self-introductory statements, including your name, age, birth date, e-mail and street address, and name of teacher.

Encounter 1   Finding out someone's age and stating your own

2.1 Getting ready: *You already know how to read and say the numbers one through ten; learning numbers through 100 is the next step. Fill in the blanks below with pinyin and Chinese characters. Pronounce each number. Note that yìbǎi (100) involves tone sandhi. Remember the rule?*

0 = líng 0

1 = yī 一	11 = shíyī 十一	21 = èrshíyī 二十一	31 = _____
2 = èr 二	12 = shí'èr 十二	22 = _____	42 = sìshí'èr 四十二
3 = sān 三	13 = shísān 十三	23 = _____	53 = _____
4 = sì 四	14 = _____	24 = _____	64 = liùshísì 六十四
5 = wǔ 五	15 = _____	25 = _____	75 = _____
6 = liù 六	16 = _____	26 = _____	86 = _____
7 = qī 七	17 = _____	27 = _____	97 = _____
8 = bā 八	18 = _____	28 = _____	98 = _____
9 = jiǔ 九	19 = _____	29 = _____	99 = jiǔshíjiǔ 九十九
10 = shí 十	20 = èrshí 二十	30 = sānshí 三十	100 = yìbǎi 一百

2.2 *With a partner or small group, take turns saying the numbers 1–100 forward, backward, by odd numbers, by even numbers, by fives, and by tens.*

yī, sān, wǔ, qī ...

2.3 加 (jiā) *means "add" or "plus";* 減／减 (jiǎn) *means "minus" or "subtract";* 等於／等于 (děngyú) *means "equals, be equal to." What do you think the following statements mean?*

一加一等於二／一加一等于二

二減一等於一／二减一等于一

Make as many of these "math statements" as you can in one minute.

2.4 *Complete the following statements using Arabic numerals.*

三十一加十等於／三十一加十等于 ＿＿＿＿＿＿＿＿＿

十九加七十八等於／十九加七十八等于 ＿＿＿＿＿＿＿＿＿

五十四加四十等於／五十四加四十等于 ＿＿＿＿＿＿＿＿＿

九十減二等於／九十减二等于 ＿＿＿＿＿＿＿＿＿

六十七減十四等於／六十七减十四等于 ＿＿＿＿＿＿＿＿＿

八十三減五十六等於／八十三减五十六等于 ＿＿＿＿＿＿＿＿＿

 2.5 *View Episode 2 of the dramatic series.*

2.6 *What would you say in English to ask someone's age and to state your own? Would you use different language with people of different ages? Make a list.*

＿＿＿＿＿＿＿＿＿＿＿＿＿＿＿＿＿＿＿＿＿＿＿＿＿＿＿＿＿＿

＿＿＿＿＿＿＿＿＿＿＿＿＿＿＿＿＿＿＿＿＿＿＿＿＿＿＿＿＿＿

＿＿＿＿＿＿＿＿＿＿＿＿＿＿＿＿＿＿＿＿＿＿＿＿＿＿＿＿＿＿

2.7 *Watch and listen to the video segment. Then fill in the blanks below.*

a. What do you think *Nǐ duō dà le* means? _____

b. Tang Yuan is _____ years old.

2.8 *Match the Chinese and English below.*

a. Nǐ duō dà le? Nǐ jǐ suì le?

你多大了？你幾歲了？／
你多大了？你几岁了？

1. *I'm eighteen years old.*

b. Wǒ shíbā suì le.

我十八歲了。／
我十八岁了。

2. *Oh, you're nineteen.*

c. Ò, nǐ shíjiǔ suì le.

噢，你十九歲了。／
噢，你十九岁了。

3. *I am, too.*

d. Nǐ ne?

你呢？

4. *I am eighteen years old, too.*

e. Wǒ yě shíbā suì le.

我也十八歲了。／
我也十八岁了。

5. *How old are you?*

f. Wǒ yě shì.

我也是。

6. *How about you?*

Grammar Bits 语法点滴

Sentences without verbs

Notice that when asking about or giving age, the number alone + *suì* suffices. No verb, such as *shì*, is required. In Chinese, when giving standard formulas such as age, price, or even one's place of origin *(Wǒ Běijīngrén)*, no verb is required, although it is not wrong to include it.

However, in the negative, a verb is always required: *Wǒ bú shì qīshíwǔ suì, wǒ qīshíliù suì.*

2.9 *Prepare to mingle:* *Write in pinyin what you would say in the following situations. Practice saying the sentences until you're comfortable with your pronunciation.*

a. Ask a classmate his or her age.

_____

b. Confirm that you understand, once someone has told you his or her age (for example, "Oh, you're 19!").

_____

c. Respond when someone asks you your age.

_____

2.10 *Mingling:* *Move around the room, asking classmates their ages and stating your own in reply.*

FYI 供你参考

Calculating age

Chinese do not calculate age as people in many other cultures do. They actually count the time in the womb, so when you're born, you're already one. And when Chinese New Year comes around (late January to mid-February)—it doesn't matter in what month you're born in your birth year—you're two! Perhaps for this reason, when Chinese ask others their age, they often include the word *jīnnián* (this year). *Nǐ jīnnián duō dà le?* (How old are you this [calendar] year? / How old are you [currently]?)

When a Chinese asks someone older than 60 his or her age, different language is used to indicate respect: *Nín (jīnnián) duō dà suìshu le? Wǒ qīshíwǔ le.*

Nín jīnnián duō dà suìshu le?

Wǒ qīshíwǔ (le).

2.11 *Watch and listen to the video segment. What is the appropriate way to ask this person his age, from what you gathered in the segment? Check one.*

☐ a. Nǐ duō dà le?

　　你多大了？

☐ b. Nín duō dà suìshu le?

　　您多大歲數了？／您多大岁数了？

☐ c. Nǐ jǐ suì le?

　　你幾歲了？／你几岁了？

2.12 *Mingling: Your teacher will hand you an image of a person. Tape this image to your chest; you now "are" this person. Move around the classroom and ask each of your classmates his or her age. Remember to be appropriately deferential to seniors.*

Grammar Bits 语法点滴

Changing things up with *le*

You may have noticed the use of the particle *le* in some of the sentences in this Encounter. *(Nǐ jīnnián duō dà **le**?)* Using *le* indicates a newly arising situation, or a change in the current state of affairs. Change is easily seen with respect to age, since our age is constantly changing over time. Therefore, a literal translation of *Nǐ jīnnián duō dà le?* might be "How old have you **gotten to be**?" or "How old are you **now**?" After the response to such a question is given, a Chinese person will often use *le* to confirm the response, as a form of endearment for a child or respect for an elder, but leave it off for someone close in age. Thus: *Ò, nǐ jiǔ suì le!* (Wow, you're 9 already; [you grew so fast!]) or *Nín jiǔshí le!* (You're 90! [Congratulations!]), but *Ò, nǐ èrshí suì* (Oh, you're 20).

Another example of a change in the current state of affairs was practiced in Unit 1. After the teacher explains a point and asks if you understand, you can reply with *Wǒ dǒng le* (I understand *now* [I didn't before]). We will discover that *le* has many uses, and you'll learn more about them in future lessons.

Encounter 2   Finding out someone's age and stating your own—Chinese style

2.13 *Getting ready:* *Have you heard about the Chinese zodiac? Each year in the zodiacal cycle is marked by a "birth sign" (*shēngxiào*) which is symbolized by one of twelve animals. The twelve signs complete a continually recurring cycle of twelve years. Can you name any Chinese zodiac signs? Close your book and write down as many as you can on a separate sheet of paper.*

 2.14 *Watch and listen to the video. Number the images below in the order in which you hear the speakers name them.*

Shí'èr shēngxiào

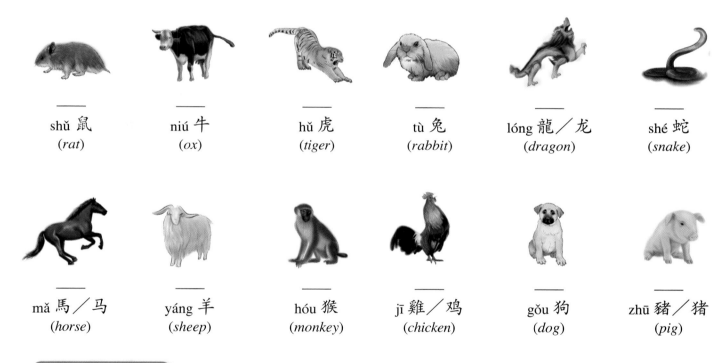

shǔ 鼠 (rat)	niú 牛 (ox)	hǔ 虎 (tiger)	tù 兔 (rabbit)	lóng 龍／龙 (dragon)	shé 蛇 (snake)
mǎ 馬／马 (horse)	yáng 羊 (sheep)	hóu 猴 (monkey)	jī 雞／鸡 (chicken)	gǒu 狗 (dog)	zhū 豬／猪 (pig)

FYI 供你参考

The Chinese zodiac

In the Chinese zodiac, the year of your birth links you to your birth sign, and you symbolically take on the characteristics of the associated animal. If you're an ox, for example, you're hard-working, loyal, warm, and sincere. In addition to its astrological uses, the Chinese zodiac has a perhaps more practical application: one can guess the year a person was born if one knows the person's birth sign. See the chart on the next page for your sign. It's interesting to note that the English word "zodiac" is derived from the Greek "zodiakos kyklos" and means, curiously enough, "circle of animals."

FYI 供你参考

What's your sign?

If you were born in January or early February, this chart may not be accurate for you, since the lunar New Year, on which the Chinese zodiac is based, does not begin until late January or February. Go to chinesezodiac.com to determine your accurate birth sign and for more information about the lore of the Chinese zodiac.

2.15 *What do you think the following question means? Write the English.*

Nǐ shǔ shénme? 你屬什麼？／你属什么？

_____

Consult the chart below and fill in the blank with your birth sign.

Wǒ shǔ ____shǔ____. 我屬／我属 _____。

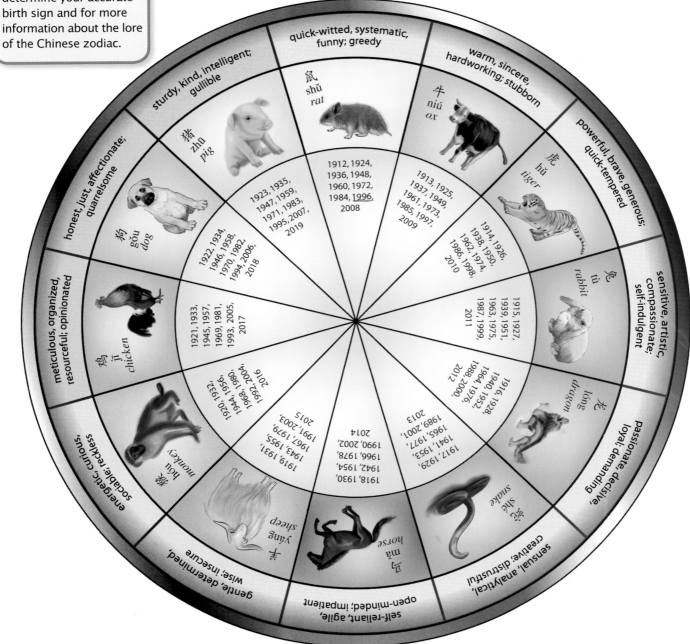

2.16 *Mingling: Walk around the room and find out your classmates' signs. Consult the chart and, using their answers, try to figure out whether they are the same age as, older than, or younger than you.*

2.17 *Homework: Outside of class, determine the birth signs of three people. Draw a picture or bring a photograph of each person, and note approximately how old each one is (for example, "in her 40s"). Use this information to report your findings to the class.*

Encounter 3 Finding out someone's birth date and stating your own

▶ Months of the year

2.18 *If January is* yīyuè *or* 一月*, write the names of the remaining eleven months in either pinyin or characters (or both) in the blanks below.*

February _____

March _____

April _____

May _____

June _____

July _____

August _____

September _____

October _____

November _____

December _____

2.19 *Pair work: With a partner, take turns saying each month of the year. After you go through the sequence once, repeat so you each have an opportunity to say every month. Repeat this process until you are both comfortable with the sequence. Finally, test each other on the Chinese names of the months by dictating random months for your partner to translate.*

▶ **Days of the month**

2.20 *If January 1 is* yīyuè yīhào *or* 一月一號／一月一号, *write the following dates in either pinyin or characters (or both) in the blanks below.*

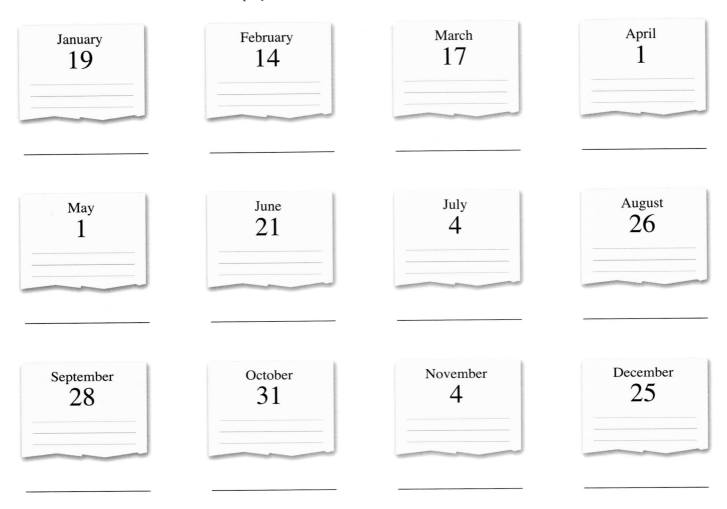

January
19

February
14

March
17

April
1

May
1

June
21

July
4

August
26

September
28

October
31

November
4

December
25

2.21 *Pair work:* With a partner, take turns saying a date in Chinese. Respond to your partner by saying the date in English.

 2.22 *Watch and listen to the video segment. Write each person's birth date in either pinyin or characters (or both) below.*

Táng Yuǎn: _____   Lynn: _____

FYI 供你参考

The Chinese calendar

For at least 4,000 years, China followed what is called a lunisolar calendar, with months determined by the phases of the moon (there are 30 days a month, from new moon on the first of the lunar month to full moon on the fifteenth and back) and "leap months" added to synchronize with the movement of the sun. On October 10, 1929, China adopted the Western (solar) calendar for official business, but informally still noted the passage of time through the traditional calendar. Chinese New Year is generally the second new moon (on very rare occasions, the third new moon) after the winter solstice; it usually falls between January 21 and February 20 in any given year and is celebrated for a full month.

 2.23 *Watch and listen to the video for exercise 2.22 again. How do you ask about the specific day of someone's birthday? Fill in the blanks.*

Nǐ de shēngrì shì ＿＿yuè ＿＿hào?

你的生日是幾月幾號？／你的生日是几月几号？

Fill in the blanks below with the appropriate numbers to indicate your birthday.

Wǒ de shēngrì shì ＿＿yuè ＿＿hào.

我的生日是 ＿月 ＿ 號／号。

2.24 *Now write the English meanings of the items below.*

shēngrì　生日　＿＿＿＿＿＿＿＿＿

jǐ 幾／几 ＿＿＿＿＿＿＿＿＿

2.25 **Mingling:** *Walk around and find out your classmates' birthdays. Then arrange yourselves in a line, organized chronologically by birthday (the student with the earliest birthday should stand at the front of the line). Once everyone has found his or her appropriate place in line, you each state your birthday, beginning with the first student in line.*

FYI 供你参考

Talking about dates

When talking about dates, the word *hào* 號 / 号 is most commonly used, as in *bāyuè wǔ hào. Bāyuè wǔ rì* is also used in speech, although it is more formal and less common. *Rì* 日 means "sun" and, by extension, "day." So, *shēng* + *rì* (birth + day) ⇒ "birthday."

2.26 *Watch and listen to the video segment. Then fill in the blanks below.*

a. What are the two numbers you hear in this exchange? _____ and _____

b. What do you think *nián* 年 means? _____

c. What do you think the following means? Write the English.

Nǐ shì něi nián shēng de? 你是哪年生的？ _____

d. Fill in the blanks with your own year of birth.

Wǒ shì _____ nián shēng de. 我是_____年生的。

Grammar Bits 语法点滴

The *shì . . . de* construction

When an event has already happened and the interest is in the specifics (when, why, where, how, etc.) of the event, Chinese uses the *shì . . . de* construction to zero in on the specifics.

The pattern is: Subject + *shì* + specific information + verb + *de*.

Examples:

Nǐ **shì** něi nián shēng **de**? Wǒ **shì** yī-jiǔ-bā-jiǔ nián shēng **de**.
(In which year were you born? I was born in 1989.
⇒ *It was in 1989 that I was born.)*

Nǐ **shì** jǐ yuè jǐ hào shēng **de**? Wǒ **shì** bāyuè shíbā hào shēng **de**.
(On which day were you born? I was born on August 18.
⇒ *It was on August 18 that I was born.)*

We will learn more about the *shì . . . de* construction in future Encounters. Notice that, in Chinese, verbs do not change form; they don't conjugate to match number, gender, tense, or anything else. Verbs are constant and invariable. You will learn to indicate tense and other grammatical points primarily by adding words. Here's an example: A Chinese might answer the question "How are you feeling?" by saying *Wǒ jīntiān hěn hǎo, zuótiān bù hǎo.* Try to figure out the meaning and, in the process, learn a bit about tense in Chinese.

2.27 *Listen and write down the birth dates as you hear them.*

Elizabeth I

Year: _____

Month: _____

Day: _____

Napoleon Bonaparte

Year: _____

Month: _____

Day: _____

Ludwig van Beethoven

Year: _____

Month: _____

Day: _____

Abraham Lincoln

Year: _____

Month: _____

Day: _____

Florence Nightingale

Year: _____

Month: _____

Day: _____

Sun Yat-Sen

Year: _____

Month: _____

Day: _____

Mahatma Gandhi

Year: _____

Month: _____

Day: _____

Jackie Chan

Year: _____

Month: _____

Day: _____

Amy Tan

Year: _____

Month: _____

Day: _____

Barack Obama

Year: _____

Month: _____

Day: _____

Zhang Ziyi

Year: _____

Month: _____

Day: _____

Rihanna

Year: _____

Month: _____

Day: _____

2.28 *Mingling: Walk around, find out your classmates' dates of birth (including year), and write them on a copy of your roster. Remember, express a year by saying it "telephone style," digit by digit, just as you would say your telephone number (diànhuà hàomǎ). 1987 = yī-jiǔ-bā-qī nián.*

Nǐ shì něi nián shēng de? Shēngrì shì jǐ yuè jǐ hào?

Wǒ shì _____ nián shēng de. Shēngrì shì ____ yuè ____ hào.

Encounter 4 Finding out someone's e-mail and street address and stating your own

▶ Asking for someone's e-mail address

2.29 *Watch and listen to the video segment. Can you figure out what each of the following means? Fill in the blanks below in English.*

e-mail dìzhǐ: _____   diànyóu dìzhǐ: _____

diànzi yóuxiāng: _____

FYI 供你参考

Translation vs. transliteration

Foreign terms, products, and names are rendered into Chinese in at least two different ways. "Hot dog" combines the Chinese words for "hot" and "dog," yielding *règǒu* 熱狗／热狗. This is <u>translation</u>. In the second process, <u>transliteration</u>, "McDonald's" becomes *Màidāngláo* 麥當勞／麦当劳, which simply combines Chinese sounds similar to the sounds of the original foreign name. Transliteration is often done with little or no meaning intended in the new Chinese word. Syllables with bad connotations are, of course, avoided. Sometimes words are both translated and transliterated. For example, "e-mail" becomes *yīmèir* 伊妹兒／依妹儿 when transliterated, and *diànzǐ yóujiàn* 電子郵件／电子邮件 (electronic mail) when translated. The latter term is now commonly abbreviated as *diànyóu* 電郵／电邮. Sometimes, the English term "e-mail" is used without translation or transliteration. If you do separate Internet searches, you'll get the most hits for "e-mail 地址," followed by "電郵地址／电邮地址," and the fewest hits for "伊妹兒地址／伊妹儿地址." This indicates that the English term "e-mail" is far more commonly used by the Chinese than either the translated term *diànyóu* or the transliterated term *yīmèir*. In this age of high-tech, rapid Westernization, and the spread of English all over the world, certain terms are more commonly used in their original English form than in the Chinese equivalent term. "E-mail" is the best example.

2.30 *Fill in your own e-mail address in the blanks below.*

Q: Nǐ de diànyóu dìzhǐ shì shénme?

你的電郵地址是甚麼？／你的电邮地址是什么？

A: Wǒ de diànyóu dìzhǐ shì _____.

我的電郵地址是 _____。

我的电邮地址是 _____。

2.31 *Mingling: Using your class roster, find out the e-mail addresses of 5–10 classmates. Helpful questions to determine if what you've written is correct include* Zhè yàng duì ma? *(Is this correct?) or* Zhè yàng duì bu duì? (Is this correct or not?)

Grammar Bits 语法点滴

Take your pick: *ma* vs. *bu*

You have already learned that questions may be formed by simply adding the query particle *ma* to a statement. Another way of asking questions is to use *bu* to provide verbal alternatives—positive and negative choices—and "invite" the other person to pick one and thus answer the question. The following are different ways to ask "Is this right?":

Zhè yàng duì ma? 這樣對嗎？／这样对吗？ *(Is this right?)* OR
Zhè yàng duì bu duì? 這樣對不對？／这样对不对？ *(Is this right or not?)*

These two question forms are interchangeable. Note that the negative adverb *bu* is not stressed in this case. To answer the question, simply reply with *Duì* OR *Bú duì*.

▶ Asking for a street address

 2.32 *Watch and listen to the video segment. How do you ask where someone lives? Write the pinyin below.*

_____

FYI 供你参考

Chinese addresses

Chinese addresses, like Chinese names, move from large to small units. To write to the President of the United States, for example, the address would appear as follows, according to Chinese custom:

USA	美國／美国
Washington, D.C.	華盛頓／华盛顿
Pennsylvania Avenue, #1600	賓夕法尼亞大道1600號／宾夕法尼亚大道1600号
To: President So-and-so	某某總統收／某某总统收

2.33 *Match the corresponding terms below.*

a. *M street*   1. 123 shì 室

b. *(single) house number 123*   2. 123 hào lóu 號樓／号楼

c. *apartment building number 123*   3. 123 hào 號／号

d. *apartment number 123*   4. M jiē 街

2.34 *Watch and listen to the video segment from exercise 2.32 again. Match the columns and then number the items by the order in which Chen Feng says them.*

_____ a. Hebei Province

_____ b. Heping Avenue

_____ c. #100

_____ d. Tangshan City

1. Tángshān shì

2. Héběi shěng

3. yì bǎi hào

4. Hépíng dàjiē

2.35 *Fill in the blanks with your own address.*

Q: Nǐ jiā zhù nǎr?

你家住哪兒？ ／ 你家住哪儿？

A: (for a single-family house)

Wǒ jiā zhù _____ jiē, _____ hào.

我家住_____街，_____號／号。

(for a multiple-unit building)

Wǒ jiā zhù _____ jiē, _____ hào lóu, _____ shì.

我家住_____街，_____號樓／号楼，_____室。

2.36 *Pair work: Exchange addresses with one or more classmates, using the question and answer formula above.*

Encounter 5 Identifying a third party's relationship to yourself

2.37 *Watch and listen to the video segment. What does* tóngxué *mean?*

☐ teacher   ☐ classmate

2.38 *Watch and listen to the video segment. Then complete each of the following sentences.*

a. The woman in pink is introducing Miss Wang, who is her . . .   ☐ good friend.   ☐ colleague.

b. Twice, the woman in the hat introduces Rongzhen, who is her . . .   ☐ good friend.   ☐ colleague.

c. Chen Feng introduces Wang Li, who is his . . .   ☐ good friend.   ☐ colleague.

2.39 *Watch and listen to the video segment. Then match the corresponding items below.*

a. *relative*   1. línjū 鄰居   A. 亲戚
b. *neighbor*   2. qīnqi 親戚   B. 邻居

 2.40 *Watch and listen to the video segment. Then match the corresponding items below.*

a. *professor* ——— 1. jiàoshòu 教授   A. 学生
b. *teacher*   2. tóngxué 同學   B. 教授
c. *student*   3. lǎoshī 老師   C. 老师
d. *classmate*   4. xuéshēng 學生   D. 同学

Grammar Bits 语法点滴

"This," "that," and some other things

Zhè (this) and *nà* (that) are called "specifiers" (SP) in Chinese. Both are used as subjects in expressions. For example: *Zhè kāfēi hěn hǎo* (This is great coffee). When followed by a measure word, *zhè* and *nà* usually appear as *zhèi* and *nèi*. For example: *Zhèi ge xuéshēng* (This [measure word] student). Measures (also called classifiers) are used to indicate or count people and things. Specific nouns usually require specific measures. For example, *wèi* is used as a polite measure to show respect for persons. Measures are always used when a noun is accompanied by a number; for example: *Nèi sān wèi lǎoshī* (Those three teachers). As you learn more nouns, you will also learn their appropriate measure words.

 2.41 *Watch and listen to the video. What do you think* Zhèi wèi shì nǐ de shénme rén *means? Write the English.*

_____

Note: The above question in its full form, as seen here, may be considered too blunt and direct. It is often shortened to simply Zhèi wèi shì . . . ? *(And this is . . . ?).*

2.42 *Mingling: Draw a simple sketch of three people you know. Walk among your classmates, sharing your pictures and looking at theirs. Ask your classmates to identify the people in their pictures, and respond to their questions in return. Use the dialogue below.*

Q: Zhèi wèi shì (nǐ de shénme rén)?
　　這位是（你的甚麽人）？／这位是（你的什么人）？

A: Zhèi wèi shì wǒ de _____. Tā jiào _____.
　　這／这位是我的 _____。他叫 _____。

> qīnqi 親戚／亲戚; péngyou 朋友; tóngxué 同學／同学; tóngshì 同事;
> lǎoshī 老師／老师; xuéshēng 學生／学生; línjū 鄰居／邻居

♫ Unit Rap

Go to the **Encounters** *website at www.EncountersChinese.com and listen to the song to review key expressions from Unit 2. Listen again and sing along!*

Encounter 6 | Reading and writing

▶ Reading familiar sentences in Chinese characters

2.43 *Pair work: Read the following dialogues (written in traditional characters) aloud with a partner, using the English as a guide. Note: In Chinese texts, numbers are almost always written in Arabic numerals, both for convenience and space-saving. However, be sure to "pronounce" them in Chinese. It's good practice. Exception: Read the e-mail address as you would normally.*

> **FYI 供你参考**
>
> **Listing things in Chinese fashion**
>
> The ancient Chinese (about 4,000 years ago) began a system with ten "Celestial Stems" (天干 *tiāngān*) and 12 "Earthly Branches" (地支 *dìzhī*) to enumerate dates in cycles of 60 years. The 天干地支 system continues to this day. "Celestial Stems" consist of the following characters:
>
> 甲 *jiǎ*, 乙 *yǐ*, 丙 *bǐng*, 丁 *dīng*, 戊 *wù*, 己 *jǐ*, 庚 *gēng*, 辛 *xīn*, 壬 *rén*, 癸 *guǐ*
>
> These characters are commonly used as a numbering system in modern China, Japan, Korea, and Vietnam, much as Roman numerals (I, II, III) or letters of the alphabet (A, B, C) are used in the West. 甲 and 乙 represent "A" and "B" in this unit's dialogues.

1 甲：你幾歲了？ *(How old are you?)*
乙：我八歲了。 *(I'm eight.)*
甲：他呢？ *(How about him?)*
乙：他兩歲，很小。 *(He's two; he's little.)*

2 甲：你多大了？ *(How old are you?)*
乙：我二十八了。 *(I'm 28.)*

3 甲：您多大歲數了？ *(How old are you?)*
乙：我七十五了。 *(I'm 75.)*

4 甲：你屬甚麼？ *(What's your sign?)*

乙：我屬＿＿＿＿。　*(I'm a ＿＿＿＿.)*

> 鼠 *(rat)*; 牛 *(ox)*; 虎 *(tiger)*; 兔 *(rabbit)*; 龍 *(dragon)*; 蛇 *(snake)*;
> 馬 *(horse)*; 羊 *(sheep)*; 猴 *(monkey)*; 雞 *(chicken)*; 狗 *(dog)*; 豬 *(pig)*

5 甲：你是哪年生的？你的生日是幾月幾號？
　　　　(Which year were you born in? When is your birthday?)

乙：我是１９７８年生的，我的生日是一月一號。
　　　(I was born in 1978; my birthday is January 1.)

6 甲：你的 e-mail 地址是甚麼？ *(What is your e-mail address?)*

乙：我的 e-mail 地址是 123abc@EncountersChinese.com.
　　　(My e-mail address is 123abc@EncountersChinese.com.)

7 甲：你家住哪兒？ *(Where do you live?)*

乙：我家住南京路１２３號。　*(I live at 123 Nanjing Road.)*

8 甲：這位是你的甚麼人？ *(What is this person's relationship to you?)*

乙：那是我的＿＿＿＿。　*(That's my ＿＿＿＿.)*

> 親戚 *(relative)*; 朋友 *(friend)*; 同學 *(classmate)*; 同事 *(colleague)*;
> 老師 *(teacher)*; 學生 *(student)*; 鄰居 *(neighbor)*

2.44 Pair work: *Read the dialogues aloud with a partner, this time without any English.*

1 甲：你幾歲了？

乙：我八歲了。

甲：他呢？

乙：他兩歲，很小。

2 甲：你多大了？

乙：我二十八了。

3 甲：您多大歲數了？

乙：我七十五了。

4 甲：你屬甚麼？

乙：我屬＿＿＿＿。

鼠，牛，虎，兔，龍，蛇，馬，羊，猴，雞，狗，豬

5 甲：你是哪年生的？你的生日是幾月幾號？

乙：我是１９７８年生的，我的生日是一月一號。

6 甲：你的 e-mail 地址是甚麼？

乙：我的 e-mail 地址是 123abc@EncountersChinese.com.

7 甲：你家住哪兒？

乙：我家住南京路１２３號。

8 甲：這位是你的甚麼人？

乙：那是我的＿＿＿＿。

親戚，朋友，同學，同事，老師，學生，鄰居

2.45 *Pair work:* *Read the dialogues aloud one more time, this time with simplified characters.*

1 甲：你几岁了？

乙：我八岁了。

甲：他呢？

乙：他两岁，很小。

2 甲：你多大了？

乙：我二十八了。

3 甲：您多大岁数了？

乙：我七十五了。

4 甲：你属什么？

乙：我属＿＿＿。

> 鼠，牛，虎，兔，龙，蛇，马，羊，猴，鸡，狗，猪

5 甲：你是哪年生的？你的生日是几月几号？

乙：我是１９７８年生的，我的生日是一月一号。

6 甲：你的 e-mail 地址是什么？

乙：我的 e-mail 地址是 123abc@EncountersChinese.com.

7 甲：你家住哪儿？

乙：我家住南京路１２３号。

8 甲：这位是你的什么人？

乙：那是我的＿＿＿。

> 亲戚，朋友，同学，同事，老师，学生，邻居

2.46 *Match the corresponding simplified characters, traditional characters, and English.*

a. 学生	1. 屬馬	A. *what day (of the month)*
b. 亲戚	2. 哪兒	B. *how old (of age)*
c. 什么	3. 鄰居	C. *classmate*
d. 几岁	4. 同學	D. *relative*
e. 同学	5. 學生	E. *age*
f. 老师	6. 歲數	F. *neighbor*
g. 岁数	7. 甚麼	G. *what*
h. 属马	8. 幾號	H. *where*
i. 邻居	9. 親戚	I. *teacher*
j. 哪儿	10. 老師	J. *student*
k. 几号	11. 幾歲	K. *be born in the Year of the Horse*

▶ Reading real-life texts

2.47 *Look at the business card and answer the following questions.*

北京外国语大学

中国语言文学学院

丁安琪

副教授

院长助理

汉语培训中心主任

地址：北京市海淀区西三环北路2号

邮编：100089

电话：(010) 88816442

传真：(010) 88818140

电子信箱：dinganqi@bfsu.edu.cn

a. Please circle and number the following.

    i. Name (Underline the last name.)

    ii. The term for "telephone"

    iii. The term for "e-mail"

b. The address is 中国 ⇒ 北京 ⇒ 西三环北路 ⇒ 二号

   Number the following items to match the Chinese sequencing.

   ___ Beijing

   ___ China

   ___ #2

   ___ West Third Ring North Road

c. What do you think the number 88818140 is? Circle one:

   fax number   home telephone number

d. Which form of Chinese characters is used? Circle one:

   simplified   traditional

2.48 *Look at the business card and answer the following questions.*

台灣華語文教學學會
Association of Teaching Chinese as a Second Language

理事長 | 信世昌 博士
國立台灣師範大學華語文教學研究所 教授

網站 | http://www.atcsl.org
電話 | 02-2341-9812 分機10   電子信箱 | hsins@ntnu.edu.tw
傳真 | 02-2341-9746   地址 | 台北市和平東路一段162號 師大華研所

a. Please circle and number the following.

　i. Name (Underline the last name.)
　ii. The term for "telephone"
　iii. The term for "fax"
　iv. The term for "e-mail address"
　v. The term for "street address"

b. The address is 台北市 ⇒ 和平東路 ⇒ 一段 ⇒ 162 號

　Number the following items to match the Chinese sequencing.

　＿＿ Heping (Peace) Road East

　＿＿ #162

　＿＿ Section 1

　＿＿ Taipei City

c. Which form of Chinese characters is used? Circle one:

　simplified   traditional

2.49 *Look at the newspaper banner and answer the following questions.*

a. Please circle and number the following:

   i. Date in English

   ii. Date in Chinese

b. Can you find and label the character for "sun"? Here, it means "day," as in "daily newspaper."

c. Can you find and label the character for "moon"? It's in an ad for moon cakes— a traditional Chinese dessert for the mid-Autumn Festival.

d. Can you find the lunar calendar date? It's different from the Western calendar date.

   Write the date in English: _____

e. Which form of Chinese characters is used? Circle one:

   simplified   traditional

2.50 *Look at the newspaper banner and answer the following questions.*

a. Please circle and number the following:

   i. Date in Chinese

   ii. Day of the week

b. What is the day of the week? Write in English: _____

c. There is an ad for an insurance company. Please circle and number the following:

   i. The address in New York

   ii. The address in China

d. Which form of Chinese characters is used? Circle one:

simplified   traditional

▶ Learning to write characters

2.51 *For stroke order and other useful information about each of the following characters from this unit, go to the* Character Writing Text. *Choose traditional or simplified characters and practice writing them until you can reproduce them on demand.*

您，多，大，小，幾／几，歲／岁，了，的，地，址
年，月，日，號／号，生，那，哪，兒／儿，這／这，位

▶ Writing a note

2.52 *Write a brief self-introduction in your choice of traditional or simplified Chinese characters. Include information about your name, age, birth date, e-mail address, street address, and the name of your teacher.*

Cultural Bits 文化点滴

Self-introduction

View the video segment "Self-introduction" and then discuss the following questions with your classmates.

- What might you want to tell a new informal Chinese acquaintance about yourself upon meeting him or her for the first time?
- What are the benefits of being "overly polite"?
- What is the role of the "social title"?
- Why do Chinese people ask each other *Nǐ shǔ shénme?* How many of the twelve animals can you name? Do you know yours?

Recap

▶ Grammar

Sentence-ending particle *le*

Use *le* at the end of a sentence to show that a change of state has occurred.

> Wǒ yǐqián bù dǒng, xiànzài dǒng le. *(I didn't understand before, [but] now I do.)*

Specifiers

Use specifiers with appropriate numbers and nouns to specify a particular thing.

> Zhè kāfēi hěn hǎo. *(This [kind of] coffee is very good.)*
> zhèi wèi lǎoshī *(this teacher)*
> nèi wèi lǎoshī *(that teacher)*
> nèi sān wèi lǎoshī *(those three teachers)*

Formulating questions

Add *ma* to the end of a statement to ask a "yes/no" question. A *ma* question is usually answered by repeating the verb either affirmatively or negatively.

> Tā hǎo ma? Tā hěn hǎo. Tā bù hǎo. *(How is he/she? He/She is well. He/She is not well.)*

Add *ne* to inquire about a topic already mentioned. This has the general meaning of asking "And what about X?"

> Wǒ jiào Chén Lǐrén. Qǐng wèn, nín ne? *(My name is Chen Liren. And yours?)*

Use unstressed *bu* to pose positive and negative alternatives and to have the listener choose between them.

> Tā hǎo bu hǎo? Bù hǎo. *(Is he/she well? [He/She is] not well.)*

The *shì . . . de* construction

Use the *shì . . . de* construction to zero in on an aspect of a past event.

> Wǒ shì yī-jiǔ-líng-líng nián shēng de. *(I was born in 1900.)*
> Wǒ shì zuótiān lái de, bú shì jīntiān lái de. *(It was yesterday that I came, not today.)*

Time words

Words expressing specific moments in time precede the verb and usually follow the subject of a sentence.

> Wǒ zuótiān bù hǎo. Jīntiān hǎo le. *(I wasn't well yesterday. Today I'm better.)*

▶ Vocabulary

Chinese zodiac

gǒu 狗 dog
hóu 猴 monkey
hǔ 虎 tiger
jī 雞／鸡 chicken/rooster
lóng 龍／龙 dragon
mǎ 馬／马 horse
niú 牛 ox
shé 蛇 snake
shǔ 鼠 rat/mouse
tù 兔 rabbit
yáng 羊 sheep/ram
zhū 豬／猪 pig/boar

Nouns

diànyóu 電郵／电邮 e-mail
dìzhǐ 地址 address, location
hào 號／号 number in a series
hàomǎ 號碼／号码 number
(as in: telephone number, room number, etc.)
jiā 家 home
jiē 街 street
lóu 樓／楼 (storied) building
shēngrì 生日 birthday
shì 室 room (as in: apartment unit)
shí'èr shēngxiào 十二生肖 twelve animals of the Chinese zodiac
suìshu 歲數／岁数 age, years of age

Common verbs

děngyú 等於／等于 be equal to
duì 對／对 be correct, be right
jiā 加 add
jiǎn 減／减 subtract
shēng 生 give birth to, bear
shǔ 屬／属 belong (to one of the 12 zodiac signs)
zhù 住 live, reside, stay

Measure word

wèi 位 [used for people of rank or status]

People

jiàoshòu 教授 professor
lǎoshī 老師／老师 teacher
línjū 鄰居／邻居 neighbor
péngyou 朋友 friend
qīnqi 親戚／亲戚 relative
tóngshì 同事 colleague, fellow worker
tóngxué 同學／同学 classmate
xuéshēng 學生／学生 student

Pronouns

nà 那 that
nèi 那 that
zhè 這／这 this
zhèi 這／这 this

Question words and associated vocabulary

dà 大 old (in age)
duō 多 how, to what extent
jǐ 幾／几 how many
něi 哪 which
suì 歲／岁 year (of age)
yàng 樣／样 kind, type, shape

Time words

jīnnián 今年 this year
nián 年 year (of time)
yuè 月 month
  Yīyuè 一月 January
  Èryuè 二月 February
  Sānyuè 三月 March
  Sìyuè 四月 April
  Wǔyuè 五月 May
  Liùyuè 六月 June
  Qīyuè 七月 July
  Bāyuè 八月 August
  Jiǔyuè 九月 September
  Shíyuè 十月 October
  Shíyīyuè 十一月 November
  Shí'èryuè 十二月 December

Numbers (11–100)

shíyī 十一 11
shí'èr 十二 12
. . .
èrshí 二十 20
èrshíyī 二十一 21
. . .
yìbǎi 一百 100

▶ Checklist of "can do" statements

After completing this unit, you should be able to perform each of the following tasks:

Listening and speaking

- ☐ Understand and say numbers from 1 to 100.
- ☐ Understand statements from others about age.
- ☐ In a culturally appropriate manner, ask a variety of persons about their age.
- ☐ Ask others about their birth sign and provide your own.
- ☐ Ask others about their birth date and provide your own.
- ☐ Understand when others say their birth year and state your own.
- ☐ Find out someone's e-mail address and provide your own.
- ☐ Find out someone's street address and provide your own.
- ☐ Specify someone's relationship to you and ask others about their relationship to a third party.

Reading and writing

- ☐ Write a brief description of yourself, providing your full name, age, birth date, e-mail address, street address, and the name of your teacher.
- ☐ Recognize printed dates.
- ☐ Understand key information on a name card.

Understanding culture

- ☐ Name four common Chinese surnames, one for each of the four tones.
- ☐ Make an accurate statement about differences in the way Westerners and Chinese count birthdays.
- ☐ Say under which "animal sign" you were born and state which personal characteristics are related to your sign.

"Don't leave before I arrive"

不見不散

Bújiànbúsàn

Making an appointment

In this unit, you will learn how to:

- ask for and say the time of day and days of the week.
- express relative time, using divisions of the day.
- find out someone's availability in terms of date and time, and state your own.
- decide on a meeting time.
- read dates and times on calendars and schedules.

- read simple written or printed messages regarding availability and appointments.
- write a simple question asking about someone's availability.
- write a simple statement confirming an appointment.

Encounter 1 Telling time

3.1 *View Episode 3 of the dramatic series.*

3.2 *Getting ready:* How would you ask for the time in English? If someone asked you the time, how would you say it was 2:20?

_____

3.3 *Watch and listen to the video segment. What do you think* Xiànzài jǐ diǎn zhōng *means? Write the English below.*

_____

3.4 *How would you say what time it is? Fill in the blanks below with pinyin and characters.*

five o'clock	= _____ diǎn zhōng	_____ 點鐘／点钟
six o'clock	= _____ diǎn zhōng	_____ 點鐘／点钟
seven o'clock	= _____ diǎn zhōng	_____ 點鐘／点钟
eight o'clock	= _____ _____ _____	_____ 點鐘／点钟
nine o'clock	= _____ _____ _____	_____ 點鐘／点钟
ten o'clock	= _____ _____ _____	_____ 點鐘／点钟

FYI 供你参考

Two words for "two"

Chinese has two words for "two." You've already learned *èr*, which is used when counting, for example. However, when stating the time "on the hour," one says *liǎng diǎn (zhōng)* for "two o'clock," not *èr diǎn zhōng*. Clock time is said with a combination of numbers and measure words. You already know the numbers. Measure words, as noted in Unit 1, are used with numbers and nouns to count everything from time to teaspoons. Most nouns have their own particular measure word. Whenever two of anything are counted or numbered with a measure word (two books, two people, etc.), *liǎng* is used to express "two."

liǎng diǎn zhōng *(two o'clock)*
liǎng běn shū *(two books)*
liǎng ge rén *(two people)*

 3.5 *Listen to the audio segment. Using a classroom clock (a clock face with moveable hands) or your fingers, indicate the time that each person is saying.*

3.6 *Pair work: With a partner, take turns asking for and telling the time, using your clock as a visual aid.*

Xiànzài jǐ diǎn zhōng?

Wǔ diǎn zhōng.

 3.7 *Watch and listen to the video segment. What is an alternate way of saying* Xiànzài jǐ diǎn zhōng? 現在幾點鐘？／现在几点钟？ *Fill in the blank below.*

Jǐ diǎn _____? 幾點了？／几点了？

3.8 *Match the corresponding times below.*

5:27	a. Wǔ diǎn shíwǔ fēn	1. 五點四十五分／五点四十五分
5:15	b. Wǔ diǎn sìshíwǔ fēn	2. 五點三十分／五点三十分
5:45	c. Wǔ diǎn sānshí fēn	3. 五點十五分／五点十五分
5:30	d. Wǔ diǎn èrshíqī fēn	4. 五點二十七分／五点二十七分

What does fēn 分 *mean? Write the English equivalent:* _____

3.9 *Listen to the audio segment. Using a classroom clock, indicate the time each person is saying.*

3.10 *Match the times with the pinyin terms in columns two and three, and the corresponding characters in column four.*

3:45	a. liù diǎn sānshí	1. yì diǎn yí kè	A. 兩點半／两点半
5:15	b. liǎng diǎn sānshí	2. liǎng diǎn bàn	B. 七點三刻／七点三刻
1:15	c. wǔ diǎn shíwǔ	3. sān diǎn sān kè	C. 六點半／六点半
6:30	d. yì diǎn shíwǔ	4. wǔ diǎn yí kè	D. 三點三刻／三点三刻
7:45	e. qī diǎn sìshíwǔ	5. liù diǎn bàn	E. 一點一刻／一点一刻
2:30	f. sān diǎn sìshíwǔ	6. qī diǎn sān kè	F. 五點一刻／五点一刻

What does bàn 半 *mean, in this context?*   *Circle one:*   *half past   quarter past*

What does yí kè 一刻 *mean?*   *Circle one:*   *half past   quarter past*

3.11 *Pair work: Work with a partner. Using the classroom clock as a visual aid, take turns asking for and telling the time. Practice saying the time in alternate ways, when possible.*

FYI 供你参考

Time measure words

The following measure words are relevant to telling time:

> **diǎn:** counts hours—*liǎng diǎn (zhōng)* (two o'clock)
> **fēn:** counts minutes—*yì fēn (zhōng)* (one minute); *liǎng diǎn èrshí fēn* (two twenty, twenty after two)
> **miǎo:** counts seconds—*yì miǎo (zhōng)* (one second)

The questions *Xiànzài jǐ diǎn zhōng?* and *Jǐ diǎn le?* literally mean "What time is it on the hour?" However, note that the expected answer to both is an exact time, including the hour and minute. Therefore, *Xiànzài jǐ diǎn zhōng?* can be answered with *Wǔ diǎn shí fēn.*

3.12 *Watch and listen to the video segment. Fill in the following blanks with the correct equivalent of each time.*

10:53 = shí diǎn wǔshísān fēn = chà _____ fēn shíyī diǎn

10:55 = shí diǎn wǔshíwǔ fēn = chà _____ fēn shíyī diǎn

10:58 = shí diǎn wǔshíbā fēn = chà _____ fēn shíyī diǎn

11:03 = shíyī diǎn líng sān fēn = shíyī diǎn guò _____ fēn

11:08 = shíyī diǎn líng bā fēn = shíyī diǎn guò _____ fēn

FYI 供你参考

Alternate ways of telling time

You may have noticed that there are many ways of saying the same time. In English, 5:05 can be "five past five," "five oh five," or "five minutes past five o'clock." Similarly, in Chinese, there are alternate ways of saying the times between ten minutes before and ten minutes after the hour. In the previous exercise, you saw that *shí diǎn wǔshísān fēn* and *chà qī fēn shíyī diǎn* are both equally acceptable ways of saying 10:53. Furthermore, it would also be acceptable to say *shíyī diǎn chà qī fēn*.

For up to ten minutes after the hour, you can use the terms *líng* (zero) and *guò* (past) interchangeably, as you also saw in the previous exercise.

Finally, you may also have noted that when the words *zhōng* (o'clock) or *fēn* (minute) appear in the final position, they may be omitted. Thus:

yì diǎn zhōng = yì diǎn

liǎng diǎn èrshí fēn = liǎng diǎn èrshí

3.13 *Listen to the audio segment. Using a classroom clock, indicate the time each person is saying.*

3.14 *Pair work: Work with a partner. Using the classroom clock as a visual aid, take turns asking for and saying any time between ten minutes before and ten minutes after the hour. Use* chà *(either before or after the hour) and* guò *or* líng.

3.15 *Group work: Work in a group. Pick any time (at random) within a 12-hour period. Ask your classmates about the times they have chosen and then line up in chronological order, beginning with 1:00. If more than one person picks exactly the same time, they should stand together and act as one person. Once the line has been formed, report your time (as the old "time callers" did in past centuries) loudly and clearly:* Xiànzài ____ diǎn ____ fēn! *If anyone is out of place, work as a group to correct the error, and then begin reporting again from the beginning. Continue until everyone has reported his or her time in order with no errors.*

> **FYI 供你参考**
>
> **Lining up units of time**
>
> Units of time in a series are expressed in the same way as many elements of Chinese grammar: largest to smallest. This is opposite of typical English conventions. Example:
>
> *Xiǎo wáwa chūshēng zài èr-líng-líng-jiǔ nián, shíyīyuè shísān hào, shí'èr diǎn èrshí fēn.*
> (The baby was born at 12:20 P.M., on November 13, 2009.)

▶ Reading practice

3.16 *Pair work:* *With a partner, take turns reading the following questions and answers aloud, with the help of the English. Then change roles.*

甲：現在幾點鐘？／现在几点钟？ *(What time is it?)*
乙：兩點鐘。／两点钟。 *(Two o'clock.)*

甲：現在幾點了？／现在几点了？ *(What time is it now?)*
乙：兩點半。／两点半。 *(Half past two.)*

甲：現在幾點了？／现在几点了？ *(What time is it now?)*
乙：兩點三刻。／两点三刻。 *(Two forty-five.)*

甲：現在幾點鐘？／现在几点钟？ *(What time is it?)*
乙：三點差十分。／三点差十分。 *(Ten to three.)*

甲：幾點了？／几点了？ *(What time is it now?)*
乙：三點過十分。／三点过十分。 *(Ten past three.)*

甲：現在幾點了？／现在几点了？ *(What time is it now?)*
乙：你去買個錶不行嗎？？？／你去买个表不行吗？？？

Nǐ qù mǎi ge biǎo bù xíng ma??? (Can't you go buy a watch???)

Encounter 2 Divisions of the day and relative time

 3.17 *Watch and listen to the video segment. Look at the following timeline. Can you tell what the conversation was about? Circle three terms you heard.*

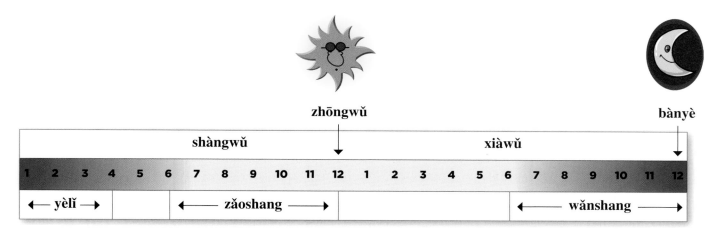

zhōngwǔ   bànyè

shàngwǔ   xiàwǔ

| 1 | 2 | 3 | 4 | 5 | 6 | 7 | 8 | 9 | 10 | 11 | 12 | 1 | 2 | 3 | 4 | 5 | 6 | 7 | 8 | 9 | 10 | 11 | 12 |

← yèlǐ →   ← zǎoshang →   ← wǎnshang →

3.18 *Match the pinyin with the corresponding English.*

a. Nǐ nàr xiànzài jǐ diǎn zhōng?   1. *A.M. or P.M.?*

b. Qī diǎn zhōng.   2. *P.M.*

c. Shì shàngwǔ háishi xiàwǔ?   3. *What time is it there now?*

d. Xiàwǔ.   4. *It's seven in the evening here.*

e. Wǒmen zhèr shì wǎnshang qī diǎn zhōng.   5. *Seven o'clock.*

Grammar Bits 语法点滴

Stating alternatives with *háishi*

You've already learned that one way to ask a question in Chinese is to pose affirmative and negative alternatives with *bu*: *Nǐ hǎo bu hǎo?* Another way is to mark the alternatives more explicitly with *háishi* in the pattern *Shì X háishi Y?* (Is it X or Y?) X and Y can be simple nouns or other expressions. Examples:

Shì shàngwǔ háishi xiàwǔ? *(Is [that] A.M. or P.M.?)*

Nǐ dà háishi tā dà? *(Are you older or is he/she older?)*

3.19 *Match the pinyin with the corresponding English.*

a. zǎoshang	1. *before noon, A.M.*
b. shàngwǔ	2. *afternoon, P.M.*
c. zhōngwǔ	3. *morning*
d. xiàwǔ	4. *at night, in the middle of the night*
e. wǎnshang	5. *midnight*
f. bànyè	6. *noon*

3.20 *Mingling: Fill in the blanks below with a time of your choice.*

Q: Nǐ nàr xiànzài jǐ diǎn zhōng?

A: Wǒmen zhèr shì _____ _____.

         (DIVISION)   (HOUR)

Now walk around the room asking and answering the above question. Line up according to the answers, from earliest to latest.

3.21 *Look at the timeline below. Match the characters with the corresponding pinyin.*

a. zǎoshang	1. 上午
b. shàngwǔ	2. 下午
c. zhōngwǔ	3. 早上
d. xiàwǔ	4. 夜裡／夜里
e. wǎnshang	5. 半夜
f. bànyè	6. 中午
g. yèlǐ	7. 晚上

▶ Reading practice

3.22 Pair work: *With a partner, take turns reading the following questions and answers aloud, using the English as a guide. Then change roles.*

甲: 你那兒現在幾點鐘？／你那儿现在几点钟？
　　(What time is it there now?)

乙: 七點鐘。／七点钟。 *(Seven o'clock.)*

甲: 是上午還是下午？／是上午还是下午？ *(A.M. or P.M.?)*

乙: 下午。我們這兒是晚上七點鐘。／下午。我们这儿是晚上七点钟。 *(P.M. It's seven in the evening here.)*

Encounter 3   Days of the week

3.23 *Watch and listen to the video segment. Match the corresponding pinyin, English, and characters below.*

a. Xīngqīyī ————	1. Monday	A. 星期一
b. Xīngqī'èr	2. Thursday	B. 星期三
c. Xīngqīsān	3. Saturday	C. 星期五
d. Xīngqīsì	4. Tuesday	D. 星期天
e. Xīngqīwǔ	5. Friday	E. 星期二
f. Xīngqīliù	6. Sunday	F. 星期六
g. Xīngqītiān	7. Wednesday	G. 星期四

Grammar Bits 语法点滴

Suggesting with *ba*

The sentence-ending particle *ba* accompanies suggestions, assumptions, or suppositions (and sometimes reluctant agreement).

Hǎo, wǒmen zǒu ba! *(OK, let's go.)*
Nǐ shì Zhāng Lǎoshī ba? *(You're Professor Zhang, right?)*
Wǔ diǎn le ba? *(It's five o'clock now, right?)*
Xiànzài jiù zǒu? Hǎo ba. *(We're leaving now, already? Oo-kay.)*

3.24 *Pair work: Work with a partner. Using a calendar, take turns asking and answering questions. Follow the model below.*

甲：五月八號是星期幾？／五月八号是星期几？

乙：五月八號是星期_____。／五月八号是星期_____。

Repeat the exchange five or six times each, until you both feel comfortable with the material.

3.25 *Mingling: Look at a calendar and see what day of the week your birthday is this year. Then walk around the class asking and answering the following question.*

你的生日是星期幾？／你的生日是星期几？

3.26 週／周 Zhōu *is a formal term meaning "week" and* 末 mò *means "end." Knowing this, can you fill in the blanks below with the correct characters?*

週末／周末 zhōumò = 星期_____ 和 hé *(and)* 星期_____

Recall that 日 *means "sun." What do you think* 週日／周日 *means? Circle one of the following:* 星期一　星期天

3.27 *As you know, "week" in Chinese is* 星期 xīngqī. *A term that is interchangeable with* 星期 *is* 禮拜／礼拜 lǐbài. *A third, more formal (written) term for "week" is* 週／周, *as you learned in the previous exercise.* 天 *and* 日 *are interchangeable when used with* 星期 *and* 禮拜／礼拜, *but you can only use* 日 *with* 週／周. *Keeping all this in mind, please match the terms below.*

a. 星期一	1. 禮拜三／礼拜三	A. 週二／周二
b. 星期二	2. 禮拜五／礼拜五	B. 週四／周四
c. 星期三	3. 禮拜二／礼拜二	C. 週六／周六
d. 星期四	4. 禮拜天（日）／礼拜天（日）	D. 週三／周三
e. 星期五	5. 禮拜一／礼拜一	E. 週日／周日
f. 星期六	6. 禮拜六／礼拜六	F. 週一／周一
g. 星期天（日）	7. 禮拜四／礼拜四	G. 週五／周五

FYI 供你參考

The workweek in China

Until the mid-1990s, the usual workweek in China was six days, from Monday through Saturday, with Sunday off. Today, the five-day workweek with the weekend off is most common. When Chinese say the days of the week, they start with *Xīngqīyī* (Monday) and end with *Xīngqītiān* (Sunday), in contrast to American patterns of expression.

Encounter 4 More time words

3.28 *Watch and listen to the video segment. Then place the following time expressions along the timeline below.*

xiànzài	gāngcái	yìhuǐr

xiànzài

_____

just a while ago   right now   in a little while

3.29 *In pinyin, complete the transcription of the conversation you just heard.*

唐母：來啊，來啊！／来啊，来啊！

Táng Mǔ: Lái a! Lái a!

(Tang Yuan's mother: Come! Come!)

琳：好的。一會兒，一會兒。／一会儿，一会儿。

Lín: Hǎo de. _____, _____.

(Lynn: OK. In a bit, in a bit.)

唐母：琳老師！休息休息吧！吃西瓜了！／琳老师！休息休息吧！吃西瓜了！

Táng Mǔ: Lín lǎoshī! Xiūxi xiūxi ba! Chī xīguā le!

(Tang Yuan's mother: Teacher Lynn! Take a break! We're having watermelon!)

琳：我寫完博客就下去，啊。／我写完博客就下去，啊。

Lín: Wǒ xiěwán bókè jiù xiàqu, a.

(Lynn: I'll come down as soon as I finish writing my blog, OK?)

唐母：你快來啊！／你快来啊！

Táng Mǔ: Nǐ kuài lái a!

(Tang Yuan's mother: _____ quickly!)

琳：好的。一會兒，一會兒。／一会儿，一会儿。

Lín: _____. _____, _____.

(Lynn: OK. In a bit, in a bit.)

...

唐：琳，快吃西瓜。

Táng: Lín, kuài chī xīguā.

(Tang: Lynn, here, have some _____.)

(The plate is empty. Lynn is perplexed.)

唐：哦，對不起。剛才有西瓜。現在沒了。都被我吃了。／哦，对不起。刚才有西瓜。现在没了。都被我吃了。

Táng: O, duìbuqǐ. _____ yǒu xīguā. _____ méi le. Dōu bèi wǒ chī le.

(Tang: Oh, sorry. There was watermelon just now. Now there isn't any more. I ate it all.)

唐母：吃吧。我给你留着呢。

Táng Mǔ: Chī ba. Wǒ gěi nǐ liú zhe ne.

(Tang Yuan's mother: Have some. I saved some for you.)

唐：吃啊。

Táng: Chī a.

(Tang: Eat up.)

3.30 *Watch and listen to the video segment. Practice saying each phrase as you make the corresponding gesture.*

3.31 *Pair work:* *With a partner, take turns saying the correct phrase in response to your partner's gesture.*

3.32 *Mingling:* *Take a blank card or a small piece of paper. Look at the time on the classroom clock and pick a time between right now (say, 9:06) and ten minutes from now (say, 9:16). Let's suppose you pick 9:11. Write this time on your card (large enough so others can read it easily). Now walk around the classroom, showing others your card and looking at the cards others hold. If both the classroom clock and a classmate's card have the same time—for example, 9:07—say,* Xiànzài *jiǔ diǎn líng (guò) qī fēn. If a classmate's card has an earlier time—for example, 9:06—say,* Gāngcái *jiǔ diǎn líng (guò) liù fēn. Your classmate would then say for your card (which has a later time),* Yìhuǐr *jiǔ diǎn shíyī fēn. Check each other and continue until you feel comfortable using all of the expressions.*

3.33 *Watch and listen to the video segment. Match the corresponding Chinese and English expressions below.*

a. zǎo yìdiǎnr   1. *a little later*
b. wǎn yìdiǎnr   2. *a little earlier*

3.34 *Pair work:* *Play the "guess the time" game with a partner. Student A writes a time on a piece of paper, and Student B tries to guess that time. If Student B guesses correctly, Student A says* Duì le! *Otherwise Student A responds by saying* Zǎo yìdiǎnr *or* Wǎn yìdiǎnr. *Continue until Student B guesses the time correctly, and then reverse roles. Play as necessary until you are comfortable with the terms in use.*

3.35 一點兒／一点儿 *are the characters for* yìdiǎnr, *meaning "a little." Here are two new characters:* 早 *and* 晚. *You can tell that they both have to do with the time of day, since the "sun" radical,* 日 rì, *appears in each. In one, the sun is higher than in the other. Can you guess what each means? Match the corresponding characters, English, and pinyin below.*

a. 早   1. *early*   A. wǎn
b. 晚   2. *late*   B. zǎo

3.36 *Watch and listen to the video segment. Then fill in the blanks below with time expressions in pinyin, to express the day relative to the circled date (that is, yesterday, two days from now, etc.).*

12 月						
週一	週二	週三	週四	週五	週六	週日
1	2	3	4	5	6	7

sān tiān yǐqián _____   _____   jīntiān   _____   _____   _____

3.37 *Match the corresponding items below.*

a. three days ago   1. qiántiān   A. 三天以後/三天以后

b. the day before yesterday   2. sān tiān yǐqián   B. 後天/后天

c. yesterday   3. hòutiān   C. 明天

d. today   4. zuótiān   D. 今天

e. tomorrow   5. sān tiān yǐhòu   E. 昨天

f. the day after tomorrow   6. míngtiān   F. 前天

g. three days from now   7. jīntiān   G. 三天以前

3.38 Pair work: *Work with a partner. On index cards, write today's day (say it's Tuesday), plus three days before (Saturday, Sunday, and Monday) and three days after (Wednesday, Thursday, and Friday). Lay the cards in order on your desk, and drill the terms by taking turns pointing at a card and having your partner say what it represents (for example, Sunday would be* qiántiān *and Wednesday would be* míngtiān*). Continue until you are both comfortable with the terms.*

3.39 *Watch and listen to the video segment. Then fill in the blanks below with pinyin.*

October						
Su	Mo	Tu	We	Th	Fr	Sa
		1	2	3	4	5
6	7	8	9	10	11	12
13	14	15	16	17	18	19
20	21	22	23	24	25	26
27	28	29	30			

_____

_____

zhèi ge xīngqī

_____

_____

> **Useful phrases**
>
> Zhè shì něi tiān?
> *(What day is this?)*
>
> Bú duì! *(Incorrect!)*
>
> Duì le! *(Correct!)*

3.40 *Match the corresponding items below.*

a. two weeks ago

b. last week

c. this week

d. next week

e. two weeks from now

1. 兩個星期以後

2. 這個星期

3. 上個星期

4. 兩個星期以前

5. 下個星期

A. 这个星期

B. 两个星期以前

C. 上个星期

D. 下个星期

E. 两个星期以后

3.41 *Pair work: Work with a partner. On index cards, write today's date (say it's 10/15), plus the dates a week ago (10/8), two weeks ago (10/1, China's National Day), a week from now (10/22), and two weeks from now (10/29). Lay the cards in order on your desk, and drill the terms by taking turns pointing to a card and having your partner say what week it represents (for example, 10/15 would be* zhèi ge xīngqī *and 10/29 would be* liǎng ge xīngqī yǐhòu *or* xià xià ge xīngqī*). Continue until you are both comfortable with the terms.*

3.42 *Mingling: Your teacher will hand you a slip. Look at the slip and circulate among your classmates, asking and answering questions according to the following pattern.*

Q: Nǐ de shì shénme shíhòu? *(When is yours?)*

A: Wǒ de shì _____. *(Mine is _____.)*

Based on the answers, line up from earliest to latest.

FYI供你参考

Chinese concepts of time

It may help to realize that Chinese people "face" and "look up to" the past, and they "go backward and downward" into the future. Consider the following terms:

xiànzài
(now)

qiántiān
the day in front
(day before yesterday)

shàng ge yuè
the month above
(last month)

yǐqián
in front of me
(the past)

hòutiān
the day behind
(day after tomorrow)

xià ge yuè
the month below
(next month)

yǐhòu
behind me
(the future)

This is tricky for speakers of English, who typically go forward into the future. However, with practice, you too can learn to turn yourself around for Chinese.

Encounter 5　Making an appointment

3.43 *Watch and listen to the video segment. When did they finally decide to meet?*
Write the day and time in English or pinyin: _____

3.44 *Match the corresponding pinyin and English below.*

a. Wǒmen shénme shíhòu jiàn?
我們甚麼時候見？／我们什么时候见？

1. *Let's meet at XX, OK?*

b. XX xíng ma?
XX 行嗎？／XX 行吗？

2. *When shall we meet?*

c. XX kěyǐ ma? _____
XX 可以嗎？／XX 可以吗？

3. *Would XX be OK?*

d. Nǐ XX yǒu kòng ma?
你 XX 有空嗎？／你 XX 有空吗？

4. *Are you busy XX?*

e. Nǐ XX yǒushì ma?
你 XX 有事嗎？／你 XX 有事吗？

5. *Would XX work?*

f. Duìbuqǐ, wǒ XX yǒushì.
對不起，我 XX 有事。／对不起，我 XX 有事。

6. *Wait a minute.*

g. Wǒmen XX jiàn, xíng ma?
我們 XX 見，行嗎？／我们 XX 见，行吗？

7. *Are you free XX?*

h. Děng yì děng.
等一等。

8. *Sorry, I'm busy XX.*

3.45 *Mingling: Walk around the room and arrange meeting times during the coming week with at least three of your classmates. Use your real appointment calendars, if possible. Write the names of the people you are meeting and the times you are meeting them.*

Meet _____ at _____

Meet _____ at _____

Meet _____ at _____

FYI 供你参考

Beijing time

Typically, things start earlier in China. While "nine to five" prevails in the United States, many employees in China are on the job as early as 7:30 or 8:00. The early-to-work habit is offset by the pleasant tradition of a two-hour midday break, observed in the workplace and in schools by workers and students sleeping at their desks. In urban areas, this "siesta" habit is on the decline, though, as China integrates into the global marketplace.

Note that there are no time zones in China, unlike other large countries, including the United States. Time across China is set to the time in Beijing. 6:00 A.M. in Beijing is 6:00 A.M. in the Gobi Desert in China's far west. Whereas the sun may have risen in Beijing, it might still be pitch black in the Gobi Desert. In winter in *Xīnjiāng*, China's westernmost province, the sun does not rise until about 10:00 in the morning, official time. However, many people in *Xīnjiāng* follow their own unofficial time, usually about two hours behind Beijing time.

♫ Unit Rap

Go to the **Encounters** *website at* www.EncountersChinese.com *and listen to the song to review key expressions from Unit 3. Listen again and sing along!*

Encounter 6 Reading and writing

▶ Reading familiar sentences in Chinese characters

3.46 *Pair work: Read the following dialogues (written in traditional characters) aloud with a partner, using the English as a guide.*

① 甲：現在幾點鐘？ *(What time is it now?)*

乙：上午九點半。 *(Nine-thirty in the morning.)*

2 甲：我們明天八點三刻見，對不對？ *(We're meeting tomorrow at 8:45, right?)*

乙：不是八點四十分嗎？ *(Isn't it 8:40?)*

甲：噢，對，八點四十分。 *(Oh, right. 8:40.)*

3 甲：現在幾點了？ *(What time is it?)*

乙：四點過五分！甚麼事？ *(Five past four! What's going on?)*

甲：四點鐘？夜裡四點鐘？ *(Four? Four o'clock at night?)*

乙：對！怎麼了？ *(Yes. What's up?)*

甲：對不起，對不起。沒事！沒事！ *(Sorry, sorry. Nothing! Nothing!)*

4 甲：我們兩點見，對不對？ *(See you at two, right?)*

乙：對，對，對，下午兩點。 我差點兒忘 (wàng) 了。 *(Right, right, right, two o'clock in the afternoon. I almost forgot.)*

5 甲：七月五號是不是星期天？ *(Is July 5th a Sunday?)*

乙：不，是星期六。 *(No, it's a Saturday.)*

甲：星期六。好。我們中午見，對不對？ *(Saturday. OK. We're meeting at noon, right?)*

乙：對。中午十二點鐘見。 *(Right. See you at twelve noon.)*

6 甲：十月九號是週末嗎？ *(Is October 9th a weekend?)*

乙：不，是禮拜一。 *(No, it's a Monday.)*

7 甲：今天星期幾？ *(What day of the week is it today?)*

乙：昨天星期六，今天星期天。 *(Yesterday was Saturday; today is Sunday.)*

8 甲：我們明天是早上六點見嗎？ *(Are we meeting at six tomorrow morning?)*

乙：不，是晚上六點。 *(No, six tomorrow evening.)*

甲：早一點兒，行嗎？ *(Can we make it earlier?)*

乙：四點半可以嗎？ *(Would four-thirty work?)*

甲：可以。明天見。 *(It would. See you tomorrow.)*

9 甲：你一會兒有沒有空？ *(Will you have some time in a little while?)*

乙：對不起，我剛才有空。一會兒有一點兒事。 *(Sorry, I was free just now. I have something to do in a little while.)*

甲：那現在有空嗎？ *(In that case, are you free now?)*

乙：有，有，有…… *(I am, I am, I am . . .)*

10 甲：你的生日是幾月幾號？ *(When is your birthday?)*

乙：是下個月的三十一號。 *(The 31st of next month.)*

3.47 Pair work: *Read the dialogues aloud with a partner, this time without any English.*

1 甲：現在幾點鐘？

乙：上午九點半。

2 甲：我們明天八點三刻見，對不對？

乙：不是八點四十分嗎？

甲：噢，對，八點四十分。

3 甲：現在幾點了？

乙：四點過五分！甚麼事？

甲：四點鐘？夜裡四點鐘？

乙：對！怎麼了？

甲：對不起，對不起。沒事！沒事！

4 甲：我們兩點見，對不對？

乙：對，對，對，下午兩點。我差點兒忘 (wàng) 了。

5 甲：七月五號是不是星期天？

乙：不，是星期六。

甲：星期六。好。我們中午見，對不對？

乙：對。中午十二點鐘見。

6 甲：十月九號是週末嗎？

乙：不，是禮拜一。

7 甲：今天星期幾？

乙：昨天星期六，今天星期天。

8 甲：我們明天是早上六點見嗎？

乙：不，是晚上六點。

甲：早一點兒，行嗎？

乙：四點半可以嗎？

甲：可以。明天見。

9 甲：你一會兒有沒有空？

乙：對不起，我剛才有空。一會兒有一點兒事。

甲：那現在有空嗎？

乙：有，有，有……

10 甲：你的生日是幾月幾號？

乙：是下個月的三十一號。

3.48 *Pair work: Read the dialogues aloud one more time, this time in simplified characters.*

1 甲：现在几点钟？

乙：上午九点半。

2 甲：我们明天八点三刻见，对不对？

乙：不是八点四十分吗？

甲：噢，对，八点四十分。

3 甲：现在几点了？

乙：四点过五分！什么事？

甲：四点钟？夜里四点钟？

乙：对！怎么了？

甲：对不起，对不起。没事！没事！

4 甲：我们两点见，对不对？

乙：对，对，对，下午两点。我差点儿忘 (wàng) 了。

5 甲：七月五号是不是星期天？

乙：不，是星期六。

甲：星期六。好。我们中午见，对不对？

乙：对。中午十二点钟见。

6 甲：十月九号是周末吗？

乙：不，是礼拜一。

7 甲：今天星期几？

乙：昨天星期六，今天星期天。

8 甲：我们明天是早上六点见吗？

乙：不，是晚上六点。

甲：早一点儿，行吗？

乙：四点半可以吗？

甲：可以。明天见。

9 甲：你一会儿有没有空？

乙：对不起，我刚才有空。一会儿有一点儿事。

甲：那现在有空吗？

乙：有,有,有……

10 甲：你的生日是几月几号？

乙：是下个月的三十一号。

3.49 *Match the corresponding simplified characters, traditional characters, and English.*

a. 现在	1. 甚麼	A. *what*
b. 几点钟	2. 對不對	B. *is that right*
c. 我们	3. 見	C. *now*
d. 对不对	4. 禮拜	D. *two o'clock*
e. 吗	5. 對不起	E. *what time (which hour)*
f. 过	6. 週末	F. *week*
g. 什么	7. 幾點鐘	G. *(particle marking a question)*
h. 两点	8. 星期幾	H. *next month*
i. 见	9. 過	I. *we, us*
j. 周末	10. 我們	J. *meet*
k. 礼拜	11. 兩點	K. *past, over (the hour)*
l. 星期几	12. 早一點兒	L. *weekend*
m. 早一点儿	13. 現在	M. *sorry*
n. 一会儿	14. 幾月幾號	N. *something to attend to*
o. 对不起	15. 一會兒	O. *what date*
p. 刚才	16. 一點兒事	P. *which day of the week*
q. 一点儿事	17. 嗎	Q. *just now*
r. 几月几号	18. 剛才	R. *a little earlier*
s. 下个月	19. 下個月	S. *in a while*

▶ Reading real-life texts

3.50 *The following is a bulletin board posting by a couple looking for childcare services. Fill in the English, based on the Chinese text.*

居住在接近東城區（交通便利，9路公車可直達）的一對夫妻尋找保姆，能講中文。每週一，三，五（星期二，四不需要）早上八點半到下午四點半，待遇面議。請有意者聯繫：王太太（手機：203-284-1166）謝謝！

A couple living near the eastern downtown district (convenient to public transportation, direct access via Route 9) seeks a childcare provider who speaks Chinese. Needed every _____ (not needed _____) from _____ to _____. Salary to be determined after interview. Interested parties please contact Mrs. Wang (_____: _____). Thank you!

3.51 *The following is a competition-day schedule for a sports team. The items listed include a wake-up call, breakfast, practice, lunch, a preparation meeting, travel, the match, and dinner. Answer the questions below.*

a. What date is posted on the schedule? Write the correct month and day in English.

_____

b. Fill in the appropriate times in the blanks below.

Breakfast (*zǎocān* 早餐) _____ A.M.

Lunch (*wǔcān* 午餐) _____ P.M.

Dinner (*wǎncān* 晚餐) _____ P.M.

6月2日日程安排
8:45 叫醒
9:00 早餐
10:00 訓練
13:00 午餐
16:00 準備會
16:45 出發
19:00 比賽
21:30 晚餐

3.52 *These two handwritten notes both arrange meeting times. Fill in the blanks below.*

Note 1:

Xiao Ming: Let's meet at the entrance to the library on _____,

                                           (DAY OF THE WEEK)

_____, at _____, OK? Tang Run.
(DATE)   (TIME)

Note 2:

我明天早上八點一刻在車站等你，行嗎？

I'll wait for you _____ at _____ at the bus stop, all right?

                     (DAY)   (TIME)

Learning to write characters

3.53 *For stroke order and other useful information about each of the following characters from this unit, go to the* **Character Writing Workbook**. *Choose traditional or simplified characters and practice writing them until you can reproduce them on demand.*

現／现, 在, 點／点, 分, 半, 上, 下, 午, 早, 晚, 今, 天, 星, 期, 時／时, 候, 有, 事, 等

Writing a note

3.54 *Write a note to a friend named* 王今, *telling her when you will meet up with her. If you need to write a term for which you don't know the characters, use pinyin.*

Cultural Bits 文化点滴

Time and timeliness

View the video segment "Time and timeliness" and then discuss the following questions with your classmates.

- How punctual would it seem the Chinese tend to be?
- What should you keep in mind regarding punctuality when you have an appointment with someone in China?
- What is the role of the cell phone in making and keeping appointments?
- What do *chàbuduō, còuhuo,* and *mǎshàngdào* imply in terms of punctuality?

Recap

Grammar

Sentence-ending particle *le*

As you learned in an earlier unit, *le* is used at the end of a sentence to show that a change of state has occurred. This is called Change-of-State (COS) *le*.

Xiànzài jǐ diǎn le? *(What time is it getting to be? [We had better get on with our plans.])*
Liǎng diǎn le! *(It's 2:00! [already—gosh it's so late!])*
Wǒ yǐqián bù dǒng, xiànzài wǒ dǒng le. *(I didn't understand before, [but] now I do.)*

Measure words (MW) and the always handy *ge*

Several new measure words were introduced in this unit, mostly relating to time on the clock.

diǎn (MW for hours) sān diǎn zhōng *(3:00)*
kè (MW for quarter hours) sān diǎn yí kè *(3:15/ quarter past three)*
fēn (MW for minutes) qī diǎn wǔ fēn *(7:05)*

An additional measure word, *ge*, is an all-purpose measure and can replace most other measures. Keep in mind that you should learn the appropriate measure word with the related noun, but *ge* can be used with almost all nouns in a "language emergency."

> yī ge xīngqī   *(one week)*
> sān ge yuè   *(three months)*
> sì ge shǒujī   *(four cell phones)*

Specifying "here" and "there"

In order to specify a particular thing in Chinese, specifiers are used with appropriate measure words, numbers, and nouns.

> Zhè shì wǒ de.   *(This is mine.)*
> nèi sān wèi lǎoshī   *(those three teachers)*

To specify "here" and "there," similar words are used: *zhèr* and *nàr*.

> Nǐ zài nàr, wǒ zài zhèr.   *(You're there and I'm here.)*
> Zhèr bù xíng, nàr hǎo.   *(This [place] will not do; it's better there.)*

Be careful to distinguish: zhè   zhèi   zhèr
nà   nèi   nàr

Forming questions

There are several ways to form questions, and their use is often dictated by context and meaning.

Add the query particle *ma* to the end of a sentence.

> Tā hǎo ma?   *(How is he/she?)*

Add the particle *ne* to the end of a sentence to indicate a follow-up question.

> Wǒ xìng Lǐ. Tā ne?   *(My last name is Li. And his/hers?)*

Use a question word.

> Shéi xìng Zhōu?   *(Who is surnamed Zhou?)*

Provide alternatives with an untoned *bu* between the same verb.

> Xīngqīyī hǎo bu hǎo?   *(Is Monday all right?)*

Provide alternatives with *háishi*.

> Nǐ gāo háishi wǒ gāo?   *(Are you tall[er] or am I tall[er]?)*

Add *zěnmeyàng* to the end of a remark.

> Xīngqītiān zěnmeyàng?   *(What about Sunday?)*

Adding tone to whole sentences

Sentence-ending particles often add tone or emotion to an entire question or statement.

Add the particle *ba* to create a tone of suggestion.

> Zǒu ba!   *(Shall we go? / Let's be off, OK?)*

Add the particle *a* to suggest a certain heartiness, especially in greetings.

> Hǎo a!   *(Hi!)*
> Zǎo a!   *(Morning!)*

Forming tenses in Chinese

All verbs in Chinese are static and unchanging. The various tenses and their complications are expressed by adding words, not by changing the verb.

> Wǒ zuótiān bù hǎo, jīntiān hǎo le, míngtiān bù zhīdào.   *(I wasn't well yesterday, [but] I'm better today; I don't know about tomorrow.)*
> Sān nián yǐqián wǒ zài Zhōngguó, míngnián wǒ hái yào qù.   *(Three years ago I was in China; next year I'm going again.)*

▶ Vocabulary

Days of the week

Xīngqīyī 星期一 Monday
Xīngqī'èr 星期二 Tuesday
Xīngqīsān 星期三 Wednesday
Xīngqīsì 星期四 Thursday
Xīngqīwǔ 星期五 Friday
Xīngqīliù 星期六 Saturday
Xīngqītiān 星期天 Sunday
zhōurì 週日／周日 Sunday
zhōumò 週末／周末 weekend

Particles

ba 吧 [particle of suggestion]
nà 那 then, in that case

Pronouns

nàr 那兒／那儿 there
zhèr 這兒／这儿 here

Telling time (on the clock)

bàn 半 half an hour
chà 差 lack ("before the hour")
diǎn zhōng 點鐘／点钟 o'clock
fēn 分 minute (clock time)
guò 過／过 exceed ("past the hour")
kè 刻 quarter of an hour
líng 零 zero
shíhou 時候／时候 time; time on the clock

Time words

bànyè 半夜 midnight
gāngcái 剛才／刚才 just a moment ago
hòutiān 後天／后天 the day after tomorrow
jīntiān 今天 today
míngtiān 明天 tomorrow
qiántiān 前天 the day before yesterday
shàng ge yuè 上個月／上个月 last month
shàngwǔ 上午 morning, A.M.
tiān 天 day
wǎn 晚 late
wǎnshang 晚上 evening (from 6 P.M. until midnight)
xià ge yuè 下個月／下个月 next month
xiànzài 現在／现在 now; at present
xiàwǔ 下午 afternoon, P.M.
yǐhòu 以後／以后 after
yìhuǐr 一會兒／一会儿 (in a) little while
yǐqián 以前 before
zǎo 早 early; Good morning.
yèli 夜裡／夜里 at night, during the night, nighttime
zǎoshang 早上 morning (until 9–10 A.M.)
zhōngwǔ 中午 noon, midday
zuótiān 昨天 yesterday

Verbs

děi 得 must; need to
děng 等 wait; wait for; await
jiàn 見／见 meet up with (someone)
kěyǐ 可以 can, may
lái 來／来 come
méiyǒu 沒有 not have; be without
xíng 行 pass muster; be OK
yǒu 有 have
yǒukòng 有空 be free, have free time
yǒushì 有事 be busy; have something to do; be occupied
zǒu 走 leave; depart

Other words and expressions

háishi 還是／还是 or; rather
jǐ 幾／几 how many
kòng 空 free time
liǎng 兩／两 two (used with measures)
shàng 上 last (in a series)
tài 太 too; excessively
xià 下 next (in a series)
xīguā 西瓜 watermelon
yìdiǎnr 一點兒／一点儿 a bit; a little; some

▶ Checklist of "can do" statements

After completing this unit, you should be able to perform each of the following tasks.

Listening and speaking

☐ Understand and formulate questions about specific clock times.

☐ Understand statements and ask questions about divisions of the day.

☐ Ask and answer questions about days of the week and calendar dates.

☐ Arrange a mutually agreeable meeting time in a culturally appropriate manner.

☐ Provide your availability in terms of time of day, day of the week, calendar date, and in times relative to the present or the future.

☐ Understand when others give their availability relative to date and time.

☐ Negotiate and confirm a meeting time.

Reading and writing

☐ Read and understand simple notes about meeting times and dates.

☐ Write a simple statement about others' availability.

☐ Write a simple note confirming an appointment.

☐ Understand the layout of a handwritten or e-mail message.

Understanding culture

☐ Explain the concept of notating time "backward and downward" in Chinese.

☐ Explain what Beijing Standard Time means to the Chinese mainland.

UNIT 4

"If only we had met sooner"

相見恨晚

Xiāngjiànhènwǎn

Talking about your nationality and background

In this unit, you will learn how to:

- ask and answer questions about nationality.
- ask and answer questions about place of birth and places lived.
- ask and answer questions about travel experiences.
- ask and answer questions about language(s) spoken.

- recognize the names of 10–15 countries on postcards and in telephone directories.
- read simple self-introductory statements about nationality, place of birth, places lived, and language(s) spoken.
- write simple self-introductory statements including nationality, place of birth, places lived, and language(s) spoken.

Encounter 1   **Expressing nationality**

 4.1 *View Episode 4 of the dramatic series.*

4.2 *Getting ready:* How would you ask someone about his or her nationality in English? If someone asked you about your nationality, what would you say?

_____

 4.3 *Watch and listen to the video segment. Write the pinyin transcription for the question "What nationality are you?"*

_____

4.4 *Match the corresponding pinyin and English for each of the following country names. Note: They are all examples of transliteration—using Chinese syllables that sound nearly the same as the pronunciation of the foreign term—except for three. Can you identify the three?*

_____   _____   _____

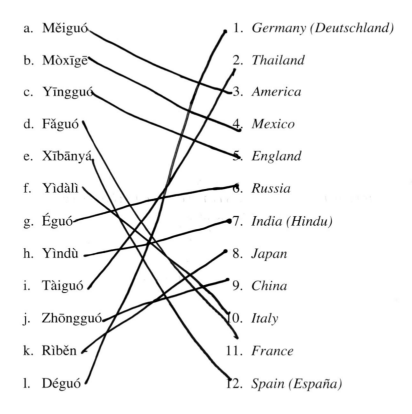

a. Měiguó   1. Germany (Deutschland)

b. Mòxīgē   2. Thailand

c. Yīngguó   3. America

d. Fǎguó   4. Mexico

e. Xībānyá   5. England

f. Yìdàlì   6. Russia

g. Éguó   7. India (Hindu)

h. Yìndù   8. Japan

i. Tàiguó   9. China

j. Zhōngguó   10. Italy

k. Rìběn   11. France

l. Déguó   12. Spain (España)

4.5 *Match the corresponding items below.*

a. Zhōngguórén 中國人
b. Měiguórén 美國人
c. Rìběnrén 日本人
d. Hánguórén 韓國人
e. Fǎguórén 法國人
f. Déguórén 德國人
g. Yīngguórén 英國人
h. Yìndùrén 印度人
i. Xībānyárén 西班牙人
j. Yìdàlìrén 意大利人
k. Tàiguórén 泰國人
l. Éguórén 俄國人

1. English
2. German
3. Spanish
4. Japanese
5. Chinese
6. Indian
7. Thai
8. Russian
9. Korean
10. Italian
11. American
12. French

A. 泰国人
B. 日本人
C. 德国人
D. 中国人
E. 英国人
F. 西班牙人
G. 法国人
H. 美国人
I. 印度人
J. 俄国人
K. 韩国人
L. 意大利人

4.6 *Write in pinyin what you would say if someone asked about your nationality. Ask your teacher if you don't know how to write the pinyin of your nationality.*

_____

4.7 Mingling: *If your class is very diverse, walk around and ask where your classmates are from, taking notes on their responses. If your class is homogeneous, choose a country (not your own) where you might like to be a citizen. Then walk around the class and find out where everyone is "from."*

▶ **Reading practice**

4.8 *Read the following country names aloud.*

中國／中国　　　　　　美國／美国　　　　　　日本

英國／英国　　　　　　印度　　　　　　　　　西班牙

韓國／韩国　　　　　　法國／法国　　　　　　德國／德国

意大利　　　　　　　　泰國／泰国　　　　　　俄國／俄国

Encounter 2　Talking about your birthplace and where you have lived

4.9 *Getting ready: How would you ask people in English where they were born and where they have lived? If someone asked you the same questions, what would you say?*

_____

_____

4.10 *Watch and listen to the video segment. Complete the English transcription of each dialogue.*

a.

A: Where were you ___born___?

B: I was born in ___Guiling___, but I grew up in ___Beijing___. How about you?

A: I ___was born in Beijing___, and my ___house___ is in Beijing, but I've also lived in ___Shanghai___.

b.

A: Where in ___America___ do you come from?

B: I was ___born___ in Washington and I've lived in many places. Now my ___home___ is in Honolulu. And you? ___Where___ have you lived?

A: I have only lived here.

4.11 *Match the pinyin with the corresponding English below.*

a. Wǒ shēngzai Běijīng.

b. Wǒ shì zài Běijīng zhǎngdà de.

c. Wǒ jiā zài Běijīng.

d. Wǒ zhùzai Běijīng.

e. Wǒ yǐqián zài Běijīng zhùguo.

1. *My home is in Beijing.*

2. *I was born in Beijing.*

3. *I've lived in Beijing before.*

4. *I grew up in Beijing.*

5. *I live in Beijing.*

4.12 *Match the questions with the appropriate answers below.*

a. Nǐ shì zài nǎr chūshēng de?

b. Nǐ shì zài nǎr zhǎngdà de?

c. Nǐ jiā zài nǎr?

d. Nǐ zài nǎr zhùguo?

e. Nǐ shì Zhōngguó nǎli rén?

1. *Wǒ yǐqián zài Běijīng zhùguo.*

2. *Wǒ shì Běijīngrén.*

3. *Wǒ shēngzai Běijīng.*

4. *Wǒ shì zài Běijīng zhǎngdà de.*

5. *Wǒ jiā zài Běijīng.*

4.13 *Match the pinyin with the corresponding characters.*

a. Nǐ shì zài nǎr chūshēng de?

b. Wǒ shēngzai Fǎguó.

c. Nǐ shì zài nǎr zhǎngdà de?

d. Wǒ shì zài Éguó zhǎngdà de.

e. Nǐ jiā zài nǎr?

f. Wǒ jiā zài Měiguó.

g. Nǐ zài nǎr zhùguo?

h. Wǒ yǐqián zài Rìběn zhùguo.

i. Nǐ shì Zhōngguó nǎli rén?

j. Wǒ shì Běijīngrén.

1. 你在哪兒住過？／你在哪儿住过？

2. 我是北京人。

3. 你是在哪兒出生的？／你是在哪儿出生的？

4. 你是在哪兒長大的？／你是在哪儿长大的？

5. 我是在俄國長大的。／我是在俄国长大的。

6. 我以前在日本住過。／我以前在日本住过。

7. 你是中國哪裡人？／你是中国哪里人？

8. 我生在法國。／我生在法国。

9. 你家在哪兒？／你家在哪儿？

10. 我家在美國。／我家在美国。

FYI 供你参考

So, where are you from?

In major cities of the Western world, people often ask where someone was born and grew up, or where a person has lived. These facts may have nothing to do with ethnicity or citizenship; an ethnically Chinese person with U.S. citizenship may have been born and raised in India, and subsequently lived all over Europe, for example. In China, these questions and the language you have learned so far in this unit are less commonly used. Instead, Chinese people often ask each other *Nǐ de lǎo jiā zài nǎr?* 你的老家在哪兒？／你的老家在哪儿？which literally means, "Where is your old home?" The response is usually where someone was born and raised. Foreigners are often confused by this question and need the specificity of the language introduced thus far. For example, how could you identify your "old home" when you were born in one place, raised for a while in another place, and then moved every two years throughout your childhood?

Another typical Chinese question about origins is *Nǐ de zǔjí zài nǎr?* 你的祖籍在哪兒？／你的祖籍在哪儿？or "Where is your ancestral home?" The response to this question is usually where someone's father's family lived for many generations. A Chinese person currently living in Beijing or Shanghai may have an ancestral home in the Shandong or Hunan countryside, for example.

4.14 *How would you describe your background—where you were born, where you grew up, where you have lived, and where you live now? Write the following statements in pinyin, using the English as a guide. If you don't know how to say the name of a town in Chinese, just write it in English, or ask your teacher.*

I was born in . . . _____

I grew up in . . . _____

I've lived in . . . _____

Right now, I live in . . . _____

4.15 *Mingling: Ask several classmates where they were born, where they grew up, where they have lived, and where they live now. Tell the same about yourself. Take some notes about your classmates below.*

Name: _____

Background: _____

Name: _____

Background: _____

Name: _____

Background: _____

4.16 *Fill in the following paragraph with details about yourself. Complete the sentences with either pinyin or English.*

我生在＿＿＿＿＿＿＿＿＿＿＿＿＿＿＿，是在＿＿＿＿＿＿＿＿＿＿＿＿＿＿＿長大的。我住過

＿＿＿＿＿＿＿＿＿＿＿＿＿＿。現在我家在＿＿＿＿＿＿＿＿＿＿＿＿＿＿＿。

Grammar Bits 语法点滴

Sharing experiences: Verb + *guo*

When you want to say that you have or haven't had an experience, use the verbal suffix *guo* (tonally neutral) in conjunction with the appropriate verb. Chinese verbs with the *guo* suffix typically mirror English expressions in the present perfect, such as "Have you ever . . . ?" The reference is always to past actions, never present or future. Therefore, verb + *guo* constructions imply a finished and complete action; it is no longer being performed. To form the negative expression, use *méi* or *méiyǒu* in conjunction with *guo*.

Nǐ qùguo Zhōngguó ma?	*(Have you ever been to China?)*
Qùguo. Qùnián qùguo.	*(Yes, I have. I went last year.)*
Méi(yǒu) qùguo, kěshì hěn xiǎng qù.	*(No, I haven't, but I'd really like to go.)*

Encounter 3　Talking about travel experiences

4.17 Getting ready: *How would you ask people in English where they have traveled or would like to travel? If someone asked you the same question, what would you say?*

_____

4.18 *Watch and listen to the video segment. Number the English translations below in the order in which the Chinese sentences occur in the dialogue.*

_____ I haven't been anywhere outside of China. How about you?

_____ I don't want to go anywhere.

_____ Suzhou, Beijing, Shanghai, Guangzhou.

_____ What places have you been to?

_____ I've gone to many places.

_____ I like staying at home. I don't like traveling.

_____ Europe, South America, Asia, Africa.

4.19 *Now complete the pinyin transcription of the dialogue.*

Lynn: Nǐ dōu dàoguo _Shénme_ dìfang?

Tang: Sūzhōu, Běijīng, Shànghǎi, Guǎngzhōu. Búguò, wǒ méiyou chūguo guó. Chúle
Zhōngguó de zhèi xiē dìfāng, wǒ nǎr dōu _méi méi_ qùguo. Nǐ ne?

Lynn: Wǒ qùguo hěn _dou_ dìfang: Ōuzhōu, Nán Měizhōu, _Yàzhōu_ ,
Fēizhōu , dōu qùguo. Kěshì, háiyǒu hěn duō dìfang méi qùguo.

Tang: Wǒ nǎr dōu bù _xiǎng_ qù. Wǒ xǐhuan dāizai jiālǐ, _bu_ xǐhuan lǚxíng.

Grammar Bits 语法点滴

The "flexible" adverb *dōu*

The adverb *dōu* operates in several language environments. First, it can mean "all."

Wǒmen dōu hǎo. *(We are all well.)*

Wǒmen dōu bù hǎo. *(All of us are not well. = None of us is well.)*

Second, *dōu* supports "all inclusive/exclusive" statements with the help of question words.

shéi + dōu ⇒ "everyone"

shéi + dōu + bù ⇒ "no one"

　Q: Shéi qù? *(Who is going?)*

　A: Shéi dōu qù. *(Everyone is going.)*

　B: Shéi dōu bú qù. *(No one is going.)*

nǎr + dōu ⇒ "everywhere"

nǎr + dōu + bù ⇒ "nowhere"

　Q: Nǐ xiǎng qù nǎr? *(Where do you want to go?)*

　A: Wǒ nǎr dōu xiǎng qù. *(I'd like to go everywhere.)*

　B: Wǒ nǎr dōu bù xiǎng qù. *(I don't want to go anywhere.)*

shénme + dōu ⇒ "everything"

shénme + dōu + bù ⇒ "nothing"

　Q: Nǐ yào shénme? *(What do you want?)*

　A: Wǒ shénme dōu yào. *(I want everything.)*

　B: Wǒ shénme dōu bú yào. *(I don't want anything.)*

Third, *dōu* acts to "totalize" when requesting and providing particulars or lists.

Nǐ dōu qùguo nǎr? *(Where all have you been to?)*

Zhōngguó, Rìběn, Hánguó, wǒ dōu qùguo. *(China, Japan, Korea—I've been to them all.)*

Always remember that, in Chinese grammar, word position is of greatest importance.

> Nǐ dōu qùguo shénme dìfang?

> Wǒ nǎr dōu méi qùguo.

4.20 *Circle the correct English translation of each term below.*

a. 都 dōu   *(all) (everywhere)*

b. 到過／到过 dàoguo   *(talked to) (been to)*

c. 甚麼地方／什么地方 shénme dìfang   *(this place) (what place)*

d. 哪兒都沒去過／哪儿都没去过 nǎr dōu méi qùguo   *(haven't been anywhere)* *(have been everywhere)*

e. 去過／去过 qùguo   *(gone to) (lived at)*

f. 歐洲／欧洲 Ōuzhōu   *(Australia) (Europe)*

g. 南美洲 Nán Měizhōu   *(North America) (South America)*

h. 非洲 Fēizhōu   *(Europe) (Africa)*

i. 哪兒都不想去／哪儿都不想去 nǎr dōu bù xiǎng qù   *(have not been anywhere)* *(don't want to go anywhere)*

j. 喜歡／喜欢 xǐhuan   *(like to) (want to)*

k. 呆在家裡／呆在家里 dāizai jiālǐ   *(live in a place) (stay at home)*

l. 旅行 lǚxíng   *(travel) (stay put)*

4.21 *Match the corresponding English and pinyin below.*

a. *What are all the places you have been to?*   1. Nǐ xiǎng qù $\begin{cases} \text{shénme dìfang?} \\ \text{nǎr?} \end{cases}$

b. *Where would you like to go?*   2. Nǐ dōu qùguo $\begin{cases} \text{shénme dìfang?} \\ \text{nǎr?} \end{cases}$

4.22 *Answer each question below by filling in the blank with either pinyin or English.*

你都去過甚麼地方？／你都去过什么地方？ Nǐ dōu qùguo shénme dìfang?

我去過／我去过 _____

你想去甚麼地方？／你想去什么地方？ Nǐ xiǎng qù shénme dìfang?

我很想去 _____

4.23 Mingling: *Speak to two or more of your classmates. Find out where they've traveled and where they would like to travel.*

Encounter 4 Talking about languages spoken

4.24 *Getting ready: How would you ask someone in English if he or she speaks a certain language? If someone asked you the same question, what would you say?*

_____

_____

 4.25 *Watch and listen to the video segment. Fill in the blank below.*

Nǐ huì shuō <u>zhōng</u> wén ma? *(Do you speak Chinese?)*

4.26 *Match the corresponding items below.*

a. 會説 huì shuō   1. *can speak*   A. 会说一点儿

b. 會説一點兒 huì shuō yìdiǎnr   2. *can't speak*   B. 会说

c. 不會説 bú huì shuō   3. *can speak a little* C. 不会说

FYI 供你参考

Deflecting a compliment

Modesty is a cardinal virtue in Chinese culture. If someone asks if you can speak a language, you might downplay your ability, as the people in the video do. Even if you were fluent, you might only say *Huì shuō yìdiǎnr* 會説一點兒／会说一点儿 or *Huì shuō* 會説／会说. Other people might compliment you, however: *Nǐ shuō de hěn hǎo!* 你説得很好!／你说得很好! (You speak very well!). The proper response to such a compliment, traditionally, is to deny it by saying something like *Bù, bù, shuō de bù hǎo* 不，不，説得不好／不，不，说得不好. A common denial is *Nǎli, nǎli* 哪裡，哪裡／哪里，哪里, which literally means "Where, where" but by extension means "How could you say that? I'm not good at all." Another popular expression is *Guòjiǎng, guòjiǎng* 過獎,過獎／过奖,过奖, which means "You flatter me." In modern, urban China, however, you'll also find some Chinese being OK with your simply accepting the compliment, as Westerners do, by saying *Xièxie* 謝謝／谢谢.

4.27 *Pair work: Compliment your partner on his or her Chinese by saying* Nǐ Zhōngwén shuō de hěn hǎo! *Your partner should respond to your compliment with a polite response. Practice a few times, each time with a different response. Then switch roles.*

4.28 *Watch and listen to the video segment. Match the corresponding pinyin and English.*

a. Zhōngwén / Zhōngguóhuà

b. Yīngwén / Yīngyǔ

c. Rìwén / Rìyǔ / Rìběnhuà

d. Hánwén / Hányǔ / Hánguóhuà

e. Fǎwén / Fǎyǔ / Fǎguóhuà

f. Déwén / Déyǔ / Déguóhuà

g. Xībānyáwén / Xībānyáyǔ / Xībānyáhuà

h. Éwén / Éyǔ / Éguóhuà

i. Yìndùwén / Yìndùyǔ / Yìndùhuà

1. *English*

2. *Chinese*

3. *Russian*

4. *Hindi*

5. *Korean*

6. *German*

7. *French*

8. *Japanese*

9. *Spanish*

 4.29 *Watch and listen to the video segment. Write, in English, the language that each of the following people speaks.*

a. German

b. English

c. Korean

d. Hindi

e. Japanese

f. Russian

g. French

h. Spanish

FYI 供你参考

Chinese languages and dialects

The language situation in China is both simple and complex, as it is in most countries as large as China. It is complex because there are many spoken languages (sometimes called "dialects") in the country, but it is also simple because nearly all Chinese people speak the national language—*Pǔtōnghuà* 普通話／普通话 (common language). It is the language taught in Chinese schools, heard in the media (on the radio, on television, and in the movies), and taught in *Encounters*. More good news is that the form of Mandarin Chinese spoken in Taiwan (called *Guóyǔ* 國語／国语, meaning "national language") and in Chinese communities throughout Southeast Asia (called *Huáyǔ* 華語／华语, meaning "Sino language") is virtually the same as *Pǔtōnghuà*. A person from Taiwan speaking the standard language has little or no difficulty speaking with someone from Mainland China. The written language, except for the differences between simplified and traditional characters, does not differ at all.

Some Chinese "dialects" include:

- *Guǎngdōnghuà* 廣東話／广东话—spoken in the southern province of Guangdong and Hong Kong; called "Cantonese" in the United States
- *Shànghǎihuà* 上海話／上海话—spoken in Shanghai and nearby communities
- *Mǐnnányǔ* 閩南語／闽南语—spoken in southern Fujian province on the coast of China opposite Taiwan; called *Táiwānhuà* 台灣話／台湾话 in Taiwan

4.30 *What languages do you speak? Fill in the blanks below with as many languages as you see fit. Write in pinyin.*

Q: Nǐ huì shuō shénme huà?

A: Wǒ huì shuō _____.

    Wǒ yě huì shuō yìdiǎnr _____, kěshì shuō de bù hǎo.

4.31 *Mingling: Make a list of all the languages you speak. (For the purposes of this exercise, if you know even one word of that language, count it.) Walk around the room and speak to at least three people. Find out which languages they speak and tell them which languages you speak.*

Nǐ huì shuō shénme huà?

Wǒ huì shuō . . .

▶ Putting it all together

4.32 *Prepare to mingle:* *Make a list of six questions you know how to ask in pinyin. For each question, write how you would answer if it were asked of you.*

_____

_____

_____

_____

_____

_____

> **Some ideas:**
> name
> age
> birth sign
> phone number
> address
> nationality
> places lived
> places traveled
> languages spoken

4.33 *Mingling:* *Mingle with your classmates. Take turns asking and answering questions. Speak to each classmate for a minute or two and then take your leave and move on. Continue until your teacher tells you time is up.*

🎵 Unit Rap

Go to the **Encounters** *website at* www.EncountersChinese.com *and listen to the song to review key expressions from Unit 4. Listen again and sing along!*

Encounter 5   Reading and writing

▶ Reading familiar sentences in Chinese characters

4.34 *Pair work:* *Read the following dialogues (written in traditional characters) aloud with a partner, using the English as a guide.*

1 甲：你是哪國人？*(What's your nationality?)*
　　乙：我是英國人。你呢？*(I'm English. And you?)*
　　甲：我是德國人。*(I'm German.)*

2 甲：你是日本人嗎？*(Are you Japanese?)*
　　乙：不，我是韓國人。你呢？*(No, I'm Korean. And you?)*
　　甲：我是泰國人。*(I'm Thai.)*

3 甲：你是西班牙人，對不對？ *(You're Spanish, right?)*

乙：不，我是印度人。 *(No, I'm Indian.)*

4 甲：你是哪國人？ *(What's your nationality?)*

乙：我是美國人，可是我是在法國出生的。 *(I'm American, but I was born in France.)*

甲：你家在哪兒？ *(Where is your home?)*

乙：在中國！我家在北京。 *(In China! My home is in Beijing.)*

5 甲：你在哪裡住過？ *(Where have you lived?)*

乙：我住過很多地方。中國，歐洲，日本──都住過。 *(I've lived many places. China, Europe, Japan—I've lived in them all.)*

甲：你去過非洲嗎？ *(Have you been to Africa?)*

乙：沒有。可是很想去。你呢？你住過甚麼地方？ *(No, but I'd really like to go. And you? Where have you lived?)*

甲：我在美國出生，美國長大的，我一直住在美國。可是我明年會去非洲。 *(I was born in the United States, [I] grew up in the United States, I've lived in the United States throughout [yìzhí]. But next year I'll go to Africa.)*

6 甲：那個人叫Alex。我想他是法國人。 *(That person's name is Alex. I think he's French.)*

乙：不對，不對。他是英國人，可是他會說法語。 *(No, no. He's English, but he can speak French.)*

7 甲：你會說日語嗎？ *(Can you speak Japanese?)*

乙：不會。我只會說中文。 *(No. I can only speak Chinese.)*

8 甲：你去過歐洲嗎？ *(Have you been to Europe?)*

乙：去過。我去過德國和法國。今年我會去俄國。 *(I have. I've been to Germany and France. This year I'm going to Russia.)*

甲：你會說俄語嗎？ *(Can you speak Russian?)*

乙：只會說一點兒。 *(I can only speak a little.)*

9 甲：老師，您去過美國嗎？ *(Teacher, have you been to the United States?)*

乙：沒有。我只去過亞洲很多國家。日本，泰國…… *(No. I've only been to many countries in Asia. Japan, Thailand . . .)*

甲：您想去美國旅行嗎？ *(Would you like to go traveling in the United States?)*

乙：想，也想去歐洲旅行。 *(Yes, I'd also like to travel in Europe.)*

⑩ 甲：你喜歡旅行嗎？ *(Do you like to travel?)*

乙：不喜歡。我哪兒都不想去。我只想呆在家裡。 *(No. I don't want to go anywhere. I just want to stay home.)*

4.35 Pair work: *Read the dialogues aloud with a partner, this time without any English.*

① 甲：你是哪國人？

乙：我是英國人。你呢？

甲：我是德國人。

② 甲：你是日本人嗎？

乙：不，我是韓國人。你呢？

甲：我是泰國人。

③ 甲：你是西班牙人，對不對？

乙：不，我是印度人。

④ 甲：你是哪國人？

乙：我是美國人，可是我是在法國出生的。

甲：你家在哪兒？

乙：在中國！我家在北京。

⑤ 甲：你在哪裡住過？

乙：我住過很多地方。中國，歐洲，日本都住過。

甲：你去過非洲嗎？

乙：沒有。可是我很想去。你呢？你住過甚麼地方？

甲：我在美國出生，美國長大的，我一直住在美國。可是我明年會去非洲。

⑥ 甲：那個人名字叫Alex。我想他是法國人。

乙：不對，不對。他是英國人，可是他會說法語。

⑦ 甲：你會說日語嗎？

乙：不會。我只會說中文。

⑧ 甲：你去過歐洲嗎？

乙：去過。我去過德國和法國。今年我會去俄國。

甲：你會說俄語嗎？

乙：只會說一點兒。

9 甲：老師，您去過美國嗎？

乙：沒有。我只去過亞洲很多國家。日本，泰國⋯⋯

甲：您想去美國嗎？

乙：想，也想去歐洲旅行。

10 甲：你喜歡旅行嗎？

乙：不喜歡。我哪兒都不想去。我只想呆在家裡。

4.36 Pair work: *Read the dialogues aloud one more time, this time in simplified characters.*

1 甲：你是哪国人？

乙：我是英国人。你呢？

甲：我是德国人。

2 甲：你是日本人吗？

乙：不，我是韩国人。你呢？

甲：我是泰国人。

3 甲：你是西班牙人，对不对？

乙：不，我是印度人。

4 甲：你是哪国人？

乙：我是美国人，可是我是在法国出生的。

甲：你家在哪儿？

乙：在中国！我家在北京。

5 甲：你在哪里住过？

乙：我住过很多地方。中国，欧洲，日本都住过。

甲：你去过非洲吗？

乙：没有。可是我很想去。你呢？你住过什么地方？

甲：我在美国出生，美国长大的，我一直住在美国。可是我明年会去非洲。

6 甲：那个人叫Alex。我想他是法国人。

乙：不对，不对。他是英国人，可是他会说法语。

7 甲：你会说日语吗？

乙：不会。我只会说中文。

8 甲：你去过欧洲吗？

乙：去过。我去过德国和法国。今年我会去俄国。

甲：你会说俄语吗？

乙：只会说一点儿。

9 甲：老师，您去过美国吗？

乙：没有。我只去过亚洲很多国家。日本，泰国……

甲：您想去美国吗？

乙：想，也想去欧洲旅行。

10 甲：你喜欢旅行吗？

乙：不喜欢。我哪儿都不想去。我只想呆在家里。

4.37 *Match the corresponding simplified characters, traditional characters, and English.*

a. 哪国	1. 去過	A. *Korea*
b. 韩国	2. 哪裡	B. *be able to speak*
c. 泰国来的	3. 韓國	C. *which country*
d. 哪里	4. 哪國	D. *come from Thailand*
e. 住过	5. 泰國來的	E. *have been to*
f. 欧洲	6. 住過	F. *where*
g. 去过	7. 甚麼地方	G. *have lived in*
h. 呆在家里	8. 會説	H. *Europe*
i. 什么地方	9. 歐洲	I. *grow up*
j. 会说	10. 長大	J. *what places*
k. 长大	11. 俄國	K. *have never been to*
l. 俄国	12. 哪兒都不想去	L. *French person*
m. 没去过	13. 法國人	M. *Russia*
n. 法国人	14. 喜歡	N. *don't want to go anywhere*
o. 喜欢	15. 呆在家裡	O. *remain at home*
p. 哪儿都不想去	16. 没去過	P. *like*

▶ **Reading real-life texts**

4.38 *Look at the sign in the window of a restaurant. Circle the characters for "India."*

4.39 *Look at the sign in the window of a restaurant. Circle the characters for "Korea."*

4.40 *This is a table of long-distance direct-dial country codes to use when you are making a call out of China.*

国际直拨电话国家代码一览表		
阿根廷 54	美国 1	西班牙 34
澳大利亚 61	墨西哥 52	新加坡 65
俄国 7	日本 81	意大利 39
法国 33	泰国 66	德国 49
加拿大 1	香港 852	英国 44

a. Write the telephone codes for the following countries:

Spain _____   France _____   Japan _____   Germany _____

b. Write the telephone codes for five more countries:

Country   Code

_____   _____

_____   _____

_____   _____

_____   _____

_____   _____

4.41 *The following is a postcard mailed to Taiwan. What does it say? Fill in the blanks below.*

Lili:

_____?

_____ is lots of fun.

_____ quickly!

Rongrong

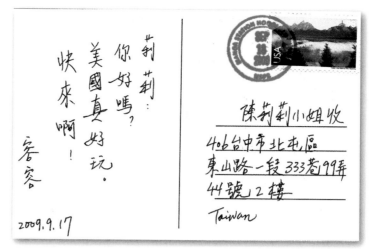

Learning to write characters

4.42 *For stroke order and other useful information about each of the following characters from this unit, go to the* Character Writing Workbook. *Choose either traditional or simplified characters and practice writing them until you can reproduce them on demand.*

國／国，中，英，美，出，會／会，說／说，話／话，
文，得，去，過／过，家，都，沒，喜，歡／欢

Writing a note

4.43 *Write a few sentences to a new friend, telling him or her your nationality, where you have lived in the past, and what language(s) you speak.*

Cultural Bits 文化点滴

Social interaction

View the video segment "Social interaction" and then discuss the following questions with your classmates.

- What is the function of the name card in establishing new relationships?
- Why might people ask where you're from? or where your parents came from?
- What is *zǔjí*?
- What do *guānxi* and *gǎnqíng* mean? What is the significance of *guānxi* and *gǎnqíng*?

Recap

▶ Grammar

The *shì . . . de* construction: Review

This pattern zeroes in on specific aspects of past actions, such as when, where, how, what, etc.

Nǐ shì zài nǎr chūshēng de? *(Where were you born?)*

Wǒ shì zài Běijīng chūshēng de. *(I was born in Beijing.)*

Verb + *guo*

Use an appropriate verb + *guo* to express having had an experience in the past.

Nǐ qùguo shénme dìfang? *(Where have you been?)*

Wǒ qùguo Měiguó hé Rìběn, méi qùguo Zhōngguó. *(I've been to the United States and Japan [but I] haven't been to China.)*

dōu + verb

Dōu, when used before a verb, means "all."

Nǐ dōu dàoguo shénme dìfang? *(What [all] places have you been to?)*

Ōuzhōu, Yàzhōu, Běi Měizhōu—dōu qùguo. *(Europe, Asia, North America—[I've] been to all [of them].)*

dōu + question word

Dōu, when used in conjunction with a question word, is "all inclusive" in an affirmative statement and "all exclusive" in a negative statement.

Wǒ nǎr dōu xiǎng qù. *(I'd like to go anywhere and everywhere.)*

Wǒ nǎr dōu méi qùguo. *(I haven't been anywhere.)*

Wǒ nǎr dōu bù xiǎng qù. *(I don't want to go anywhere.)*

▶ Vocabulary

Continents

Běi Měizhōu 北美洲 North America
Fēizhōu 非洲 Africa
Nán Měizhōu 南美洲 South America
Ōuzhōu 歐洲／欧洲 Europe
Yàzhōu 亞洲／亚洲 Asia

Country names and nationalities

[Asia]

Hánguó / Hánguórén 韓國／韓國人 ||
韩国／韩国人 Korea / Korean
Rìběn / Rìběnrén 日本／日本人 Japan / Japanese
Tàiguó / Tàiguórén 泰國／泰國人 || 泰国／泰国人 Thailand / Thai
Yìndù / Yìndùrén 印度／印度人 India / Indian
Zhōngguó / Zhōngguórén 中國／中國人 || 中国／中国人 China / Chinese

[North America]

Měiguó / Měiguórén 美國／美國人 || 美国／美国人 America / American

[Europe]

Déguó / Déguórén 德國／德國人 || 德国／德国人 Germany / German
Éguó / Éguórén 俄國／俄國人 || 俄国／俄国人 Russia / Russian
Fǎguó / Fǎguórén 法國／法國人 || 法国／法国人 France / French
Xībānyá / Xībānyárén 西班牙／西班牙人 Spain / Spanish
Yìdàlì / Yìdàlìrén 意大利／意大利人 Italy / Italian
Yīngguó /Yīngguórén 英國／英國人 || 英国／英国人 England / English

Languages

Déwén / Déyǔ / Déguóhuà 德文／德語／德國話 || 德文／德语／德国话 German

Éwén / Éyǔ / Éguóhuà 俄文／俄語／俄國話 || 俄文／俄语／俄国话 Russian

Fǎwén / Fǎyǔ / Fǎguóhuà 法文／法語／法國話 || 法文／法语／法国话 French

Hánwén / Hányǔ / Hánguóhuà 韓文／韓語／韓國話 || 韩文／韩语／韩国话 Korean

Rìwén / Rìyǔ / Rìběnhuà 日文／日語／日本話 || 日文／日语／日本话 Japanese

Xībānyáwén / Xībānyáyǔ / Xībānyáhuà 西班牙文／西班牙語／西班牙話 || 西班牙文／西班牙语／西班牙话 Spanish

Yìndùwén / Yìndùyǔ / Yìndùhuà 印度文／印度語／印度話 || 印度文／印度语／印度话 Hindi

Yīngwén / Yīngyǔ 英文／英語 || 英文／英语 English

Zhōngwén / Zhōngguóhuà 中文／中國話 || 中文／中国话 Chinese

Verbs

chūshēng 出生 be born
dāizai 呆在 stay (at)
dàoguo 到過／到过 been to
lái 來／来 come
lǚxíng 旅行 travel
qù 去 go
qùguo 去過／去过 gone to

shēngzai 生在 be born in
shuō 説／说 speak, say
xǐhuan 喜歡／喜欢 like, prefer
zhǎngdà 長大／长大 grow up
zhù 住 reside, live
zhùzai 住在 reside (at), live (at)

Auxiliary (helping) verbs

huì 會／会 can, be able to; be likely/sure to, will
xiǎng 想 want to; would like to; feel like

Adverbs

dōu 都 all
hái 還／还 still
háiyǒu 還有／还有 in addition there is
zhǐ 只 only

Other words and expressions

cóng 從／从 from
dìfang 地方 place
hé 和 and (connects nouns only, not clauses)
huà 話／话 words, speech; language
kěshì 可是 but, yet, however
míngnián 明年 next year
nǎli, nǎli 哪裡, 哪裡／哪里, 哪里 (polite rejection of a compliment)
yǐqián 以前 in the past, some time ago, formerly
yìzhí 一直 all along (in time or place)
zài 在 in, on, at

▌ Checklist of "can do" statements

After completing this unit, you should be able to perform each of the following tasks.

Listening and speaking
(Starred items are for review.)

- ☐ Ask questions about nationality.
- ☐ Understand when others tell their nationality.
- ☐ Ask others where their home is and provide information about your own home.
- ☐ Understand statements and ask questions about place of birth.
- ☐ Ask and answer questions about where you grew up.
- ☐ Pose questions to others about their travel experiences.
- ☐ Respond to questions about your own travel experiences.
- ☐ Ask and answer questions about places lived.
- ☐ Respond to and ask questions about languages spoken.
- ☐ *Tell others when your birthday is.

Reading and writing

- ☐ Recognize the names of 10–15 countries of the world.
- ☐ Read simple self-introductory statements about nationality, place of birth, places you have lived, and languages you can speak.
- ☐ Write simple self-introductory statements about your nationality, places you have lived, and languages you can speak.

Understanding culture

- ☐ Say what the standard national language of China is called and name two Chinese dialects.
- ☐ Give an example to explain how modesty is reflected in Chinese expressions.

In this unit, you will learn how to:

- respond to and make introductory statements about family members.

- ask and answer questions about birth order.

- describe the physical appearance of family members.

- read photo captions and simple statements describing family members.

- write simple statements about members of your family.

Encounter 1 Talking about nuclear family members

5.1 *View Episode 5 of the dramatic series.*

5.2 *Getting ready: How would you ask someone about his or her family members? If someone asked you about yours, what would you say?*

_____

_____

5.3 *Watch and listen to the video segment. How do you ask, "Who are the members of your family?" Fill in the blanks with pinyin.*

Nǐ _____ dōu yǒu shénme _____?

5.4 *Match the corresponding pinyin and English below.*

a. fùmǔ   1. mother (mom)

b. bàba   2. parents

c. māma   3. older brother

d. jiějie   4. father (dad)

e. gēge   5. older sister

f. mèimei   6. younger brother

g. dìdi   7. sisters

h. jiěmèi   8. younger sister

i. xiōngdì   9. siblings

j. xiōngdìjiěmèi   10. brothers

5.5 *Produce an approximate description of your family with check marks or numbers on the lines below. (You may also create an imaginary family, if you'd like.)*

Wǒ jiālǐ yǒu __5__ ge rén: __1__ bàba, __1__ māma, __1__ ge gēge, __1__ ge jiějie, __0__ ge dìdi, __0__ ge mèimei, hái yǒu wǒ.

5.6 Pair work: *Ask your partner about his or her family members and tell about yours. Take notes below.*

_____

_____

_____

_____

_____

Nǐ jiālǐ dōu yǒu shénme rén?

Wǒ jiālǐ yǒu . . .

Grammar Bits 语法点滴

To have (*yǒu*) and to have not (*méiyǒu*)

All Chinese verbs can become negative with the addition of *bù* (for example, *bù xǐhuan*), with the exception of *yǒu* (have). Never say ~~*bù yǒu*~~; always say *méiyǒu* (not have, be without). When *méiyǒu* is used in connected speech, *-you* is often unstressed: *Wǒ méiyou xiōngdìjiěmèi* (I don't have any siblings).

To *de* or not to *de*

You have already learned how to form the possessive in Chinese: *wǒ de shǒujī* (my cell phone); *Zhāng Lǎoshī de diànhuà hàomǎ* (Professor Zhang's telephone number). However, constructions without *de* are common when one talks of personal relationships: *Wǒ tóngxué xìng Lǐ* (My classmate is surnamed Li); *Tā gēge shì wǒ de péngyou* (Her older brother is my friend). Recall that, in other constructions, when the noun directly relates to oneself and to no one else, *de* can also be omitted: *Wǒ míngzi jiào Lynn* (My name is Lynn).

The most versatile measure word: *ge*

Recall that measure words are used with nouns in combination with specifiers (*zhèi, zhè, nèi, nà*) and numbers (*zhèi sān ge rén*). You have already learned that the measure word *ge* is used with common objects (*yí ge shǒujī*) and certain time words (*yí ge zhōngtóu, yí ge zǎoshang, yí ge wǎnshang, yí ge xīngqī, yí ge yuè* [but NOT with *yì tiān* or *yì nián*, as *tiān* and *nián* are themselves measure words]). In this unit, you'll see that it is also used with people: *liǎng ge dìdi, sān ge péngyou, wǔ ge tóngxué*. However, many nouns have their own particular measure word that relates to a specific class of nouns. In some respects, this is similar to English, as in three <u>loaves</u> of bread; six <u>slices</u> of pizza; two <u>skeins</u> of yarn; a <u>flock</u> of ducks. Chinese has many measure words, as you will see in later units. While you should learn the measure word that relates to each particular noun, you will find that *ge* is used with more nouns than any other measure word—therefore, when in doubt, use *ge*. However, don't use *ge* indiscriminately; use the proper measure word whenever you can. A "loaf of yarn" sounds as strange in Chinese as it does in English.

▶ Reading practice

5.7 *Read the following family terms aloud, using the English as a guide.*

媽媽 ／ 妈妈 *mother (mom)*

弟弟 *younger brother*

爸爸 *father (dad)*

妹妹 *younger sister*

父母 *parents*

姐妹 *sisters*

哥哥 *older brother*

兄弟 *brothers*

姐姐 *older sister*

兄弟姐妹 *siblings*

Encounter 2   Talking about immediate family members

5.8 *Look at the following words.*

shēng 生 *give birth*

jì 繼 ／ 继 *continue, follow after*

yǎng 養 ／ 养 *raise*

Based on what you know, can you figure out the meanings of the terms below? Match each Chinese word with the corresponding English equivalent.

a. shēngfù 生父

1. *foster/adoptive mother*

b. shēngmǔ 生母

2. *stepfather*

c. jìfù 繼父 ／ 继父

3. *birth mother*

d. jìmǔ 繼母 ／ 继母

4. *foster/adoptive father*

e. yǎngfù 養父 ／ 养父

5. *stepmother*

f. yǎngmǔ 養母 ／ 养母

6. *birth father*

5.9 *Circle any terms in the previous activity that apply to your family.*

FYI供你参考

Addressing family members—Chinese style

Chinese children call their father *bàba* and their mother *māma*, just as American children might call their parents "mommy" and "daddy." In a family with several children, both male and female, siblings address one another not by their given names but rather by birth order and relationship combinations. Younger children will call the oldest brother *dàgē* (eldest brother), the next oldest *èrgē* (second brother), and so on. Oldest sisters are called *dàjiě*, *èrjiě*, etc., while younger ones are called *èrmèi*, *sānmèi*, etc. In a home with two children, brothers will still address each other according to their relationship—the younger addressing the older as *gē* or *gēge* and the older addressing the younger as *dì* or *dìdi*. In a one-child family (more and more common because of China's one-child policy), parents often address children with *háizi* (child) or an endearing nickname, such as *máomáo* (little fuzzy [head]) or *bèibèi* (little precious).

5.10 *Now look at the following words.*

tóng 同 *same* (Recall that *tóngxué* means "classmate.")

yì 異／异 *different*

Can you figure out the meaning of the following sentence? Check the correct translation below.

Tā shì wǒ tóngmǔ-yìfù de mèimei.

她是我同母異父的妹妹。／她是我同母异父的妹妹。

☐ She is my half sister (we have the same father and different mothers).

☐ She is my half sister (we have the same mother and different fathers).

To simplify things, you can drop the first half of the hyphenated term; thus, a tóngmǔ-yìfù de mèimei can be simply a yìfù de mèimei.

5.11 *If you have any half siblings, write a complete sentence explaining the relationship. For example:* Wǒ yǒu yí ge yìmǔ de gēge, yí ge yìfù de dìdi.

_____

Stepbrothers and stepsisters are generally not acknowledged as siblings, but as "my stepmother's daughter," for example. If you have any stepsiblings, describe them here.

_____

5.12 *Now, can you rewrite the description of your family with greater accuracy? If you don't have any "step," "half," or adoptive relationships to report, copy your statement from exercise 5.5.*

_____

_____

_____

5.13 *Mingling: Walk around the room and ask your classmates* Nǐ jiālǐ dōu yǒu shénme rén? 你家裡都有甚麼人？／你家里都有什么人？ *Write in English what you can understand of their responses.*

名字：＿＿＿＿＿ 家人：＿＿＿＿＿＿＿＿＿＿＿＿＿＿＿＿＿＿

名字：＿＿＿＿＿ 家人：＿＿＿＿＿＿＿＿＿＿＿＿＿＿＿＿＿＿

名字：＿＿＿＿＿ 家人：＿＿＿＿＿＿＿＿＿＿＿＿＿＿＿＿＿＿

名字：＿＿＿＿＿ 家人：＿＿＿＿＿＿＿＿＿＿＿＿＿＿＿＿＿＿

名字：＿＿＿＿＿ 家人：＿＿＿＿＿＿＿＿＿＿＿＿＿＿＿＿＿＿

Encounter 3 Talking about birth order

5.14 *Getting ready: How would you ask someone about his or her birth order? If someone asked you about yours, what would you say?*

＿＿＿＿＿＿＿＿＿＿＿＿＿＿＿＿＿＿＿＿＿＿＿＿＿＿＿＿＿＿＿

 5.15 *Watch and listen to the video segment. What is the birth order of each person? Check the correct boxes and fill in the correct numbers, if necessary.*

a. ☐ only child

☐ eldest

☐ #＿＿＿

☐ youngest

b. ☐ only child

☐ eldest

☐ #＿＿＿

☐ youngest

c. ☐ only child

☐ eldest

☐ #＿＿＿

☐ youngest

d. ☐ only child

☐ eldest

☐ #＿＿＿

☐ youngest

5.16 *How would you ask someone about his or her birth order? Fill in the blanks in the two questions below, which can be used interchangeably.*

Nǐ shì lǎo_____? 你是老幾？／你是老几？

OR

Nǐ zài jiālǐ shì lǎo_____? 你在家裡是老幾？／你在家里是老几？

5.17 *Tell something about your birth order. Which of the following are you? Circle one.*

dúshēngzǐ 獨生子／独生子 *an only son*

dúshēngnǚ 獨生女／独生女 *an only daughter*

lǎodà 老大 *the eldest*

lǎo'èr 老二 *the second child*

lǎosān 老三 *the third child*

lǎosì 老四 *the fourth child*

. . .

lǎoyāo 老么／老幺 *the youngest child* (In northern China, people also say *lǎoxiǎo* 老小 for the youngest child.)

To preface a statement about your birth order, you can say *Wǒ shì* _____ OR *Wǒ* _____.

5.18 *Pair work: Ask your partner about his or her birth order. If your partner is not an only child, ask about his or her siblings.*

Nǐ shì lǎojǐ?

Wǒ shì . . .

Encounter 4 Describing family members

5.19 *Getting ready: How would you describe your family?*

_____

5.20 *Watch and listen to the video segment. Write at least one fact about each speaker's family, in English or in pinyin.*

1. _____

2. _____

3. _____

5.21 *Pair work: Tell your partner again who is in your family, this time in Chinese. Give one or more facts about each person, such as name, age, birthday, birth sign, where he or she lives, what language he or she speaks, etc. Write some information about your partner's family members.*

_____

_____

_____

5.22 *Watch and listen to the video segment. Match the corresponding pinyin and English terms.*

a. gāo   1. *fat*

b. ǎi   2. *neither fat nor thin (average)*

c. bù gāo (yě) bù ǎi   3. *tall*

d. pàng   4. *neither tall nor short (average)*

e. shòu   5. *short*

f. bú pàng (yě) bú shòu   6. *thin*

5.23 *Complete the following chart about physical appearances. Write the name or relationship of family members on each line and then check the appropriate physical characteristics.*

family member	gāo	ǎi	bù gāo (yě) bù ǎi	pàng	shòu	bú pàng (yě) bú shòu
	☐	☐	☐	☐	☐	☐
	☐	☐	☐	☐	☐	☐
	☐	☐	☐	☐	☐	☐
	☐	☐	☐	☐	☐	☐
	☐	☐	☐	☐	☐	☐
	☐	☐	☐	☐	☐	☐

5.24 *Using the chart from the previous exercise, make statements about the physical appearance of several people in your family. Follow the model to the right.*

_____

_____

_____

Wǒ māma hěn shòu. Wǒ bàba yě hěn shòu. Wǒ bú pàng bú shòu. Wǒ dìdi yòu ǎi yòu pàng.*

*yòu X yòu Y = *both X and Y*

▶ Reading practice

5.25 *Read the following expressions aloud, using the English as a guide.*

我媽媽很瘦。／我妈妈很瘦。　*My mother is thin.*

我爸爸也很瘦。　*My father is also thin.*

我不胖不瘦。　*I'm neither fat nor thin.*

我弟弟又矮又胖。　*My little brother is short and fat.*

FYI 供你参考

Understanding cultural differences

Although cultural differences may be diminishing with the growth of the global village, differences in habits and perspectives may still be noticeable between cultures. What might be considered pushy, intrusive, nosy, or downright rude in the United States may be no more than a demonstration of concern, caring, and intimacy by your Chinese friends. Examples include: "How old are you?" "How much are you earning these days?" "Do you have a boyfriend/girlfriend yet? Why not?" "You're getting fat! You should watch what you eat!" Conversely, conversation topics and behavior quite acceptable in the United States might strike Chinese as shockingly antisocial or disharmonious. Examples include: "No, I don't feel like going, so I'm not going to go." "None of your business! I don't want to talk about it." "Why do you put up with this rule? It's such a hassle!" While a certain amount of tension is likely to be inevitable, awareness of cultural differences can help create the sought-after sense of harmony.

Encounter 5 More family and personal relationships

 5.26 *Watch and listen to the video segment. Write* W *before the term that means "wife" and* H *before the term that means "husband."*

a. _____ qīzi 妻子

b. _____ lǎopó 老婆

c. _____ zhàngfu 丈夫

d. _____ lǎogōng 老公

e. _____ xiānsheng 先生

f. _____ àiren 愛人／爱人

g. _____ tàitai 太太

FYI 供你参考

From *xiānsheng/tàitai* to *àiren* and back again: Language reflecting culture

Language terms are in a constant state of flux in all societies, and they reflect political as well as cultural trends. The fact that Chinese society has always been particularly sensitive to age and status and proper forms of address makes matters even more complicated for the language student.

For decades, *xiānsheng* 先生 was used as a general term of address for "Mr." as well as "husband," while *tàitai* 太太 was used for "Mrs." as well as "wife." In the past, *xiǎojiě* 小姐 was the common term for "Miss." All three terms indicated individuals with a degree of social status.

After the birth of the People's Republic in 1949, however, *tóngzhì* 同志 "comrade" replaced *xiānsheng* 先生, *tàitai* 太太, and *xiǎojiě* 小姐, becoming the general term of address for all three. This reflected the newfound prestige of the proletariat as well as the social ideal of gender equality. In the same fashion, *àiren* 愛人／爱人 "beloved person" was used to mean both "husband" and "wife." Now it appears the pendulum has swung once again. Both *tóngzhì* 同志 and *àiren* 爱人／愛人 are now used less, and older titles are regaining their place, to some extent. Especially in Chinese communities outside of the PRC, it's still quite common to use *xiānsheng* 先生 and *tàitai* 太太 for "husband" and "wife," and *xiǎojiě* 小姐 for "Miss," regardless of social status. However, in the PRC *xiǎojiě* 小姐 is now sometimes used to indicate a bargirl or prostitute, and *tóngzhì* 同志 is now used to mean a gay man or a lesbian. Both terms should be used with extreme caution.

As for "husband" and "wife," the Chinese can be rather cagey about these potentially embarassing terms, presumably because the spousal relationship implies sexual activity. The informal terms *lǎogōng* 老公 ("old man") and *lǎopó* 老婆 ("old lady") are commonly used; *zhàngfu* 丈夫 (spouse, male) and *qīzi* 妻子 (spouse, female) are used only in formal situations; and such terms as *wǒ de nèi wèi* 我的那位 (that fellow/gal of mine) or *háizi tā bà / mā* 孩子他爸／媽（妈）(the child's dad/mom) abound in casual conversation. Look for the scene in Episode 4 of the dramatic series, for example, in which Tang Yuan's mother addresses her husband as "*Tā bà!*" ([His] Dad!).

5.27 Mingling: *Draw a picture of your spouse (or an imaginary spouse, if you're not married). Walk around the class and introduce your "spouse" to your classmates by saying, "Zhè shì wǒ ___." Then add another piece of information about your "spouse."*

5.28 *Watch and listen to the video segment. Then write the English equivalent of each of the following terms.*

男朋友 nánpéngyou _____

女朋友 nǚpéngyou _____

5.29 *How do you ask if someone has a girlfriend or boyfriend? Write the pinyin (or appropriate characters) here.*

_____

5.30 Pair work: *Ask your partner whether he or she has a* 男朋友 *or* 女朋友. *If so, try to find out more about that boyfriend or girlfriend. If not, make small talk with your partner until you run out of time. Take some notes about what your partner said.*

_____

_____

5.31 *Watch and listen to the video segment. How many children does each speaker have? Fill in the correct numbers in the blanks below.*

a. _____   b. _____   c. _____

5.32 *Match the corresponding items.*

a. háizi   1. *daughter*   A. 孩子

b. nǚhái   2. *girl*   B. 男孩兒／男孩儿

c. nánhái   3. *child(ren)*   C. 女孩兒／女孩儿

d. érzi   4. *boy*   D. 女兒／女儿

e. nǚ'ér   5. *son*   E. 兒子／儿子

Note: *Háizi* 孩子 and *hái r* 孩兒／孩儿 are interchangeable for "child." *Hái r* 孩兒／孩儿 tends to be used in northern China, and *háizi* 孩子 everywhere else.

5.33 *How do you ask if someone has any children? Write the pinyin (or appropriate characters) here.*

_____

5.34 *Pair work: Draw a portrait of your children (real or imaginary) on a piece of paper. Turn to your partner and find out how many children he or she has, as well as something about each child. Then turn to another classmate and tell him or her about your partner's children.*

Encounter 6 Extending the family

5.35 Getting ready: *What would you say if someone asked you about your extended family?*

_____

_____

 5.36 *Watch and listen to the video segment. Then match the corresponding items below.*

a. *uncle: father's older brother*

b. *aunt: father's older brother's wife*

c. *uncle: father's younger brother*

d. *aunt: father's sister*

e. *uncle: mother's brother*

f. *aunt: mother's sister*

g. *paternal grandfather*

h. *paternal grandmother*

i. *maternal grandfather*

j. *maternal grandmother*

k. *grandparents*

1. bóbo de qīzi = bómǔ 伯母

2. bàba de gēge = bóbo 伯伯

3. māma de xiōngdì = jiùjiu 舅舅

4. māma de jiěmèi = āyí 阿姨

5. fùmǔ de fùmǔ = zǔfùmǔ 祖父母

6. bàba de dìdi = shūshu 叔叔

7. bàba de bàba = yéye 爺爺／爷爷

8. bàba de jiěmèi = gūgu 姑姑

9. bàba de māma = nǎinai 奶奶

10. māma de māma = wàipó 外婆

    or lǎolao 姥姥

11. māma de bàba = wàigōng 外公

    or lǎoye 姥爺／姥爷

FYI 供你参考

Chinese terms for family members

If you find that Chinese family terms are complicated, it's because they are! And the list in exercise 5.36 isn't even complete. For example, *shěnshen* 嬸嬸／婶婶 is the wife of 叔叔, *yízhàng* 姨丈 is the husband of 阿姨, *gūzhàng* 姑丈 is the husband of 姑姑, and *jiùmā* 舅媽 is the wife of 舅舅—not to mention their children! Names for cousins (and nieces and nephews) differ depending on whether they are on the father's or mother's side of the family. Cousins on the father's side are *tánggē* 堂哥, *tángjiě* 堂姐, *tángdì* 堂弟, and *tángmèi* 堂妹. The character 堂 means "hall," and these terms imply that all cousins by patrilineal descent (following the father) share the same ancestral hall (and the father's last name). Cousins on the mother's side are *biǎogē* 表哥, *biǎojiě* 表姐, *biǎodì* 表弟, and *biǎomèi* 表妹, with the character 表 implying a relationship "outside" the patrilineal clan. Note that there is also differentiation by age and gender. One generation down, a brother's son is a *zhízi* 侄子 and his daughter is a *zhínǚ* 侄女, while a sister's son is a *wàisheng* 外甥 and her daughter is a *wàishengnǚ* 外甥女. Two generations down, children of a son are the *sūnzi* 孫子／孙子 and *sūnnǚ* 孫女／孙女, while children of a daughter are the *wàisūn* 外孫／外孙 and *wàisūnnǚ* 外孫女／外孙女. Again, these terms reflect direct descent through the male line and relegate the female line of descent to an indirect, external status (the character 外 means "outside").

For the learner, it does not simplify matters that there are also regional distinctions to consider. One regional variance presented here is for maternal grandparents. Many Chinese people living overseas have the terms *gōnggong* 公公 and *pópo* 婆婆 lodged firmly in their vocabularies as general terms of address for grandparents or anyone of their grandparents' generation. These are the terms for maternal grandparents that are widely used in southern China (where many overseas Chinese have ancestral roots). In modern standard parlance, however, *gōngpó* 公婆 is what a wife would call her husband's parents.

5.37 *Write the Chinese terms for any grandparents, aunts, and uncles you have, together with what you call them in English.*

_____

_____

5.38 *Pair work: Take three index cards and draw a person on one side of each card. On the other side, write down your relationship to that person. Then work with a partner to perform the following dialogue multiple times. Switch roles between pictures.*

A: Tā shì nǐ de shénme rén? *(What is he/she to you?)*

B: Nǐ cāicai kàn. *(Take a guess.)*

A: Tā shì nǐ de _____. *(He/She is your _____.)*

B: Duì. / Bú duì. *(Right. / Wrong.)*

Continue guessing until student B answers Duì. *Repeat for the next picture.*

Grammar Bits 语法点滴

Repeating verbs for effect

Verbs can be said twice in a row for effect, in which case the two verbs together form one word, such as *cāicai* (take a guess). This makes the verb less forceful or imperative, and more tentative and polite, as suggested by such English formations as "give it a try, have a look, try [VERB + -ing] a bit." The verb *kàn* (see) is sometimes added to enhance the informal, polite flavor. Here are some examples.

Nǐ cāicai kàn. *(Take a guess—and let's see what you come up with.)*

Nǐ chīchi kàn ba. *(Here, have a taste. Try some.)*

Nǐ shuōshuo kàn. *(Try telling me. Try saying it.)*

Nǐ kànkan ba. *(Why don't you take a look and see?)*

Nǐ wènwen Lǐ Lǎoshī ba. *(Try asking Professor Li.)*

5.39 Socializing: *Bring some family pictures to class. Introduce family members to your classmates in Chinese, and ask questions about people your classmates introduce to you.*

FYI 供你参考

How people address one another in the community

Respect for age and status is shown both within the Chinese home and in the wider community. People often treat each other as members of one big extended family, even when there's no real family relationship involved. All children are called *xiǎo mèimei* 小妹妹 or *xiǎo dìdi* 小弟弟. Children call adults *shūshu* 叔叔 or *āyí* 阿姨. Young or middle-aged adults may call each other *gē* 哥 or *jiě* 姐, and older adults may call each other *bóbo* 伯伯 or *bómǔ* 伯母. Adults and children call elderly people (about 70 years old or older) *yéye* 爺爺／爷爷 and *nǎinai* 奶奶. In youth slang, young men call each other *gēmenr* 哥們兒／哥们儿.

♫ Unit Rap

Go to the **Encounters** *website at* www.EncountersChinese.com *and listen to the song to review key expressions from Unit 5. Listen again and sing along!*

Encounter 7 Reading and writing

▶ Reading familiar sentences in Chinese characters

5.40 Pair work: *Read the following dialogues (written in traditional characters) aloud with a partner, using the English as a guide.*

1 甲：你家裡都有甚麼人？ *(Who all are in your family?)*

乙：只有我和我父母。你呢？ *(Just [zhǐ yǒu] my parents and me. And you?)*

甲：我家有我媽媽，我繼父，我，三個姐姐，兩個妹妹，還有我繼父的弟弟，我們家人很多！
(For my family, there's my mother, my stepfather, me, three older sisters, two younger sisters, and my stepfather's younger brother. There are a lot of people in my family!)

2 甲：你有哥哥姐姐嗎？ *(Do you have [older] brothers or sisters?)*

乙：沒有。我沒有兄弟姐妹。你呢？ *(No, I don't have any siblings. What about you?)*

甲：我也是獨生子。 *(I'm an only child too.)*

3 甲：你們家有幾個人？ *(How many are there in your family?)*

乙：我們家有四個人。我媽媽，我，一個妹妹，一個弟弟。我沒有爸爸。 *(There are four in my family. My mother, me, a younger sister, and a younger brother. I don't have a father.)*

甲：你妹妹弟弟幾歲了？ *(How old are your little brother and sister?)*

乙：妹妹十歲了，弟弟才一歲。 *(My sister's 10, my brother's only [cái] 1.)*

4 甲：Lynn 的父親是她的生父還是養父啊？ *(Is Lynn's father her birth father or adoptive father?)*

乙：我想是她生父，不是嗎？ *(I think he's her birth father, right?)*

5 甲：你家人都在哪裡？ *(Where is everyone in your family?)*

乙：我父母在英國，我姐姐和他丈夫在印度，我弟弟在美國。可是我爺爺奶奶，外公外婆都在中國。 *(My parents are in England, my older sister and her husband are in India, and my younger brother is in the United States. But my [paternal and maternal] grandparents are all in China.)*

6 甲：你是老幾？ *(Which child are you in your family?)*

乙：我是老大。你呢？ *(I'm the eldest. What about you?)*

甲：我是老么。 *(I'm the youngest.)*

7 甲：你很高。你父母也都很高嗎？ *(You're tall. Are both your parents tall too?)*

乙：我母親高，我父親很矮。我母親又高又瘦；我父親又矮又胖。 *(My mother's tall, and my father's short. My mother is tall and skinny, and my father is short and fat.)*

8 甲： Alejandro 有老婆嗎？ *(Does Alejandro have a wife?)*

乙：有。他妻子叫 April。 *(Yes. His wife's name is April.)*

甲：你呢？你有太太嗎？ *(How about you? Do you have a wife?)*

乙：沒有。可是我有個女朋友。 *(No. But I have a girlfriend.)*

9 甲：你和你先生有孩子嗎？ *(Do you and your husband have children?)*

乙：沒有。你們呢？ *(No. How about you?)*

甲：我和我太太有兩個孩子。 *(My wife and I have two children.)*

乙：男孩兒還是女孩兒？ *(Boys or girls?)*

甲：我們有一個女兒，一個兒子。 *(We have a daughter and a son.)*

10 甲：爺爺，奶奶！你們來了！ *(Grandpa, Grandma! You're here!)*

乙：小毛。你又高了啊！ *(Xiao Mao. You've grown taller!)*

甲：爸，媽！爺爺，奶奶來了！ *(Dad, Mom! Grandpa and Grandma are here!)*

乙：你伯伯，伯母來了嗎？ *(Have your uncle and aunt [paternal] come yet?)*

甲：還沒呢。阿姨舅舅來了。 *(Not yet, but Auntie and Uncle [maternal] are here.)*

11 甲：叔叔阿姨，你們好！ *(Hello, Uncle and Auntie!)*

乙：小妹妹，你好！你媽呢？ *(Hi, little girl! Where's your mother?)*

甲：在我姥姥，姥爺家！ *(She's at my [maternal] grandma and grandpa's home!)*

5.41 Pair work: *Read the dialogues aloud with a partner, this time without any English.*

1 甲：你家裡都有甚麼人？

乙：只有我和我父母。你呢？

甲：我家有我媽媽，我繼父，我，三個姐姐，兩個妹妹，還有我繼父的弟弟，我們家人很多！

2 甲：你有哥哥姐姐嗎？

乙：沒有。我沒有兄弟姐妹。你呢？

甲：我也是獨生子。

3 甲：你們家有幾個人？

乙：我們家有四個人。我媽媽，我，一個妹妹，一個弟弟。我沒有爸爸。

甲：你妹妹弟弟幾歲了？

乙：妹妹十歲了，弟弟才一歲。

4 甲：Lynn 的父親是她的生父還是養父啊？

乙：我想是她生父，不是嗎？

5 甲：你家人都在哪裡？

乙：我父母在英國，我姐姐和他丈夫在印度，我弟弟在美國。可是我爺爺奶奶，外公外婆都在中國。

6 甲：你是老幾？

乙：我是老大。你呢？

甲：我是老么。

7 甲：你很高。你父母也都很高嗎？

乙：我母親高，我父親很矮。我母親又高又瘦；我父親又矮又胖。

8 甲：Alejandro 有老婆嗎？

乙：有。他妻子叫 April。

甲：你呢？你有太太嗎？

乙：沒有。可是我有個女朋友。

9 甲：你和你先生有孩子嗎？

乙：沒有。你們呢？

甲：我和我太太有兩個孩子。

乙：男孩兒還是女孩兒？

甲：我們有一個女兒，一個兒子。

10 甲：爺爺，奶奶！你們來了！

乙：小毛。你又高了啊！

甲：爸，媽！爺爺，奶奶來了！

乙：你伯伯，伯母來了嗎？

甲：還沒呢。阿姨舅舅來了。

11 甲：叔叔阿姨，你們好！

乙：小妹妹，你好！你媽呢？

甲：在我姥姥，姥爺家！

5.42 Pair work: *Now try it once again, this time in simplified characters.*

1 甲：你家里都有什么人？

乙：只有我和我父母。你呢？

甲：我家有我妈妈，我继父，我，三个姐姐，两个妹妹，
　　还有我继父的弟弟，我们家人很多！

2 甲：你有哥哥姐姐吗？

乙：没有。我没有兄弟姐妹。你呢？

甲：我也是独生子。

3 甲：你们家有几个人？

乙：我们家有四个人。我妈妈，我，一个妹妹，一个弟弟。
　　我没有爸爸。

甲：你妹妹弟弟几岁了？

乙：妹妹十岁了，弟弟才一岁。

4 甲：Lynn 的父亲是她的生父还是养父啊？

乙：我想是她生父，不是吗？

5 甲：你家人都在哪里？

乙：我父母在英国，我姐姐和他丈夫在印度，我弟弟在美
　　国。可是我爷爷奶奶，外公外婆都在中国。

6 甲：你是老几？

乙：我是老大。你呢？

甲：我是老幺。

7 甲：你很高。你父母都很高吗？

乙：我母亲高，我父亲很矮。我母亲又高又瘦；我父亲又矮又胖。

8 甲：Alejandro 有老婆吗？

乙：有。他妻子叫 April。

甲：你呢？你有太太吗？

乙：没有。可是我有个女朋友。

9 甲：你和你先生有孩子吗？

乙：没有。你们呢？

甲：我和我太太有两个孩子。

乙：男孩儿还是女孩儿？

甲：我们有一个儿子，一个女儿。

10 甲：爷爷，奶奶！你们来了！

乙：小毛。你又高了啊！

甲：爸，妈！爷爷，奶奶来了！

乙：你伯伯，伯母来了吗？

甲：还没呢。阿姨舅舅来了。

11 甲：叔叔阿姨，你们好！

乙：小妹妹，你好！你妈呢？

甲：在我姥姥，姥爷家！

5.43 *Match the corresponding simplified characters, traditional characters, and English.*

a. 妈妈	1. 繼父	A. *only child (girl)*
b. 继父	2. 獨生女	B. *"same father, different mother"*
c. 继母	3. 爺爺	C. *mother*
d. 同父异母	4. 同父異母	D. *adoptive father*
e. 同母异父	5. 同母異父	E. *paternal grandfather*
f. 独生女	6. 媽媽	F. *"same mother, different father"*
g. 养父	7. 養母	G. *stepfather*
h. 养母	8. 養父	H. *adoptive mother*
i. 爷爷	9. 繼母	I. *stepmother*

▶ Reading real-life texts

5.44 *This is a family photo taken when Allan Yu (余毅廉) was a boy. Read the descriptions of his family members, and then answer the following questions.*

我的名字叫余毅廉。我今年十岁。这是我的全家福。坐着的那两位是我妈妈和爸爸。我站在我妈的右边，靠后。我小妹妹站在我前面。顺着时钟排的还有我嫂嫂，我侄子，大哥，二哥，弟弟，和小侄女。我父母，两个哥哥，嫂嫂，和我都生在中国。我弟弟，妹妹，侄子和侄女都是在美国出生的。我属虎。我是1950年，四月十八日生的。我大哥比我大十五岁，他属猪。他和我嫂嫂有两个孩子：一个男孩儿，一个女孩儿。我二哥属鼠，弟弟属马，妹妹属猴。我觉得我妈妈很漂亮，我爸爸脾气很好。

a. What is Allan's birth date? Write in English: _____

b. What is Allan's birth order? _____

c. When was this picture taken? _____

d. Check the choice that correctly completes the sentence:

Allan's eldest brother has _____.

☐ two sons   ☐ two daughters   ☐ a son and a daughter

e. What do you think the term 嫂嫂 (*sǎosao*) means? Check the correct answer.

☐ younger brother's wife   ☐ older brother's wife   ☐ sister's husband

f. What is each person's birth sign? Write in English.

Allan: _____

Allan's younger brother: _____

Allan's younger sister: _____

g. Can you figure out each person's age at the time the picture was taken, based on his or her birth sign? Consult the chart on page 48, if necessary.

Allan's second eldest brother: _____

Allan's younger brother: _____

Allan's younger sister: _____

h. On the photo, label persons born in China with "C." Label persons born in America with "A."

Learning to write characters

5.45 *For stroke order and other useful information about each of the following characters from this unit, go to the* Character Writing Workbook. *Choose either traditional or simplified characters and practice writing them until you can reproduce them on demand.*

裡／里，個／个，和，爸，媽／妈，哥，姐，弟，妹，兄，
男，女，父，母，親／亲，才，兩／两

Writing a note

5.46 *Write a detailed note to accompany a family photo (draw your family if no photo is available). Identify each person and add a detail or two about each.*

Cultural Bits 文化点滴

Changing families

View the video segment "Changing families" and then discuss the following questions with your classmates.

- What is the significance of the family in China?
- What does "paternal lineage" mean and imply?
- What are some implications of being female in China?
- Name some members of a family in which there are "four generations under one roof" *(sìshì-tóngtáng)*.
- What have been some of the consequences of the "one-child" policy?

Recap

Grammar

The unique negative: *méi*

Always use the special negative *méi* for *méiyǒu*.

Wǒ yǒu yí ge jiějie. Wǒ méiyǒu mèimei. *(I have an older sister. I don't have a younger sister.)*

Possessives without *de*

When the relationship is close, constructions without *de* are common with personal pronouns.

Wǒ tàitai xìng Lǐ. *(My wife is surnamed Li.)*

BUT

Tā de péngyou jiào Mǎkè. *(Her friend is named Mark.)*

The versatile measure word: *ge*

Use the measure word *ge* to talk about people, including family members and personal relationships.

liǎng ge rén *(two people)*

sì ge péngyou *(four friends)*

jǐ ge háizi? *(how many children?)*

Use of *dōu* in lists: Review

When lists of things are asked for or given, the adverb *dōu* is regularly used. Note its position in the following examples.

> Nǐ jiālǐ dōu yǒu shénme rén? *(Who do you have in your family?)*

> Zhōngguó, Měiguó, Fǎguó, Déguó, wǒ dōu qùguo. *(I've been to China, the United States, France, and Germany.)*

Repeating the verb to lessen effect

Verbs can be repeated and said as one word to lessen the force of the verb and make it more of a suggestion. *Kàn* (see) is often added for increased effect. The sentence-ending particle *ba* is also often seen in this pattern.

> Nǐ cāicai kàn. *(Take a guess and see [what you come up with].)*

> Nǐ kànkan ba. *(Why don't you take a look and see?)*

▶ Vocabulary

Immediate family members

bàba 爸爸　father (dad)
dìdi 弟弟　younger brother
fùmǔ 父母　parents
gēge 哥哥　older brother
jiějie 姐姐　older sister
jiěmèi 姐妹　sisters
māma 媽媽／妈妈　mother (mom)
mèimei 妹妹　younger sister
xiōngdì 兄弟　brothers
xiōngdìjiěmèi 兄弟姐妹　brothers and sisters

Extended family members

āyí 阿姨　aunt (mother's sister)
bóbo 伯伯　uncle (father's older brother)
bómǔ 伯母　aunt (wife of father's older brother)
gūgu 姑姑　aunt (father's sister)
jìfù 繼父／继父　stepfather
jìmǔ 繼母／继母　stepmother
jiùjiu 舅舅　uncle (mother's brother)
lǎolao / wàipó 姥姥／外婆　(maternal) grandmother
lǎoye / wàigōng 姥爺／外公 || 姥爷／外公　(maternal) grandfather
nǎinai 奶奶　(paternal) grandmother

shēngfù 生父　birth father
shēngmǔ 生母　birth mother
shūshu 叔叔　uncle (father's younger brother)
(tóngfù-)yìmǔ de xiōngdìjiěmèi (同父-) 異母的兄弟姊妹／(同父-) 异母的兄弟姐妹　half sibling (same father)
(tóngmǔ-)yìfù de xiōngdìjiěmèi (同母-) 異父的兄弟姊妹／(同母-) 异父的兄弟姐妹　half sibling (same mother)
yǎngfù 養父／养父　foster / adoptive father
yǎngmǔ 養母／养母　foster / adoptive mother
yéye 爺爺／爷爷　(paternal) grandfather

Birth order

dúshēngzǐ 獨生子／独生子　only child (boy)
dúshēngnǚ 獨生女／独生女　only child (girl)
lǎodà 老大　oldest child
lǎo'èr 老二　second child
lǎoyāo 老么／老幺　youngest child

Other family relationships

àiren 愛人／爱人　spouse
érzi 兒子／儿子　son
háizi 孩子　child(ren)

lǎogōng 老公　husband
lǎopó 老婆　wife
nánháir 男孩兒／男孩儿　boy
nǚ'ér 女兒／女儿　daughter
nǚháir 女孩兒／女孩儿　girl
qīzi 妻子　wife
tàitai 太太　wife
xiānsheng 先生　husband
zhàngfu 丈夫　husband

Descriptive words

ǎi 矮　short
bù gāo (yě) bù ǎi 不高(也)不矮　neither tall nor short
bú pàng (yě) bú shòu 不胖(也)不瘦　neither fat nor thin
gāo 高　tall
pàng 胖　fat
shòu 瘦　thin
yòu . . . yòu 又……又　both . . . and
yòu ǎi yòu pàng 又矮又胖　both short and fat
yòu gāo yòu shòu 又高又瘦　both tall and thin

Other words and expressions

cāicai kàn 猜猜看　guess
méiyǒu 没有　not have, be without
yǒu 有　have

▶ **Checklist of "can do" statements**

After completing this unit, you should be able to perform each of the following tasks.

Listening and speaking

☐ Give details about the composition of your immediate family.

☐ Ask a friend about the members of his or her family.

☐ Ask and answer questions about extended family members.

☐ Be able to describe, in simple terms, some of your family members.

Reading and writing

☐ Understand the relationship of family members listed in simple photo captions.

☐ Read simple self-introductory statements about a family and family members.

☐ Write a simple statement about your family composition, and provide an additional descriptive statement for each member.

Understanding culture

☐ Test your new knowledge about Chinese families with a Chinese friend or acquaintance. Find out how he or she refers to immediate family members.

☐ Make two or three accurate statements in English about how China's patrilineal family structure is manifested in the Chinese language.

UNIT 6

"Happy at home and work"

安居樂業

Ānjūlèyè

Discussing school, professions, and careers

In this unit, you will learn how to:

- ask and answer questions about school and grade level.
- ask and answer questions about future professions.
- ask and answer questions about the reasons behind a future career choice.
- talk about the professions of family members and friends.

- read and understand information on want ads and help wanted signs.
- read and understand simple self-introductory statements about professions.
- write simple self-introductory statements about professions for yourself, your family, and your friends.

Encounter 1 Talking about school and grade level

 6.1 *View Episode 6 of the dramatic series.*

6.2 *Getting ready: If someone asks what you do and you're a student, what would you say? Write two to three details in English about your studies.*

_____

_____

 6.3 *Watch and listen to the video segment. Then match the questions with the responses.*

a. Nǐ shì xuéshēng ma?

你是學生嗎？／你是学生吗？

b. Nǐ zài nǎr niànshū?

你在哪兒念書？／你在哪儿念书？

c. Nǐ niàn jǐ niánjí?

你念幾年級？／你念几年级？

1. Wǒ zài _____ dàxué dúshū.

我在_____大學讀書。／我在_____大学读书。

2. Wǒ shì xuéshēng.

我是學生。／我是学生。

3. Sān niánjí.

三年級。／三年级。

6.4 *Write the pinyin for "Are you a student?"*

_____

6.5 *Check the statement below that pertains to you.*

☐ Wǒ niàn yánjiūshēngyuàn. Wǒ shì yánjiūshēng. 我念研究生院。我是研究生。
 (I am in graduate school. I am a graduate student.)

☐ Wǒ niàn dàxué. Wǒ shì dàxuéshēng. 我念大學。我是大學生。／我念大学。我是大学生。
 (I am in college. I am a college student.)

☐ Wǒ niàn gāozhōng. Wǒ shì gāozhōngshēng. 我念高中。我是高中生。
 (I am in high school. I am a high school student.)

☐ Wǒ niàn chūzhōng. Wǒ shì chūzhōngshēng. 我念初中。我是初中生。
 (I am in middle school. I am a middle school student.)

☐ Wǒ niàn xiǎoxué. Wǒ shì xiǎoxuéshēng. 我念小學。我是小學生。／我念小学。我是小学生。
 (I am in elementary school. I am an elementary school student.)

☐ Wǒ bú shì xuéshēng. Wǒ yǒu gōngzuò. 我不是學生。我有工作。／我不是学生。我有工作。
 (I am not a student. I have a job.)

Grammar Bits 语法点滴

Flexing your verbal muscles: Verb-object combinations

Niànshū 念書／念书 and *dúshū* 讀書／读书 both mean "to study." Both are examples of Chinese verbs that express action on a generalized object—called verb-object (VO) combinations. So, "to study" is "study-books" or *niànshū*, "to speak" is "say-words" or *shuōhuà*, "to earn" is "earn-money" or *zhuànqián*.
All verb-object combinations can:

- be split and made specific: *niàn wǒ de Zhōngwén shū* (study <u>my Chinese</u> book)
- be split and minimized: *zhuàn yìdiǎnr qián* (earn <u>a little</u> money)
- be split and maximized: *zhuàn hěn duō qián* (earn <u>lots of</u> money)
- shift their object: *niànshū* ⇒ *niàn dàxué* (study <u>in college</u>)

6.6 *Match the corresponding English, pinyin, and characters.*

a. *graduate school*   1. gāozhōng   A. 初中

b. *college*   2. xiǎoxué   B. 大學／大学

c. *high school*   3. dàxué   C. 高中

d. *middle school*   4. yánjiūshēngyuàn   D. 小學／小学

e. *elementary school*   5. chūzhōng   E. 研究生院

Note: In Taiwan, graduate school is called *yánjiùsuǒ* 研究所.

Based on these terms, can you guess the meaning of the following characters? Fill in the blanks, using English.

大 _____   中 _____   小 _____

FYI 供你参考

The Chinese educational system

Preschool*	*Tuō'érsuǒ*			
Kindergarten*	*Yòuzhìyuán* [Taiwan] / *Yòu'éryuán* [PRC]			
Grade 1	*Xiǎoxué*	*Chūxiǎo*	*Xiǎoxué yī niánjí*	
Grade 2			*Xiǎoxué èr niánjí*	
Grade 3			*Xiǎoxué sān niánjí*	
Grade 4		*Gāoxiǎo*	*Xiǎoxué sì niánjí*	
Grade 5			*Xiǎoxué wǔ niánjí*	
Grade 6			*Xiǎoxué liù niánjí*	
Grade 7	*Zhōngxué*	*Chūzhōng*	*Chūzhōng yī niánjí*	(*Chūyī*)
Grade 8			*Chūzhōng èr niánjí*	(*Chū'èr*)
Grade 9			*Chūzhōng sān niánjí*	(*Chūsān*)
Grade 10		*Gāozhōng*	*Gāozhōng yī niánjí*	(*Gāoyī*)
Grade 11			*Gāozhōng èr niánjí*	(*Gāo'èr*)
Grade 12			*Gāozhōng sān niánjí*	(*Gāosān*)
First-year college	*Dàxué*		*Dàxué yī niánjí*	(*Dàyī*)
Second-year college			*Dàxué èr niánjí*	(*Dà'èr*)
Third-year college			*Dàxué sān niánjí*	(*Dàsān*)
Fourth-year college			*Dàxué sì niánjí*	(*Dàsì*)
Graduate school	*Yánjiùsuǒ* [Taiwan] / *Yánjiūshēngyuàn* [PRC]			

*Preschool children are generally two years old. By age three, children enter kindergarten, where they remain for three years. Children in first grade are usually six years old.

6.7 *What do you think the following means? Write the English.*

a. Nǐ niàn jǐ niánjí? 你念幾年級？／你念几年级？ _____

If you are in school, answer by underlining one choice and filling in the blank below.

b. Wǒ niàn
| yánjiūshēngyuàn |
| dàxué |
| gāozhōng |
| chūzhōng |
| xiǎoxué |
_____ niánjí.

Do this again for the same statement in characters.

c. 我念
| 研究生院 |
| 大學／大学 |
| 高中 |
| 初中 |
| 小學／小学 |
_____ 年級。

6.8 Pair work: *Ask your partner whether he or she, or anyone in his or her family, is in school. If the answer is "yes," press for details. Answer any questions your partner asks, then switch roles.*

> Nǐ shì xuéshēng ma?

> Shì de. Wǒ . . .

6.9 Mingling: *Now ask others in your class for the same information, asking and answering appropriate questions.*

Encounter 2 Discussing career choices

6.10 Getting ready: *How would you ask a fellow student what he or she wants to be in the future? Write a question as well as your own response to it.*

_____

_____

6.11 *Watch and listen to the video segment. Then answer each question by checking the appropriate column.*

	an actor	a doctor	doesn't know
a. What does the man in the grey T-shirt want to be?	☐	☐	☐
b. What do his parents want him to be?	☐	☐	☐
c. What does the man in the orange T-shirt want to be?	☐	☐	☐

6.12 *Listen to the audio. What do you think each person's profession is? Circle one.*

1. 醫生／医生
   - (a.) yīshēng
     doctor
   - b. yùndòngyuán
     athlete
   - c. jiàoshòu
     professor

2. 護士／护士
   - a. sījī
     driver
   - (b.) hùshi
     nurse
   - c. gēxīng
     singer

3. 秘書／秘书
   - (a.) mìshū
     secretary
   - b. nóngmín
     farmer
   - c. gōngrén
     laborer

4. 律師／律师
   - a. gōngrén
     laborer
   - b. jǐngchá
     police officer
   - (c.) lùshī
     lawyer

5. 建築師／建筑师
   - (a.) jiànzhùshī
     architect
   - b. jiùhuǒyuán
     firefighter
   - c. fúwùyuán
     waiter, salesclerk

6. 工程師／工程师
   - a. mìshū
     secretary
   - (b.) gōngchéngshī
     engineer
   - c. jūnrén
     soldier

7. 演員／演员
   - (a.) yǎnyuán
     actor
   - b. jīnglǐ
     manager
   - c. jiànzhùshī
     architect

8. 歌星
   - a. jiàoshòu
     professor
   - b. fúwùyuán
     waiter, salesclerk
   - (c.) gēxīng
     singer

9. 運動員／运动员
   - a. jūnrén
     soldier
   - b. gōngrén
     laborer
   - (c.) yùndòngyuán
     athlete

10. 經理／经理
    - (a.) jīnglǐ
      manager
    - b. jiànzhùshī
      architect
    - c. yīshēng
      doctor

11. 工人
    - a. lùshī
      lawyer
    - b. yīshēng
      doctor
    - (c.) gōngrén
      laborer

12. 司機／司机
    - a. kuàijìshī
      accountant
    - (b.) sījī
      driver
    - c. hùshi
      nurse

13. 服務員／服务员
   a. gēxīng
   singer
   b. fúwùyuán
   waiter, salesclerk
   c. jiànzhùshī
   architect

14. 警察
   a. jǐngchá
   police officer
   b. gōngrén
   laborer
   c. sījī
   driver

15. 軍人／军人
   a. jūnrén
   soldier
   b. yǎnyuán
   actor
   c. gōngchéngshī
   engineer

16. 救火員／救火员
   a. yùndòngyuán
   athlete
   b. jiùhuǒyuán
   firefighter
   c. gōngrén
   laborer

17. 農民／农民
   a. nóngmín
   farmer
   b. yǎnyuán
   actor
   c. yīshēng
   doctor

18. 教授
   a. sījī
   driver
   b. jǐngchá
   police officer
   c. jiàoshòu
   professor

19. 會計師／会计师
   a. jiùhuǒyuán
   firefighter
   b. yīnyuèjiā
   musician
   c. kuàijìshī
   accountant

20. 作家
   a. zuòjiā
   writer
   b. gōngrén
   laborer
   c. gēxīng
   singer

21. 音樂家／音乐家
   a. yīnyuèjiā
   musician
   b. lǜshī
   lawyer
   c. hùshi
   nurse

22. 藝術家／艺术家
   a. gōngchéngshī
   engineer
   b. yùndòngyuán
   athlete
   c. yìshùjiā
   artist

23. 老師／老师
   a. gēxīng
   singer
   b. lǎoshī
   teacher
   c. jūnrén
   soldier

Note: Did you notice overlaps in the professional titles? For example, *shī* 師／师 in *lǜshī, jiànzhùshī, gōngchéngshī, kuàijìshī,* and *lǎoshī* refers to white-collar professionals; *yuán* 員／员 in *yùndòngyuán, jiùhuǒyuán, yǎnyuán,* and *fúwùyuán* implies a degree of physicality or refers to a member of a team or troupe, while *jiā* 家 in *zuòjiā, yīnyuèjiā,* and *yìshùjiā* denotes creativity.

FYI 供你参考

What's in a job?

In traditional China, the primary occupations were gentry, peasant, artisan, and merchant, with the gentry (scholar-officials who achieved their positions by studying hard and passing exams) at the top rung of society, and merchants at the bottom (because they produced nothing but merely lived off the labor of others). The greatest proportion of the population was involved in farming and crafts. In modern China, people like to comment that this order has been flipped upside down. Nowadays, businesspeople have the potential to earn the greatest wealth and social power, whereas the erudite scholarly class (e.g., teachers, writers) is generally less well paid. Although farmers in China still make up the bulk of the population, this proportion is shrinking rapidly as modernization leads to urbanization.

6.13 *What professions would you like to pursue? Write at least three terms in pinyin. If the profession you seek is not among those already introduced, ask your teacher for help, or try to find a translation online.*

Wǒ jiānglái xiǎng dāng _____, huòzhě _____, huòzhě _____.

(*huòzhě* 或者 means "or"; *jiānglái* 將來／将来 means "in the future")

Grammar Bits 语法点滴

Expressing "or" one way OR the other

Háishi 還是／还是, meaning "or," introduces alternatives in a question.

> Nǐ niànshū háishi gōngzuò? (*Do you work or study?*)
> Nǐ yào zhèi ge háishi nèi ge? (*Do you want this one or that one?*)

Huòzhě 或者, also meaning "or," introduces alternatives in a statement.

> Niànshū huòzhě gōngzuò dōu kěyǐ. (*Either studying or working is fine.*)
> Zhèi ge huòzhě nèi ge dōu xíng. (*Either this one or the other one will do.*)

6.14 *Mingling: Find out something about the career goals of as many of your classmates as you can in the time given.*

Nǐ xiǎng dāng shénme?

Wǒ xiǎng dāng . . .

Encounter 3　Talking about occupations of family and friends

6.15 *Getting ready:* *If someone asks about the occupations of people in your family, what would you say?*

_____

6.16 *Watch and listen to the video segment. For each speaker, identify the relationship between the speaker and the persons mentioned, as well as the professions named. Write in English or pinyin.*

a. _____

_____

b. _____

_____

c. _____

_____

Wǒ māma shì jūnrén.

Wǒ de péngyou Todd shì yǎnyuán.

6.17 *Are any of your family members or friends engaged in one of the occupations you've learned to say so far? Write at least five sentences, following the examples.*

_____

_____

_____

_____

_____

6.18 *Mingling:* *Find out something about the occupations of several of your classmates' family members. Ask and answer questions such as the following.*

> Nǐ fùmǔ shì zuò shénme de?
>
> 你父母是做甚麼的？／你父母是做什么的？
>
> Nǐ yǒu xiōngdìjiěmèi ma? Tāmen shì zuò shénme de?
>
> 你有兄弟姐妹嗎？他們是做甚麼的？／你有兄弟姐妹嗎？他们是做什么的？
>
> Nǐ jiālǐ yǒu méiyǒu rén dāng yīshēng?
>
> 你家裡有沒有人當醫生？／你家里有没有人当医生？

Take some notes about what your classmates tell you.

_____

_____

_____

_____

Encounter 4   Discussing reasons behind your career choice

6.19 *Getting ready:* *If someone were to ask why you chose your career, what would you say?*

_____

 6.20 *Watch and listen to the video. What do you think is the meaning of* Nǐ wèishénme xiǎng dāng lǎoshī? 你為甚麼想當老師？／你为什么想当老师？ *Write the English below.*

_____

6.21 *Watch and listen to the video again. Match each reason with the person who said it.*

1. ____   2. ____   3. ____

4. ____   5. ____   6. ____

a. Yīnwèi dāng ____ hěn zhuàn qián.

因為當____很賺錢。／因为当____很赚钱。

Because being a ___ can earn you a lot of money.

b. Yīnwèi dāng ____ hěn yǒu yìsi.

因為當____很有意思。／因为当____很有意思。

Because being a ___ is very interesting.

c. Yīnwèi dāng ____ néng bāng biéren.

因為當____能幫別人。／因为当____能帮别人。

Because being a ___ enables you to help others.

d. Yīnwèi wǒ mǔqīn shì ____, suǒyǐ wǒ yě xiǎng dāng ____.

因為我母親是 ____, 所以我也想當____。／

因为我母亲是 ____, 所以我也想当____。

Because my mother is a ____; therefore I'd like to be a _____ too.

e. Yīnwèi wǒ fùmǔ yào wǒ dāng ____.

因為我父母要我當____。／因为我父母要我当____。

Because my parents want me to be a ____.

f. Wǒ bù zhīdào wèishénme.

我不知道為甚麼。／我不知道为什么。

I don't know why.

6.22 *Complete the following conversation with your own career choice and the reasons behind it, using pinyin.*

Q: Nǐ jiānglái xiǎng dāng shénme?

A: Wǒ xiǎng dāng _____.

Q: Nǐ wèishénme xiǎng dāng _____?

A: _____.

6.23 *Mingling: Speak to several of your classmates, using the dialogue in exercise 6.22 as a model. Learn about their career choices and the reasons behind those choices. Take some notes below.*

_____

_____

_____

FYI 供你参考

From "work unit" to want ads: Changes in modern China

As globalization pushes change in China, as Chinese socialism becomes influenced by Western capitalism, and as technology "flattens" the entire world, the life and career choices of the average Chinese citizen are changing as well. It was not so long ago that words like *dānwèi* ([assigned] work unit/place of work) and *tiě fànwǎn* (iron rice bowl—signifying guaranteed lifelong employment) were used to describe the lives and aspirations of all people on the Chinese mainland. Both phrases have now become part of an increasingly long list of things that "used to be" in China. The *dānwèi*, or work unit to which each person was assigned, used to be every citizen's source of assigned employment, health care, housing, and a host of other social benefits. The "iron rice bowl" guaranteed benefits from the *dānwèi* for life. Today, the "iron rice bowl" has cracked, and the work unit's importance in the average person's life has almost vanished. Looking for a job suitable to one's interests and training has become part of the fabric of working in modern China. Where there was previously no private enterprise, entrepreneurship is now thriving. Today, roughly 10 percent of the world's billionaires are Chinese. Very likely, this figure will increase steadily as China's standard of living surges upward.

♫ Unit Rap

Go to the **Encounters** *website at* www.EncountersChinese.com *and listen to the song to review key expressions from Unit 6. Listen again and sing along!*

Encounter 5　Reading and writing

▶ Reading familiar sentences in Chinese characters

Note: In modern Mandarin (PRC), a distinction is made in writing between "he" 他, "she" 她, and "it" 它, all of which are pronounced *tā*. In Taiwan, 它 is further distinguished from 牠, used for animals, and also pronounced *tā*. Beginning here, the three forms used in Mainland China—他, 她, and 它—will appear in reading exercises.

6.24 Pair work: *Read the following dialogues (written in traditional characters) aloud with a partner, using the English as a guide.*

1 甲：你是學生嗎？　*(Are you a student?)*

乙：是的。我念高中二年級。　*(Yes. I'm a sophomore in high school.)*

甲：才高二啊！　*(Only a high school sophomore!)*

乙：你呢？你念幾年級？　*(How about you? What grade are you in?)*

甲：我讀大一！　*(I'm a college freshman!)*

2 甲：你有弟弟妹妹嗎？　*(Do you have younger brothers and sisters?)*

乙：有，兩個妹妹。　*(I do, two younger sisters.)*

甲：都上學了嗎？　*(Have they both started school [by now]?)*

乙：上學了。我大妹妹上初中一年級，小妹妹上小學二年級。
　　(Yes, they have. The older one is in grade 7, and the younger one is in grade 2.)

3 甲：你是大學生還是研究生？　*(Are you an undergraduate or graduate student?)*

乙：大學生。我明年想上研究生院。　*(Undergrad. I'd like to go to graduate school next year.)*

4 甲：你將來想當甚麼？　*(What do you want to be in the future?)*

乙：我想當演員或者運動員。可是我父母要我當醫生。你呢？　*(I'd like to be an actor or an athlete. But my parents want me to be a doctor. What about you?)*

甲：我還不知道呢。　*(I don't know yet.)*

5 甲：你父母是做甚麼的？　*(What do your parents do?)*

乙：我爸爸是老師，我媽媽是律師。　*(My father is a teacher, and my mother is a lawyer.)*

甲：哦，我爸爸也是律師。　*(Oh, my father is a lawyer too.)*

乙：那麼你媽媽呢？　*(What about your mother then?)*

甲：我媽媽不工作。　*(My mother doesn't work.)*

6 甲：警察，救火員，還是經理……當哪個最好？ *(Which is best: a police officer, firefighter, or business manager?)*

乙：我怎麼知道呢？為甚麼要問這個？ *(How would I know? Why do you ask?)*

甲：我爺爺，伯伯，和爸爸都是警察。我兩個舅舅都是救火員。我媽媽是經理。我不知道我要當甚麼。 *(My grandfather, uncle, and father are all police officers. My mother's brothers are both firefighters. My mother is a business manager. I don't know what I want to be.)*

乙：我呢，我想當司機！ *(Me, I want to be a driver!)*

甲：司機有甚麼好？ *(What's good about being a driver?)*

乙：司機很賺錢！ *(Drivers make [a lot of] money!)*

甲：是嗎？ *(They do?)*

乙：是啊！我姐姐的男朋友是個歌星的司機，他一個月賺的錢可不少啊！ *(Yes! My sister's boyfriend is the chauffeur for a famous singer; he makes quite a lot of money every month!)*

7 甲：你先生是做甚麼的？ *(What does your husband do?)*

乙：他是個軍人。你的呢？ *(He's a soldier. What about yours?)*

甲：我沒有先生，有男朋友。他是個服務員。 *(I don't have a husband; I have a boyfriend. He's a waiter.)*

8 甲：王老師，您家人都是做甚麼的？ *(Professor Wang, what do the people in your family do?)*

乙：他們都是農民。 *(They're all farmers.)*

9 甲：你有沒有秘書？ *(Do you have a secretary?)*

乙：我是工人，我沒有秘書！ *(I'm a laborer; I don't have a secretary!)*

甲：你不是工程師嗎？ *(Aren't you the engineer?)*

乙：我太太才是工程師。她有秘書。 *(My wife is the engineer. She has a secretary.)*

10 甲：我不知道我將來要當甚麼！ *(I don't know what I want to be in the future!)*

乙：你想賺錢還是想幫別人還是…… *(Do you want to make money or help others or . . .)*

甲：都要！又想賺錢又想幫別人又要有意思的工作。 *(I want it all! To make money and help people and have an interesting job.)*

乙：那你去當醫生或者護士吧。 *(Then go be a doctor or a nurse.)*

甲：不，不。我不想當醫生或者護士。 *(No. I don't want to be a doctor or a nurse.)*

乙：為甚麼不？　　*(Why not?)*

甲：不知道。我就是不要。　　*(I don't know. I just don't want to.)*

6.25 Pair work: *Read the dialogues aloud with a partner, this time without any English.*

1 甲：你是學生嗎？

乙：是的。我念高中二年級。

甲：才高二啊！

乙：你呢？你念幾年級？

甲：我讀大一！

2 甲：你有弟弟妹妹嗎？

乙：有，有兩個妹妹。

甲：都上學了嗎？

乙：上學了。我大妹妹上初中一年級，小妹妹上小學二年級。

3 甲：你是大學生還是研究生？

乙：大學生。我明年想上研究生院。

4 甲：你將來想當甚麼？

乙：我想當演員或者運動員。可是我父母要我當醫生。
　　你呢？

甲：我還不知道呢。

5 甲：你父母是做甚麼的？

乙：我爸爸是老師，我媽媽是律師。

甲：哦，我爸爸也是律師。

乙：那麼你媽媽呢？

甲：我媽媽不工作。

6 甲：警察，救火員，還是經理……當哪個最好？

乙：我怎麼知道呢？為甚麼要問這個？

甲：我爺爺，伯伯，和爸爸都是警察。我兩個舅舅都是救火
　　員。我媽媽是經理。我不知道我要當甚麼。

乙：我呢，我想當司機！

甲：司機有甚麼好！

乙：司機很賺錢！

甲：是嗎？

乙：是啊！我姐姐的男朋友是個歌星的司機，他一個月賺的錢可不少啊！

7 甲：你先生是做甚麼的？

乙：他是個軍人。你的呢？

甲：我沒有先生，有男朋友。他是個服務員。

8 甲：王老師，您家人都是做甚麼的？

乙：他們都是農民。

9 甲：你有秘書嗎？

乙：我是工人，我沒有秘書。

甲：你不是工程師嗎？

乙：我太太才是工程師。她有秘書。

10 甲：我不知道我將來要當甚麼！

乙：你想賺錢還是想幫別人還是……

甲：都要！又想賺錢又想幫別人又要有意思的工作。

乙：那你去當醫生或者護士吧。

甲：不，不。我不想當醫生或者護士。

乙：為甚麼不？

甲：不知道。我就是不要。

6.26 Pair work: *Now try it once again, this time in simplified characters.*

1 甲：你是学生吗？

乙：是的。我念高中二年级。

甲：才高二啊！

乙：你呢？你念几年级？

甲：我读大一！

2 甲：你有弟弟妹妹吗？

乙：有，有两个妹妹。

甲：都上学了吗？

乙：上学了。我大妹妹上初中一年级，小妹妹上小学二年级。

3 甲：你是大学生还是研究生？

乙：大学生。我明年想上研究生院。

4 甲：你将来想当什么？

乙：我想当演员或者运动员。可是我父母要我当医生。你呢？

甲：我还不知道呢。

5 甲：你父母是做什么的？

乙：我爸爸是老师，我妈妈是律师。

甲：哦，我爸爸也是律师。

乙：那么你妈妈呢？

甲：我妈妈不工作。

6 甲：警察，救火员，还是经理……当哪个最好？

乙：我怎么知道呢？为什么要问这个？

甲：我爷爷，伯伯和爸爸都是警察。我两个舅舅都是救火员。我妈妈是经理。我不知道我要当什么。

乙：我呢，我想当司机！

甲：当司机有什么好！

乙：司机很赚钱！

甲：是吗？

乙：是啊！我姐姐的男朋友是个歌星的司机，他一个月赚的钱可不少啊！

7 甲：你先生是做什么的？

乙：他是个军人。你的呢？

甲：我没有先生，有男朋友。他是服务员。

8 甲：王老师，您家人都是做什么的？

乙：他们都是农民。

9 甲：你有秘书吗？

乙：我是工人，我没有秘书。

甲：你不是工程师吗？

乙：我太太才是工程师。她有秘书。

10 甲：我不知道我将来要当什么！
⠀⠀⠀⠀乙：你想赚钱还是帮别人还是……
⠀⠀⠀⠀甲：都要！又想赚钱又想帮别人又要有意思的工作。
⠀⠀⠀⠀乙：那你去当医生或者护士吧。
⠀⠀⠀⠀甲：不，不。我不想当医生或者护士。
⠀⠀⠀⠀乙：为什么不？
⠀⠀⠀⠀甲：不知道。我就是不要。

6.27 *Match the corresponding simplified characters, traditional characters, and English.*

a. 帮别人	1. 老師	A. *in the future*
b. 几年级	2. 將來	B. *which year in school*
c. 读书	3. 運動員	C. *be in what job/profession*
d. 小学	4. 醫生	D. *doctor*
e. 大学生	5. 演員	E. *athlete*
f. 将来	6. 幾年級	F. *undergraduate student*
g. 当什么	7. 護士	G. *nurse*
h. 演员	8. 大學生	H. *help others*
i. 运动员	9. 幫別人	I. *actor*
j. 医生	10. 當甚麼	J. *teacher*
k. 老师	11. 讀書	K. *elementary school*
l. 护士	12. 小學	L. *attend school*

6.28 *Match the corresponding simplified characters, traditional characters, and English.*

a. 律师	1. 律師	A. *farmer*
b. 救火员	2. 服務員	B. *or [in questions]*
c. 还是	3. 經理	C. *earn money*
d. 经理	4. 還是	D. *driver/chauffeur*
e. 司机	5. 秘書	E. *waiter/attendant/clerk*
f. 赚钱	6. 軍人	F. *manager*
g. 军人	7. 農民	G. *engineer*
h. 服务员	8. 賺錢	H. *lawyer*
i. 农民	9. 救火員	I. *secretary*
j. 秘书	10. 司機	J. *firefighter*
k. 工程师	11. 工程師	K. *soldier*

▶ **Reading real-life texts**

6.29 *Look at the employment agency ad. Fill in the blanks in the English version of this ad.*

上海第一职业介绍所

正规职介：国家批准
服务保证：高效，周到，诚心
求职／找工作：021-62342534
免费代理招聘：021-62342645

浦东投资公司急招会计师，5000元
实业有限公司招建筑师，6388元
贸易公司急招司机，2200元

_____ **Number One Employment Agency**

Proper placements: government certified

Service guaranteed to be effective, considerate, and honest

Career/job seekers: 021-62342534

Free service to potential employers: 021-62342645

Pudong Investment Company urgently seeks _____, 5000 _____

Enterprise Corporation seeks _____, 6388 _____

Trade Company urgently seeks _____, 2200 _____

6.30 *Look at the photo and answer the following questions.*

a. What does the sign above the door say? Apartments for _____

b. At what time is the front entrance locked at night? _____

6.31 *Look at the help wanted sign.* 招聘 *zhāopìn literally means "seek to hire."*

What sort of employee does this store seek to hire?

_____

▶ Learning to write characters

6.32 *For stroke order and other useful information about each of the following characters from this unit, go to the* Character Writing Workbook. *Choose either traditional or simplified characters and practice writing them until you can reproduce them on demand.*

做，將／将，來／来，想，要，念，級／级，為／为，因，
當／当，也，意，思，賺／赚，錢／钱，幫／帮，別，或，
者，還／还，知，道，她

▶ Writing a note

6.33 *Write a brief self-introduction in your choice of traditional or simplified Chinese characters. Include information about what you do or what you would like to do and why; also include what members of your family and your friends do.*

Cultural Bits 文化点滴

Education and careers

View the video segment "Education and careers" and then discuss the following questions with your classmates.

- Do you agree with the commentary that going to college is much more important to the future of a young person in China than in the United States?

- Summarize what you know about the Chinese 高考 *gāokǎo* (college entrance exam).

- Discuss some differences in the process of getting into college in China compared to the process in the United States.

- What are some changes underway in the Chinese educational system and in its link to today's marketplace for careers?

Recap

▶ Grammar

Verb-object (VO) combinations

Certain verbs are combined with an object to express a generalized verbal action.

> niànshū (*study*)
>
> shàngxué (*attend school*)
>
> zhuànqián (*earn money*)

All verb-object combinations can have their object shifted or modified.

> shàngxué (*attend school*) ⇒ shàng gāozhōng (*attend high school*) ⇒ shàng yì suǒ zhùmíng de gāozhōng (*attend a famous high school*)

Háishi vs. *huòzhě*

Use *háishi* in a question to state alternatives.

> Nǐ xiǎng shàng dàxué háishi xiǎng gōngzuò? (*Do you intend to go to college or work?*)

Use *huòzhě* in a statement to state alternatives.

> Shàng dàxué huòzhě gōngzuò dōu hǎo. (*Going to college or working—either is fine.*)

▶ Vocabulary

Schools

chūzhōng 初中 middle school

dàxué 大學／大学 college, university

gāozhōng 高中 high school

xiǎoxué 小學／小学 elementary school

yánjiūshēngyuàn 研究生院 graduate school

Professions

fúwùyuán 服務員／服务员 waiter, attendant, salesclerk

gēxīng 歌星 singer

gōngchéngshī 工程師／工程師 engineer

gōngrén 工人 laborer

hùshi 護士／护士 nurse

jiànzhùshī 建築師／建筑师 architect

jiàoshòu 教授 professor

jǐngchá 警察 police officer

jīnglǐ 經理／经理 manager

jiùhuǒyuán 救火員／救火员 firefighter

jūnrén 軍人／军人 soldier

kuàijìshī 會計師／会计师 accountant

lǎoshī 老師／老师 teacher

lǜshī 律師／律师 lawyer

mìshū 秘書／秘书 secretary

nóngmín 農民／农民 farmer

sījī 司機／司机 driver, chauffeur

yǎnyuán 演員／演员 actor, actress

yīnyuèjiā 音樂家／音乐家 musician

yīshēng 醫生／医生 doctor

yìshùjiā 藝術家／艺术家 artist

yùndòngyuán 運動員／运动员 athlete

zuòjiā 作家 writer

Verbs

bāng 幫／帮 help, assist

dāng 當／当 be (in position of), serve as

dú 讀／读 study

dú (gāozhōng) 讀高中／读高中 attend (high school)

dú (sān niánjí) 讀三年級／读三年级 be in (Grade 3)

dúshū 讀書／读书 attend school

gōngzuò 工作 work

niàn 念 study

niàn (gāozhōng) 念高中／念高中 attend (high school)

niàn (sān niánjí) 念三年級／念三年级 be in (Grade 3)

niànshū 念書／念书 attend school

shàng 上 go to (school)

shàng (gāozhōng) 上高中 attend (high school)

yào 要 want, want to

zhuàn 賺／赚 earn (money)

zuò 做 do

Stative verbs

méi(yǒu) yìsi 没（有）意思
uninteresting, dull

yǒu yìsi 有意思 interesting, fun

zuìhǎo 最好 best

Adverbs

cái 才 only

hái 還／还 still, yet

zuì 最 most

Auxiliary (helping) verbs

xiǎng 想 would like to, intend to

yào 要 want to, will

Nouns

biéren 別人 other people

niánjí 年級／年级 year (in school)

qián 錢／钱 money

Verb phrases and conjunctions

suǒyǐ 所以 therefore

wèishénme 為甚麼／为什么 why

yīnwèi 因為／因为 because

▶ Checklist of "can do" statements

After completing this unit, you should be able to perform each of the following tasks.

Listening and speaking

☐ Tell someone that you're a student and specify what school you attend.

☐ Specify your year or grade level.

☐ Ask someone what he or she does for a living.

☐ Specify two occupations in which you are now interested.

☐ Introduce family members and friends by their profession.

☐ Ask a friend what he or she wants to be in the future.

☐ Describe your career aspirations.

☐ State your reasons for selecting a particular career.

☐ Ask a friend why he or she has chosen a particular career.

Reading and writing

☐ Read and understand simple statements about year or grade level.

☐ Read and understand simple statements about professional affiliations.

☐ Read and understand professional affiliations in advertisements.

☐ Write a simple statement about family members, giving their ages and occupations/professions.

Understanding culture

☐ State one difference between the Chinese school system and your own.

☐ Comment on the difference between traditional social classes in China and modern job realities.

☐ Explain the impact of globalization on the career choices of modern Chinese youth.

"Meeting our needs"

各有所求
Gèyǒusuǒqiú

Discussing personal needs

In this unit, you will learn how to:

- talk about physical and mental conditions.
- ask about someone's well-being.
- make and respond to suggestions about specific physical or mental conditions.
- express urgency.
- interpret signs for food, drink, sanitary facilities, etc.

- interpret simple declarative statements about physical perceptions and needs.
- write simple declarative statements about physical needs and responses to those needs.

Encounter 1 Stating how you feel

 7.1 *View Episode 7 of the dramatic series.*

7.2 Getting ready: *What are some physical sensations you have had in the past day or two? Have you felt hot, cold, hungry, or tired? Take some notes about these sensations.*

_____

_____

 7.3 *Watch and listen to the video segment. Then circle how each person is feeling.*

a.

lěng *(cold)*   rè *(hot)*

b.

lěng *(cold)*   rè *(hot)*

7.4 *What do you think the following sentences mean? Fill in the blanks in the English translations.*

Nǐ juéde lěng ma? Wǒ bìng bù juéde lěng. Wǒ juéde tǐng rè ne.

你覺得冷嗎？我並不覺得冷。我覺得挺熱呢。／
你觉得冷吗？我并不觉得冷。我觉得挺热呢。

Do you _____? I don't really _____. I (actually) _____ rather hot.

7.5 *Number the English sentences below to match the order of the Chinese sentences.*

Nǐ bìng le ma?
你病了嗎？／你病了吗？

Fāshāo le ma?
發燒了嗎？／发烧了吗？

Wǒ méi bìng!
我没病！

Nǐ yào bu yao hē diǎnr rè de?
你要不要喝點兒熱的？／
你要不要喝点儿热的？

Qù chīfàn?
去吃飯／去吃饭？

<u>4</u> Do you want to drink something hot?

<u>1</u> Are you sick?

<u>2</u> Do you have a fever?

<u>5</u> Do you want to go eat?

<u>3</u> I'm not sick!

Grammar Bits 语法点滴

The noun that is and isn't there

You have already learned that *de* helps to describe or modify the noun that it precedes. Examples include:

> wǒ de péngyou (*my friend*)
>
> wǒ de dōngxi (*my things*)
>
> Měiguó de xuéxiào (*American schools*)

In all of these examples, the noun is present. However, *de* also plays a role when the noun is missing or implied. For example:

> rè de dōngxi (*something that's hot*) ⇒ rè de (*something hot*)
>
> lěng de (*something that's cold, something cold*)
>
> wǒ de (*something belonging to me, mine*)
>
> hǎo de (*something that's good, a good one*)
>
> shéi de? (*of who ⇒ whose?*)
>
> chī de (*something to eat*)
>
> hē de (*something to drink*)

"Rising intonation" questions without *ma*

You've already learned that, in Chinese, you can turn a statement into a question by adding the particle *ma* to the end of it. The overall intonation in a *ma* question is higher than in the statement. In addition, just as in English, questions in Chinese can also be formed without *ma*—simply by saying a phrase, in the proper context, in a higher and rising intonation, as in the video segment for exercise 7.3: *Qù chīfàn?* ([Shall we] go eat?)

 7.6 *Watch and listen to the video segment. Then match the corresponding items below.*

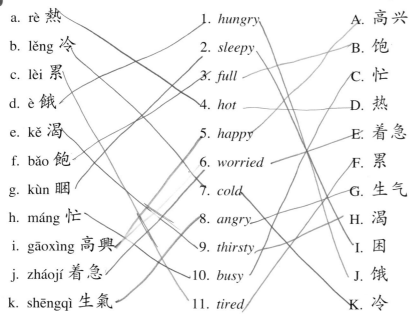

a. rè 熱	1. *hungry*	A. 高兴
b. lěng 冷	2. *sleepy*	B. 饱
c. lèi 累	3. *full*	C. 忙
d. è 饿	4. *hot*	D. 热
e. kě 渴	5. *happy*	E. 着急
f. bǎo 饱	6. *worried*	F. 累
g. kùn 睏	7. *cold*	G. 生气
h. máng 忙	8. *angry*	H. 渴
i. gāoxìng 高興	9. *thirsty*	I. 困
j. zháojí 着急	10. *busy*	J. 饿
k. shēngqì 生氣	11. *tired*	K. 冷

7.7 *Pair work:* *With a partner, drill these vocabulary items by playing "charades" or "twenty questions." The person guessing could ask, for example, "Nǐ rè ma?" or "Nǐ máng ma?" The person pantomiming would say "Bú duì" until the correct question is asked. The response would then be, "Duì! Duì! Wǒ hěn ___!"*

7.8 *Mingling:* *Fill in the blank below to express how you are feeling right now. Then walk around the room asking how everyone is; address your classmates by name and take notes (on a class roster) on each person's response.*

Q: Nǐ xiànzài juéde zěnmeyàng? *(How are you feeling right now?)*

A: Wǒ hěn _____.

 7.9 *Watch and listen to the video segment. Fill in the blanks (in pinyin) with the words you hear.*

Husband:	È _____ ma?
Wife:	Wǒ è _____. Zánmen chīfàn ba. *(Let's eat.)*
Zhao:	Chībǎo _____ ma?
Alejandro:	Chībǎo _____.
Zhao:	Yào bu yao huíqù shuì yí ge wǔjiào? *(Do you want to go back and take an afternoon nap?)*
April:	Bú yào. *(No.)*

Grammar Bits 语法点滴

Le: **Review and extension**

You've probably noticed that the sentence particle *le* is used throughout the exchange in this video segment. It roughly means "to have become _____ (when you weren't before)." In other words, *le* indicates a change in status: You weren't this way before, but now you are.

> Wǒ è le. *(I'm hungry.)* *(Literally: I've gotten hungry. I wasn't before.)*
> Bǎo le ma? *(Full?)* *(Literally: Have you become full now? You were hungry before.)*

You may recall this construction from Unit 1: *Wǒ dǒng le.* (Now I understand [after your explanation].)

If you want to answer a *le* question in the negative—in other words, when there's NO change in status—you can use *bù* or *méi.* Consider these examples:

> Xiànzài è le ma? *(Are you hungry now?)*
> Bú è. Háishi bú è. *(No, I'm not. I'm still not hungry.)*
> Bìng le ma? *(Are you sick?)*   Méi bìng. *(I'm not sick.)*
> Dǒng le ma? *(Do you understand now?)*
> Háishi bù dǒng. *(I still don't understand.)*

The negative form *bù . . . le,* on the other hand, indicates a status that once existed but no longer does.

> Wǒ gāngcái hěn kùn, xiànzài bú kùn le. *(I was sleepy just now; now I'm not sleepy anymore.)*
> Wǒ gāngcái hěn lěng, xiànzài bù lěng le. *(I was cold just now; now I'm not cold anymore.)*

7.10 *Match the corresponding items below.*

a. Wǒ dǒng le.	1. *She's become angry.*	A. 我好了。
b. Wǒ bìng le.	2. *He's gotten worried.*	B. 我懂了。
c. Wǒ hǎo le.	3. *I've gotten sick.*	C. 她生氣了。 ／ 她生气了。
d. Tā shēngqì le.	4. *Now I understand.*	D. 他著急了。 ／ 他着急了。
e. Tā zháojí le.	5. *I'm well now.*	E. 我病了。

7.11 *Write the English meanings of the sentences below.*

a. Wǒ bù dǒng. _____

b. Wǒ méi bìng. _____

c. Wǒ bú tài *(too)* hǎo. _____

d. Tā bù shēngqì. _____

e. Tā bù zháojí. _____

7.12 *Fill in the blanks with pinyin to match the English sentences.*

a. *I'm no longer angry.* Wǒ bù _____ le.

b. *I'm no longer hungry.* Wǒ bú _____ le.

c. *I'm no longer tired.* Wǒ bú _____ le.

d. *I'm no longer cold.* Wǒ bù _____ le.

7.13 *Fill in the blanks below with the last time you felt the following way.*

Examples: Wǒ <u>jīntiān zǎoshang</u> è le.

Wǒ <u>liǎng ge xīngqī yǐqián</u> bìng le.

Wǒ <u>zuótiān wǎnshang</u> shēngqì le.

a. Wǒ _____ è le.

b. Wǒ _____ bìng le.

c. Wǒ _____ shēngqì le.

d. Wǒ _____ zháojí le.

e. Wǒ _____ lèi le.

f. Wǒ _____ dǒng le. [*Try using* xiànzài *(now)*.]

7.14 ***Pair work:*** *Work with a partner. Compare each sentence you wrote with each of your partner's. If the time you wrote is earlier, give your partner a thumbs-up sign. If the time your partner wrote is earlier, he or she gives you a thumbs-up sign. If you and your partner wrote the same time, shake hands.*

Encounter 2 Asking about someone's well-being

7.15 *Watch and listen to the video segment. Using the English as a guide, write the pinyin for the following expressions. (Note: Not all the expressions below appear in the video segment.)*

Asking about someone's well-being

a. 你怎麼樣？好嗎？_____

 (How are you? [Are] things OK?)

b. 有甚麼事嗎？_____

 (Is anything wrong?)

c. 怎麼了？_____

 (What's going on?)

d. 你呢？你怎麼樣？_____

 (What about you? What's up with you?)

Stating one's own well-being

a. 還好。馬馬虎虎。_____

 (OK. So-so.)

b. 沒事，沒事。_____

 (No, nothing's wrong.)

c. 沒事，沒事，真的。_____

 (No, nothing's wrong. Really.)

d. 沒事。很好。老樣子。_____

 (Nothing's up. Things are fine. The same as ever.)

FYI 供你參考

Restraint as a social virtue

If harmony within a group is a key social objective, then it often behooves an individual to downplay personal feelings. Not complaining about one's own problems can be a sign of maturity, or it can be an indication that one has learned to put the needs of others or of a group before one's own needs. Furthermore, there is the expectation that with increasing age, one becomes more skillful in cooperating with others and maintaining harmony (including within one's own physical body). Complaints can sometimes be seen as an admission of failure, leading to disharmony. Of course, struggling to maintain a reasonable balance between the needs of the individual and those of others is a challenge in any society. In the video segment you just watched, while one person resists burdening another with his personal issues, the other presses out of concern for the well-being of her friend. The reluctance to "unburden oneself" may be more pronounced in China than in many Western societies. However, as with many other issues, change is in the air.

7.16 *Match the corresponding traditional and simplified characters.*

a. 你呢？你怎麼樣？　　　　1. 你怎么样？好吗？

b. 你怎麼樣？好嗎？　　　　2. 还好。马马虎虎。

c. 還好。馬馬虎虎。　　　　3. 怎么了？

d. 有甚麼事嗎？　　　　　　4. 你呢？你怎么样？

e. 老樣子。　　　　　　　　5. 有什么事吗？

f. 怎麼了？　　　　　　　　6. 老样子。

▶ Reading practice

7.17 *Pair work:* *Work together with your partner. The following dialogue is written in simplified characters. Practice reading it aloud with your partner. Then change roles and read it again.*

甲：嗨，老朋友。你怎么样？好吗？

乙：还好。马马虎虎。

甲：有什么事吗？

乙：没事，没事。

甲：怎么了？

乙：没事，没事，真的。你呢？你怎么样？

甲：没事。很好。老样子。

Now try reading it in traditional characters.

甲：嗨，老朋友。你怎麼樣？好嗎？

乙：還好。馬馬虎虎。

甲：有甚麼事嗎？

乙：沒事，沒事。

甲：怎麼了？

乙：沒事，沒事，真的。你呢？你怎麼樣？

甲：沒事。很好。老樣子。

7.18 *Tang Yuan in the previous video segment wasn't feeling happy but didn't want to admit it at first. If he had been really unwell, he might have used one or more of the following phrases. Watch and listen to the video. Then number the English translations below in the order in which the Chinese statements appear in the segment.*

_3_ *I have a headache.*

_1_ *I'm not feeling well.*

_6_ *I'm angry.*

_2_ *I've gotten sick.*

_4_ *I'm in a bad mood.*

_7_ *I'm not doing too well.*

_5_ *I'm worried.*

7.19 *Now complete the pinyin transcription of each statement.*

a. Wǒ _bu_ shūfu.

b. Wǒ _bìng_ le.

c. Wǒ _tóu téng_

d. Wǒ xīnqíng _bù_ _hǎo_.

e. Wǒ hěn _zháojí_.

f. Wǒ hěn _shēngqì_

g. Wǒ bú _tài_ _hǎo_.

7.20 *Match the corresponding English, pinyin, and characters.*

a. *I'm not feeling well.*   1. Wǒ tóu téng.   A. 我心情不好。

b. *I've gotten sick.*   2. Wǒ bù shūfu.   B. 我病了。

c. *I have a headache.*   3. Wǒ hěn shēngqì.   C. 我很生氣。／我很生气。

d. *I'm in a bad mood.*   4. Wǒ bìng le.   D. 我不舒服。

e. *I'm worried.*   5. Wǒ xīnqíng bù hǎo.   E. 我不太好。

f. *I'm angry.*   6. Wǒ bú tài hǎo.   F. 我頭疼。／我头疼。

g. *I'm not doing too well.*   7. Wǒ hěn zháojí.   G. 我很著急。／我很着急。

7.21 *Pair work: Work together with your partner. Write a dialogue of at least four exchanges between you and your partner, making small talk about how you are feeling. Write the script in pinyin below.*

甲 : _____

乙 : _____

甲 : _____

乙 : _____

甲 : _____

乙 : _____

甲 : _____

乙 : _____

7.22 *Using the dialogue from exercise 7.21, perform a skit for another pair or the entire class.*

Encounter 3 Suggesting a course of action

 7.23 *Watch and listen to the video segment. Check the actions illustrated below that you hear mentioned.*

☐ chī dōngxi ☐ hē kāfēi huò chá ☐ sànbù ☐ liáotiānr ☐ huíjiā

☐ xǐzǎo ☐ shuìjiào ☐ dǎ diànhuà ☐ guàngjiē ☐ xiūxi

7.24 *Match the pinyin and traditional characters with the corresponding English equivalents.*

a. sànbù 散步   1. *go shopping*

b. chī dōngxi 吃東西   2. *take a shower/bath*

c. hē kāfēi huò chá 喝咖啡或茶   3. *go to sleep*

d. liáotiānr 聊天兒   4. *make a phone call*

e. huíjiā 回家   5. *eat something*

f. xǐzǎo 洗澡   6. *rest*

g. shuìjiào 睡覺   7. *drink coffee or tea*

h. guàngjiē 逛街   8. *take a walk*

i. dǎ diànhuà 打電話   9. *chat*

j. xiūxi 休息   10. *go home*

7.25 *Match the corresponding traditional and simplified characters.*

a. 散步　　　　　　　　1. 吃东西

b. 吃東西　　　　　　　2. 聊天儿

c. 喝咖啡或茶　　　　　3. 洗澡

d. 聊天兒　　　　　　　4. 打电话

e. 回家　　　　　　　　5. 逛街

f. 洗澡　　　　　　　　6. 休息

g. 睡覺　　　　　　　　7. 回家

h. 逛街　　　　　　　　8. 散步

i. 打電話　　　　　　　9. 睡觉

j. 休息　　　　　　　　10. 喝咖啡或茶

Grammar Bits 语法点滴

"Duping" your verbs: Review and extension

Sometimes in conversation a speaker will "soften" or minimize an action by duplicating the verb or by adding *yìdiǎnr* "a little" (or its shortened form *diǎnr*) before the object.

- duplicating a one-syllable verb:

    wèn *(ask)* ⇒ wènwen *(pose a question)*
    kàn *(look)* ⇒ kànkan *(take a look)*

- duplicating a verb-object combination:

    sànbù *(take a walk)* ⇒ sànsanbù *(take a little walk)*
    liáotiānr *(chat)* ⇒ liáoliaotiānr *(have a little chat)*

- with [*yì*]*diǎnr:*

    chī dōngxi *(eat something)* ⇒ chī diǎnr dōngxi *(have a little something to eat)*
    hē kāfēi *(drink coffee)* ⇒ hē diǎnr kāfēi *(drink a bit of coffee)*

One cannot "dup" all verbs. The verb must denote an action over which you have some control, such as *kàn* (look) => *kànkan* (take a look); that is, the action must be volitional. Therefore, you can choose to *kànkan* (take a look), but you cannot *wàngwang* (forget-forget) because you have no real control over forgetting.

By the way, the *r* sound in (*yì*)*diǎnr* is a Beijing habit. Don't pronounce the *n*. When *r* is added to a word, the *n* sound disappears, but the letter is retained in standard pinyin spelling.

7.26 *Pair work: Working with a partner, make a list of four to six terms that describe how you feel right now (hungry, tired, worried, etc.). Then tell your partner how you feel: for example,* Wǒ hěn lèi. *Your partner should respond by making a suggestion:* Nà nǐ xiūxi-xiūxi ba. *(Remember to add the particle* ba *for suggestions.) Switch roles and continue until you have both used all your terms. Practice two or three of your favorite exchanges to perform for another pair or the entire class.*

Grammar Bits 语法点滴

Zánmen 咱們／咱们 **vs.** *wǒmen* 我們／我们

You've already learned the pronoun *wǒmen* (we). *Zánmen* also means "we," but it is a narrower sense of "we" in that it includes only the speaker and the person(s) being addressed. It is equivalent to "you and I."

   Zánmen zǒu ba! *(Let's [you and I] go!)*

Wǒmen, on the other hand, has a wider application. *Wǒmen* includes the speaker and others, but not necessarily the person being addressed.

   Wǒmen zǒu le, zàijiàn a! *(We are leaving now. Good-bye then!)*

Zánmen is particularly suited to suggesting a shared course of action because of its narrower focus. It also creates a more intimate feeling between the speaker and the person(s) addressed. However, keep in mind that although *zánmen* is widely used in northern China, it is less used in the south. By the way, the first *n* in *zánmen* is silent but is still retained in the pinyin spelling.

Encounter 4 **Expressing urgency**

 7.27 *Watch and listen to the video. Focus only on what the second person says. Then number the terms below from the least urgent (1) to the most urgent (4).*

_____ děi

_____ yào

_____ bìxū

_____ xiǎng

7.28 *Match the corresponding items below.*

a. Wǒ xiǎng shàng cèsuǒ.

1. 我必须上廁所。／
我必须上厕所。

A. I want to go to the bathroom.

b. Wǒ yào shàng cèsuǒ.

2. 我想上廁所。／
我想上厕所。

B. I must go to the bathroom!

c. Wǒ děi shàng cèsuǒ.

3. 我得上廁所。／
我得上厕所。

C. I'd like to go to the bathroom.

d. Wǒ bìxū shàng cèsuǒ.

4. 我要上廁所。／
我要上厕所。

D. I have to go to the bathroom.

Of course, if you don't need to go to the bathroom, you can say:

Wǒ bú yòng shàng cèsuǒ.   我不用上廁所。／我不用上厕所。

Write a sentence (in pinyin) stating your degree of urgency regarding a trip to the bathroom.

FYI 供你参考

Chinese terms for "restroom"

As in other countries, the issue of the toilet is a delicate one in China. There are various ways of referring to this place; some are direct and some are more polite. Some of the more popular expressions, in addition to *cèsuǒ* 廁所／厕所 (toilet), include *wèishēngjiān* 衛生間／卫生间 (literally, "hygienic room"), *xǐshǒujiān* 洗手間／洗手间 (literally, "washroom" or "room to wash your hands"), and *huàzhuāngshì* 化妝室／化妆室 (literally, "makeup room" or "powder room"). Public toilets are usually called *gōnggòng cèsuǒ* 公共廁所／公共厕所 (public toilet) and are usually separated by gender: *nán* 男 (male) and *nǚ* 女 (female). Just as in the United States and elsewhere, a visit to a *gōnggòng cèsuǒ* can be an adventure.

7.29 *Complete the following sentences to state your own "degree of urgency" right now.*

> chī dōngxi   hē shuǐ   shuìjiào   sànbù   shàng cèsuǒ   qù guàngjiē
>
> huíjiā   qù zhǎo ge péngyou *(call on a friend)*   chī yào *(take medicine)*

1. Wǒ xiǎng _____.
2. Wǒ yào _____.
3. Wǒ děi _____.
4. Wǒ bìxū _____.
5. Wǒ bú yòng _____.

7.30 *Pair work: Find out what your partner wrote about his or her "degree of urgency." Take some notes below.*

_____

_____

Nǐ xiànzài xiǎng zuò shénme?

Wǒ xiànzài xiǎng . . .

7.31 Group work: *Work with two or three classmates to come up with five sentences that you all agree on, regarding urgent (or not so urgent) things you want to do right now.*

Example: Wǒmen dōu hěn xiǎng qù chī diǎnr dōngxi! *(We'd all really like to go eat something!)*

_____

_____

_____

_____

_____

♫ Unit Rap

Go to the **Encounters** website at www.EncountersChinese.com *and listen to the song to review key expressions from Unit 7. Listen again and sing along!*

Encounter 5 Reading and writing

▶ Reading familiar sentences in Chinese characters

7.32 *Pair work:* *Read the following dialogues (written in traditional characters) aloud with a partner, using the English as a guide.*

1 甲：哎 (ài)，冷啊，冷啊。 *(Wow, it's cold, it's cold.)*

乙：冷嗎？我不覺得冷。要不要喝點熱的？ *(Is it? I'm not cold. You want to drink something hot?)*

甲：要要要。我們去喝點熱的吧！ *(Yes, yes, yes. Let's go get something hot to drink!)*

2 甲：累了嗎？ *(Tired?)*

乙：不累。就是有點兒餓。你餓了嗎？ *(No. I'm just a little hungry. Are you hungry yet?)*

甲：我並 (bìng) 不餓。有點兒渴。 *(I'm not really hungry. I'm a little thirsty.)*

乙：那我們去喝點兒東西？ *(Then shall we go get something to drink?)*

甲：好啊。你也可以吃點兒東西。 *(OK. And you can eat something too.)*

3 甲：我飽了。你吃飽了嗎？ *(I'm full. Are you full yet?)*

乙：我也吃飽了。吃飽了就 (jiù) 睏！ *(I'm full too. As soon as I'm full, I get sleepy!)*

4 甲：忙不忙？ *(Are you busy?)*

乙：很忙，很忙。我姐姐跟他先生要回來了！ *(I'm really very busy. My sister and her husband are coming back very soon!)*

甲：甚麼時候來？ *(When are they returning?)*

乙：後天來。我真 (zhēn) 高興！ *(The day after tomorrow. I'm really happy!)*

5 甲：你是著急還是生氣？ *(Are you worried or are you angry?)*

乙：生氣。我女兒還沒回家。我叫她早回來…… *(I'm angry. My daughter's not home yet. I told her to come back early . . .)*

甲：哦，你著急嗎？ *(Oh, are you worried?)*

乙：也著急。 *(Yes, I'm worried too.)*

6 甲：昨天晚上我媽媽生氣了。 *(My mother got angry last night.)*

乙：為甚麼？ *(Why?)*

甲：我回家晚了。我就是不懂她為甚麼會那麼著急。 *(I got home late. I just don't understand why she gets so worried.)*

乙：父母嘛 (ma—*pause marker*)……都會著急的！ *(They're parents . . . all parents worry!)*

7 甲：嗨，老朋友。你最近怎麼樣？還好嗎？ *(Hi, old friend. How have you been? [Are] things OK?)*

乙：不太好。我心情不好。 *(Not too good. I'm in a bad mood.)*

甲：甚麼事啊？ *(Is something wrong?)*

乙：我生我男朋友的氣。真頭疼！ *(I'm angry at my boyfriend. [He's a] real headache!)*

甲：不要生氣啦！我們去散散步，聊聊天兒，好不好？ *(Don't be mad! Let's go for a walk and have a chat, OK?)*

乙：好吧。我先給我男朋友打個電話…… *(OK. Let me call my boyfriend first . . .)*

甲：生你男朋友的氣，為甚麼還要給他打電話呢？ *(If you're mad at your boyfriend, why would you want to call him?)*

8 甲：我今天晚上有事，要見個朋友。我得回家洗澡。對不起，我走了！ *(I have something to do tonight. I'm meeting with a friend. I have to go home and take a bath/shower. Sorry, I'm leaving now!)*

乙：我也走了。 *(I'll leave too.)*

甲：你去哪兒？ *(Where are you going?)*

乙：先必須上個衛生間，然後回家睡覺！我累了！明天見。 *(First I have to go to the bathroom, and then I'm going home to bed! I'm tired! See you tomorrow.)*

7.33 Pair work: *Read the dialogues aloud with a partner, this time without any English.*

1 甲：哎 (ài)，冷啊，冷啊。

乙：冷嗎？我不覺得冷。要不要喝點熱的？

甲：要要要。我們去喝點熱的吧！

2 甲：累了嗎？

乙：不累。就是有點兒餓。你餓了嗎？

甲：我並 (bìng) 不餓。有點兒渴。

乙：那我們去喝點兒東西？

甲：好啊。你也可以吃點兒東西。

3 甲：我飽了。你吃飽了嗎？

乙：我也吃飽了。吃飽了就 (jiù) 睏！

4 甲：忙不忙？

乙：很忙，很忙。我姐姐跟他先生要回來了！

甲：甚麼時候來？

乙：後天來。我真 (zhēn) 高興！

5 甲：你是著急還是生氣？

乙：生氣。我女兒還沒回家。我叫她早回來……

甲：哦，你著急嗎？

乙：也著急。

6 甲：昨天晚上我媽媽生氣了。

乙：為甚麼？

甲：我回家晚了。我就是不懂她為甚麼會那麼著急。

乙：父母嘛 (ma) ……都會著急的！

7 甲：嗨，老朋友。你最近怎麼樣？還好嗎？

乙：不太好。我心情不好。

甲：甚麼事啊？

乙：我生我男朋友的氣。真頭疼！

甲：不要生氣啦！我們去散散步，聊聊天兒，好不好？

乙：好吧。我先給我男朋友打個電話……

甲：生你男朋友的氣，為甚麼還要給他打電話呢？

8 甲：我今天晚上有事，要見個朋友。我得回家洗澡。對不起，我走了！

乙：我也走了。

甲：你去哪兒？

乙：先必須上個衛生間，然後回家睡覺！我累了！明天見。

7.34 *Pair work: Now try it once again, this time in simplified characters.*

1 甲：哎 (ài)，冷啊，冷啊。

乙：冷吗？我不觉得冷。要不要喝点热的？

甲：要要要。我们去喝点热的吧！

2 甲：累了吗？

乙：不累。就是有点儿饿。你饿了吗？

甲：我并 (bìng) 不饿。有点儿渴。

乙：那我们去喝点儿东西？

甲：好啊。你也可以吃点儿东西。

3 甲：我饱了。你吃饱了吗？

乙：我也吃饱了。吃饱了就 (jiù) 困！

4 甲：忙不忙？

乙：很忙，很忙。我姐姐跟他先生要回来了！

甲：什么时候来？

乙：后天来。我真 (zhēn) 高兴！

5 甲：你是着急还是生气？

乙：生气。我女儿还没回家。我叫她早回来……

甲：哦，你着急吗？

乙：也着急。

6 甲：昨天晚上我妈妈生气了。

乙：为什么？

甲：我回家晚了。我就是不懂她为什么会那么着急。

乙：父母嘛 (ma) ……都会着急的！

7 甲：嗨，老朋友。你最近怎么样？还好吗？

乙：不太好。我心情不好。

甲：什么事啊？

乙：我生我男朋友的气。真头疼！

甲：不要生气啦！我们去散散步，聊聊天儿，好不好？

乙：好吧。我先给我男朋友打个电话……

甲：生你男朋友的气，为什么还要给他打电话呢？

8 甲：我今天晚上有事，要见个朋友。我得回家洗澡。对不
　　　起，我走了！

　　乙：我也走了。

　　甲：你去哪儿？

　　乙：先必须上个卫生间，然后回家睡觉！我累了！明天见。

7.35 *Match the corresponding simplified characters, traditional characters, and English.*

a. 觉得	1. 吃點東西	A. *a little hungry*
b. 喝点热的	2. 有點餓	B. *really happy*
c. 有点饿	3. 飽了	C. *full (after eating)*
d. 吃点东西	4. 喝點熱的	D. *feel*
e. 饱了	5. 真高興	E. *become sleepy*
f. 困了	6. 生氣	F. *angry*
g. 真高兴	7. 覺得	G. *drink something hot*
h. 生气	8. 睏了	H. *meet with a friend*
i. 头疼	9. 見朋友	I. *have a headache*
j. 见朋友	10. 上衛生間	J. *eat something*
k. 上卫生间	11. 頭疼	K. *go to the bathroom*

▶ Reading real-life texts

7.36 飲／饮 *yǐn means "drink." What kinds of drinks are being advertised?*

Answer: _____ and _____

7.37 *Match the photos with the captions. Write the letter on the line.*

a.

b.

c.

___ Open for business   ___ Restroom   ___ Men's room/Women's room

7.38 *Read the following note and fill in the blanks.*

> 李华：
>
> 我不舒服. 发烧.
> 头疼. 先回去了.
>
> 姚丽

Li Hua:

I'm _____. I have a fever

and _____. I've gone home early.

Yao Li

▶ Learning to write characters

7.39 *For stroke order and other useful information about each of the following characters from this unit, go to the* Character Writing Workbook. *Choose either traditional or simplified characters and practice writing them until you can reproduce them on demand.*

熱／热，冷，累，餓／饿，飽／饱，忙，怎，樣／样，吧，吃
飯／饭，東／东，西，坐，走，回，高，興／兴，著／着，急

▶ Writing a note

7.40 *Write a brief description of yourself in your choice of traditional or simplified Chinese characters. Include information about how you feel at different times, and what you do in response to these feelings.*

Cultural Bits 文化点滴

Meeting our needs

View the video segment "Meeting our needs" and then discuss the following questions with your classmates.

- What are some challenges you might face in China?
- What might be easier in China than in your home country?
- What are some steps you might take to "get underway" in China?
- What are some things you might need to be careful about?

Recap

▶ Grammar

Sentence-ending particles: Review

Use *ba* to make a suggestion or mild command or to express agreement.

> Zánmen zǒu ba! *(Let's go, OK?)*
> Hǎo ba. *(OK then.)*

Use *a* to soften a question.

> Lǎoshī, nín hǎo a? *(How are you, Teacher?)*

Use *ma* to ask a question.

> Nǐ lěng ma? *(Are you cold?)*

Use *ne* to ask a follow-up question.

> Tāmen hěn máng. Nǐmen ne? *(They're busy. How about you [all]?)*

Use *le* to show a change in the situation.

> Wǒ zuótiān bìng le. Jīntiān hǎo le. *(Yesterday I was sick. I'm better today.)*

Rising intonation questions without *ma*

Questions in Chinese can be formed without *ma* at the end of the inquiry by simply using rising intonation, just as you do in English.

> Chīfàn? *([Shall we go] eat?)*
> Rè? *([You're] hot?)*

Possessive *de* with and without nouns

The possessive *de* modifies the noun it precedes.

> wǒ de shǒujī *(my cell phone)*

When the noun modified by *de* is understood or implied, it can be omitted.

> Nǐ yào hē diǎnr rè de ma? *(Will you have a little [something] hot to drink?)*

Zánmen vs. *wǒmen*

Zánmen is used when the speaker refers to himself or herself and the person(s) addressed.

> Zánmen zǒu ba! *(Let's [you and I] go.)*

Wǒmen includes the speaker and others, but not necessarily the person(s) addressed.

> Wǒmen zuótiān qù guàngjiē le, nǐ wèishénme méiyǒu lái? *(We [all] went shopping yesterday; why didn't you come?)*

"Softening" an action

In conversation, you can "soften" or minimize the impact of an action by duplicating the verb or adding *(yì)diǎnr*.

> Zánmen qù kànkan, hǎo ma? *(Let's go take a look, OK?)*
> Zánmen qù chī diǎnr dōngxi, xíng bu xíng? *(Let's go have a bite to eat, OK?)*

▶ Vocabulary *(Starred items are for review.)*

Physical and mental states
(all stative verbs)

bǎo 飽／饱 full, not hungry

è 餓／饿 hungry

gāoxìng* 高興／高兴 happy, pleased, in good spirits

hǎo* 好 well, in good health

kě 渴 thirsty

kùn 睏／困 sleepy

lèi 累 tired, weary

lěng 冷 cold (in temperature)

máng 忙 busy

rè 熱／热 hot (in temperature, not flavor)

shēngqì 生氣／生气 angry, upset

shūfu 舒服 feeling well, comfortable

wǎn* 晚 late

zháojí 著急／着急 worried, anxious

Verb objects
(verbs with generalized objects)

chīfàn 吃飯／吃饭 have a meal, eat

fāshāo 發燒／发烧 have a fever

guàngjiē 逛街 go shopping

liáotiānr 聊天兒／聊天儿 have a chat

sànbù 散步 take a walk/stroll

shuìjiào 睡覺／睡觉 sleep, go to sleep

tóuténg 頭疼／头疼 have a headache

xǐzǎo 洗澡 take a bath/shower

Verbs

bìng le 病了 become ill, sick

chī 吃 eat

chībǎo 吃飽／吃饱 eat to fullness

dǎ diànhuà 打電話／打电话 make a phone call

děng 等 wait

hē 喝 drink

huíjiā 回家 return home

huíqu 回去 return

jiàn (péngyou) 見(朋友)／见(朋友) meet, meet up with (a friend)

qù 去 go to

shàng 上 go to

shuì 睡 sleep

shuō 説／说 speak, say

xiūxi 休息 rest, take a rest, take it easy

zǒu 走 leave/depart from (a place)

Auxiliary (helping) verbs

bìxū 必須／必须 must

búyòng 不用 no need to

děi 得 have to

huì 會／会 be likely to, will

juéde 覺得／觉得 feel, think

xiǎng* 想 would like to, feel like

yào* 要 want to, will, be about to

Adverbs

bú yào 不要 don't; don't want

hái 還／还 still, yet; fairly

jiù 就 right after, then

tài 太 too, extremely

tǐng 挺 very, rather, quite (stronger than *hěn*)

zhēn 真 really, truly, indeed

Time words

gāngcái* 剛才／刚才 a moment ago, just now

ránhòu 然後／然后 thereafter, then

xiān 先 first, in advance of

xiànzài* 現在／现在 now, at present

Conjunctions

háishi* 還是／还是 or (in questions)

huòzhě* 或者 or (in statements)

nà 那 in that case, then

suǒyǐ* 所以 therefore, so

yīnwèi* 因為／因为 because

Nouns

cèsuǒ 廁所／厕所 toilet

chá 茶 tea

diànhuà* 電話／电话 telephone; phone call

dōngxi 東西／东西 (material) thing, things

kāfēi 咖啡 coffee

nánpéngyou* 男朋友 boyfriend

nǚpéngyou* 女朋友 girlfriend

shì 事 matter, affair

tiānqi 天氣／天气 weather

wǔjiào 午覺／午觉 afternoon nap

xīnqíng 心情 mood, feeling, state of mind

xuéxiào 學校／学校 school

yào 藥／药 medicine

Phrases

Bìng bu lěng/rè. 並不冷／熱。‖ 并不冷／热。 Not really cold/hot.

Chī diǎnr dōngxi. 吃點兒東西。／吃点儿东西。 Have something to eat.

Hái hǎo. 還好。／还好。 I'm OK. I'm fairly well.

Mǎma-hūhū. 馬馬虎虎。／马马虎虎。 Fair to middling. So-so.

Méishì. 没事。 Nothing's wrong; it doesn't matter; never mind.

Wǒ lǎo yàngzi. 我老樣子。／我老样子。 I'm the same as usual.

Xīngqīyī jiàn! 星期一見!／星期一见! See you Monday!

Zánmen zǒu ba! 咱們走吧!／咱们走吧! Let's (you and I) go/leave!

Zěnme le? 怎麼了?／怎么了? What's going on? What happened?

Zěnmeyàng? 怎麼樣?／怎么样? How's it going?

Zěnme zhème lěng/rè? 怎麼這麼冷／熱? ‖ 怎么这么冷／热? How come it's so cold/hot?

Zhēn de ma? 真的嗎?／真的吗? Really? Is that true?

▌ Checklist of "can do" statements

After completing this unit, you should be able to perform each of the following tasks.

Listening and speaking

☐ Find out how someone is feeling.

☐ Respond to questions about your own physical condition.

☐ Ask and respond to questions about mental states (worried, anxious, etc.).

☐ Be able to suggest a remedy for specific physical or mental conditions.

☐ Be able to express degrees of urgency of action. (For example, "I have to go to the bathroom.")

☐ Courteously express your need to take leave of a friend.

Reading and writing

☐ Demonstrate your ability to read simple signs indicating sources of food, drink, and sanitary facilities.

☐ Be able to read simple statements regarding the physical needs of others.

☐ Write simple statements expressing your physical needs and mental state.

Understanding culture

☐ Explain why one might wish to demonstrate restraint in expressing personal feelings.

"Early to bed, early to rise . . . "

早睡早起身體好

Zǎo shuì zǎo qǐ shēntǐ hǎo

Discussing daily routines

In this unit, you will learn how to:

- discuss daily routines for weekdays.
- discuss daytime and evening activities.
- discuss weekend activities.
- talk about when and how often you do things.
- express actions that occur before, during, or after other actions.

- read key items on signs advertising services around town.
- read simple written statements regarding daily routines.
- write a simple note describing your own daily routines.

一百八十七

Encounter 1 Discussing morning routines

 8.1 *View Episode 8 of the dramatic series.*

8.2 *Getting ready:* What do you do in the morning to get ready for the day?

_____

_____

 8.3 *Watch and listen to the video segment. What do you think the following questions mean? Write the English below.*

a. Nǐ zǎoshang dōu zuò xiē shénme?

你早上都做些甚麼？／你早上都做些什么？

_____

b. Nǐ jǐ diǎn zhōng qǐ chuáng?

你幾點鐘起床？／你几点钟起床？

_____

 8.4 *Watch and listen to the video segment again. Circle the appropriate time each person gives in response.*

a.

5:30
7:00, 8:00, or 9:00
doesn't say

b.

5:30
7:00, 8:00, or 9:00
doesn't say

c.

5:30
7:00, 8:00, or 9:00
doesn't say

8.5 *How would you answer for yourself? Fill in the blanks below.*

Wǒ měitiān _____ diǎn qǐ chuáng.

我每天_____點起床。／我每天_____点起床。

8.6 *Pair work: Tell your partner what time you get up in the morning, and then listen to what time he or she tells you. If you have time, ask other classmates as well.*

Grammar Bits 语法点滴

Expressing how an action was done

To express how an action is performed, use "adverbs of manner"—get up <u>early</u>, run <u>fast</u>, sing <u>well</u>, etc.—with the particle *de* (得). Here is the basic pattern:

subject + verb + *de* (得) + adverb

Nǐ qǐ de hěn zǎo. 你起得很早。 *(You get up early.)*

Nǐ shuō de hěn hǎo. 你說得很好。／你说得很好。 *(You speak well.)*

- Nǐ shuō de bú gòu màn. 你說得不夠慢。／你说得不够慢。 *(You don't speak slowly enough.)* (夠 gòu = enough)

Note that this *de* (得) is NOT the same as the possessive particle *de* (的).

8.7 *Guess what the following phrases mean, and then match the corresponding Chinese and English phrases. Hint:* bǐ (比) *means "compared to."*

a. Māma zǎoshang qǐ de hěn zǎo: tā liù diǎn jiù qǐ le.

媽媽早上起得很早：她六點就起了。／
妈妈早上起得很早：她六点就起了。

b. Bàba měitiān qǐ de hěn wǎn: tā shí diǎn cái qǐ.

爸爸每天起得很晚：他十點才起。／
爸爸每天起得很晚：他十点才起。。

c. Mā bǐ wǒ qǐ de zǎo, Bà bǐ wǒ qǐ de wǎn.

媽比我起得早，爸比我起得晚。／
妈比我起得早，爸比我起得晚。

1. *Dad gets up very late every day—not until ten.*

2. *Mom gets up earlier (while) Dad gets up later than I do.*

3. *Mom gets up very early; she's already up at six.*

8.8 *Mingling:* *Find out what time everyone in your class gets up. Write your classmates' names in the first column and then check the appropriate boxes in the chart below, based on their answers.*

姓名	bǐ wǒ qǐ de zǎo	bǐ wǒ qǐ de wǎn	gēn wǒ yíyàng shíjiān qǐ *(gets up the same time as I)*
	☐	☐	☐
	☐	☐	☐
	☐	☐	☐
	☐	☐	☐
	☐	☐	☐

Grammar Bits 语法点滴

Expressing similarities and differences

To talk about similarities and differences, use:

X gēn Y (bù) yíyàng

Gēn 跟 means "and, with, as" and *yíyàng* 一樣／一样 means "the same." Thus:

Wǒ gēn nǐ yíyàng. *(I am the same as you.)*
Zhōngwén gēn Yīngwén bù yíyàng. *(Chinese and English are different.)*
Wǒ gēn nǐ yíyàng shíjiān qǐ chuáng. *(I get up at the same time as you.)*

To compare one thing to another, use:

X bǐ Y + stative verb or other verbal expression

Wǒ bǐ nǐ hǎo. *(I'm better than you.)*
Jīntiān bǐ zuótiān lěng. *(Today is colder than yesterday.)*
Wǒ bǐ nǐ qǐ de zǎo. *(I get up earlier than you.)*

To negate a comparison, there are two alternatives, one with *bù* (<u>preceding</u> *bǐ*) and the other with *méiyǒu* (. . . *nàme*) (<u>replacing</u> *bǐ*). However, note that the meanings are significantly different.

Wǒ bù bǐ nǐ hǎo. *(I am not better than you.)*
Wǒ méiyǒu nǐ hǎo. *(I am not as good as you.)*
Wǒ bù bǐ nǐ zǎo qǐ chuáng. *(I don't get up earlier than you.)*
Wǒ méiyǒu nǐ nàme zǎo qǐ chuáng. *(I don't get up as early as you.)*

8.9 *Watch and listen to the video segment. The words beneath the ten illustrations below describe typical morning activities, some of which are mentioned in the segment, some not. Under the picture of each speaker at the bottom of the page, circle the letters that correspond to the activities he or she mentions.*

a. xǐ liǎn

b. shuāyá

c. shū tóufa

d. guā húzi

e. huàzhuāng

f. pǎobù

g. zuò zǎocāo

h. zuò yújiā

i. xǐzǎo

j. chī zǎofàn

1. a b c d e
   f g h i j

2. a b c d e
   f g h i j

8.10 *Check the activities you do every morning. Then match the corresponding items in the columns.*

a. ☐ xǐ liǎn 洗臉
b. ☐ shuāyá 刷牙
c. ☐ shū tóufa 梳頭髮
d. ☐ guā húzi 刮鬍子
e. ☐ huàzhuāng 化妝
f. ☐ pǎobù 跑步
g. ☐ zuò zǎocāo 做早操
h. ☐ zuò yújiā 做瑜珈
i. ☐ xǐzǎo 洗澡
j. ☐ chī zǎofàn 吃早飯

1. 梳头发
2. 化妆
3. 做早操
4. 刷牙
5. 做瑜珈
6. 吃早饭
7. 洗脸
8. 洗澡
9. 跑步
10. 刮胡子

A. *jog*
B. *do yoga*
C. *eat breakfast*
D. *do morning calisthenics*
E. *comb hair*
F. *wash face*
G. *shave (a beard)*
H. *brush teeth*
I. *bathe / take a shower*
J. *put on makeup*

8.11 *Match the corresponding Chinese and English phrases.*

a. měitiān pǎobù 每天跑步
b. cónglái bù xǐzǎo 從來不洗澡／从来不洗澡
c. yì tiān xǐ liǎng cì zǎo 一天洗兩次澡／一天洗两次澡

1. *bathes twice a day*
2. *jogs every day*
3. *never takes a bath/shower*

Based on the previous exercise, fill in each blank with an appropriate English equivalent.

d. měitiān 每天 = _____

e. yì tiān liǎng cì 一天兩次／一天两次 = _____

f. cónglái bù 從來不／从来不 = _____

Grammar Bits 语法点滴

Counting nouns—and now, counting verbs!

You have learned that nouns are counted in Chinese with measure words: *sān běn shū* (three books); *sān ge rén* (three people); *sān wèi lǎoshī* (three teachers). The word order is: number + measure word + noun. Verbal actions can be "counted" as well. In this unit, you will practice this using *cì* (times). For example:

Wǒ yì zhōu zuò yí cì yújiā. (*I do yoga once a week.*)
Wǒ yì tiān xǐ liǎng cì zǎo. (*I shower twice a day.*)

In these examples, the verbal form is verb + object, as in *xǐzǎo* and *zuò yújiā*. In this construction, *zǎo* (bath) and *yújiā* (yoga) are the objects of the verbs *xǐ* (wash) and *zuò* (do), respectively. With VO (verb-object) combinations, the pattern to express number of occurrences is:

verb + number + measure word (*cì* 次) + noun
xǐ + sān + cì + zǎo   *take three showers*

8.12 *Check the appropriate boxes or fill in the blanks to indicate how often you do each of the following activities. Remember:* yì zhōu 一週／一周 = *"one week."*

	從來不／从来不	一週／一周 　X　 次	每天
梳頭髮／梳头发	☐	＿＿＿ 次	☐
化妝／化妆	☐	＿＿＿ 次	☐
做早操	☐	＿＿＿ 次	☐
刷牙	☐	＿＿＿ 次	☐
做瑜珈	☐	＿＿＿ 次	☐
吃早飯／吃早饭	☐	＿＿＿ 次	☐
洗臉／洗脸	☐	＿＿＿ 次	☐
洗澡	☐	＿＿＿ 次	☐
跑步	☐	＿＿＿ 次	☐
刮鬍子／刮胡子	☐	＿＿＿ 次	☐

8.13 *Pair work: Choose the best response to answer your partner, based on what you checked in the previous exercise.*

Q: Nǐ duō cháng shíjiān shū yí cì tóufa? *(How often do you comb your hair?)*

A:　a. Wǒ měitiān shū tóufa.

　　b. Wǒ yì zhōu shū (sān) cì tóufa.

　　c. Wǒ cónglái bù shū tóufa.

Now find out how often your partner does the activities listed in the previous exercise, using this Q & A as a model. Record your partner's answers, using a different color pen or pencil to distinguish them from your own answers.

8.14 *Fill in each blank with an appropriate English translation. Then check the sentence that best corresponds to your own habits.*

a. ☐ 我早上洗澡。　　　＿＿＿＿＿＿＿＿＿＿＿＿＿＿＿＿＿

b. ☐ 我晚上洗澡。　　　＿＿＿＿＿＿＿＿＿＿＿＿＿＿＿＿＿

c. ☐ 我早上洗一次，晚上洗一次。　＿＿＿＿＿＿＿＿＿＿＿＿

d. ☐ 我不是每天洗澡。　＿＿＿＿＿＿＿＿＿＿＿＿＿＿＿＿＿

8.15 *Mingling: Go around the room and ask your classmates the following questions:*

Nǐ yì tiān xǐ jǐ cì zǎo? 你一天洗幾次澡？／你一天洗几次澡？
Nǐ shénme shíhou xǐzǎo? 你甚麼時候洗澡？／你什么时候洗澡？

While you're at it, find out one other detail about their daily routines. Note their answers on your copy of the class roster.

Encounter 2 Discussing daytime activities

8.16 *Getting ready: What do you generally do during the day on a weekday? Write your answer below in English.*

_____

_____

8.17 *Watch and listen to the video segment. Check which of the speakers is doing, or intends to do, each of the activities listed below: the father, the daughter, or both.*

	爸爸	女兒／女儿	兩個都／两个都
a. shàngbān	☐	☐	☐
b. shàngxué	☐	☐	☐
c. chī zhōngfàn (wǔfàn)	☐	☐	☐
d. fàngxué	☐	☐	☐
e. xiàbān	☐	☐	☐
f. huíjiā	☐	☐	☐

Note: The final two entries in the table are not in the segment, but you should be able to guess what they mean.

8.18 *Match the corresponding items below.*

a. *go to work*	1. xiàbān 下班	A. 放学
b. *go to school*	2. huíjiā 回家	B. 上学
c. *eat lunch*	3. fàngxué 放學	C. 下班
d. *get out of school*	4. chī zhōngfàn (wǔfàn) 吃中飯（午飯）	D. 上班
e. *get out of work*	5. shàngbān 上班	E. 回家
f. *return home*	6. shàngxué 上學	F. 吃中饭（午饭）

8.19 *Using the vocabulary in exercise 8.18 and following the pattern below, write five sentences about your schedule or about that of someone in your family.*

Example:　**subject + time expression + verb phrase**

　　　　　Wǒ Xīngqīyī hé Xīngqīsān qī diǎn bàn shàngxué.

	subject	+ time expression	+ verb phrase
1.			
2.			
3.			
4.			
5.			

8.20 *Pair work: Find out five facts about your partner's daily schedule or about that of someone in his or her family, and write them down below.*

Nǐ měitiān jǐ diǎn zhōng chī zhōngfàn?

1. _____

2. _____

3. _____

4. _____

5. _____

Encounter 3 Discussing evening activities

8.21 *Getting ready:* What do you generally do in the evening?

_____

_____

8.22 *Watch and listen to the video segment. Then check the appropriate activities, according to what each person says he or she does.*

	1.	2.	3.	4.
a. kànbào *read the paper*	☐	☐	☐	☐
b. zuò wǎnfàn (nòng wǎnfàn) *make dinner*	☐	☐	☐	☐
c. chī wǎnfàn *eat dinner*	☐	☐	☐	☐
d. zuò gōngkè (xiě zuòyè) *do homework*	☐	☐	☐	☐
e. kànshū *read*	☐	☐	☐	☐
f. tīng yīnyuè *listen to music*	☐	☐	☐	☐
g. kàn diànshì *watch TV*	☐	☐	☐	☐
h. shàngwǎng (chá e-mail) *go online (check e-mail)*	☐	☐	☐	☐
i. wán diànzǐ yóuxì *play video games*	☐	☐	☐	☐

8.23 *Match the corresponding items below.*

a. kànbào 看報
b. zuò wǎnfàn 做晚飯
c. chī wǎnfàn 吃晚飯
d. zuò gōngkè 做功课
e. kànshū 看書
f. tīng yīnyuè 聽音樂
g. kàn diànshì 看電視
h. shàngwǎng 上網
i. wán diànzǐ yóuxì 玩電子遊戲

1. 上网
2. 看电视
3. 看书
4. 做晚饭
5. 听音乐
6. 做功课
7. 看报
8. 玩电子游戏
9. 吃晚饭

FYI 供你参考

Many terms for meals

There are a number of alternative terms for the meals of the day. For each of the following terms, the parenthetical English translations are literal. Breakfast is *zǎofàn* 早飯／早饭 ("early rice"), *zǎodiǎn* 早點／早点 ("early tidbits"), or *zǎocān* 早餐 ("early meal"). Lunch is *wǔfàn* 午飯／午饭 ("noon rice"), *zhōngfàn* 中飯／中饭 ("middle rice") or *wǔcān* 午餐 ("noon meal"). Dinner is *wǎnfàn* 晚飯／晚饭 ("late rice") or *wǎncān* 晚餐 ("late meal"). There are no "tidbits" for lunch or dinner. *Fàn* and *diǎn* are more conversational; *cān* is used more in writing. Interestingly, *zhōngcān* 中餐 means "Chinese food" rather than "lunch."

8.24 *What do you do during the evening on weekdays? Using pinyin, fill in the blanks below with activities from the previous list or any other activities you know how to say in Chinese.*

a. Wǒ měitiān wǎnshang huíjiā yǐhòu děi _____.

我每天晚上回家以後得……／我每天晚上回家以后得……

Every evening after I get home, I have to . . .

b. Wǒ měitiān wǎnshang huíjiā yǐhòu xǐhuan _____.

我每天晚上回家以後喜歡……／我每天晚上回家以后喜欢……

Every evening after I get home, I like to . . .

c. Wǒ měitiān wǎnshang huíjiā yǐhòu huì _____.

我每天晚上回家以後會……／我每天晚上回家以后会……

Every evening after I get home, I will . . .

8.25 *Pair work: Find out what your partner does during the evening on weekdays. Ask:*

Q: Nǐ wǎnshang dōu zuò xiē shénme?

你晚上都做些甚麼？／你晚上都做些什么？

What (all) do you do in the evening?

A: (write your partner's name in the blank on the left)

_____ děi _____, _____, _____;

          xǐhuan _____, _____, _____;

          huì _____, _____, _____.

Grammar Bits 语法点滴

Yes, you can signal the plural in Chinese!

You've learned that to make the plural form in Chinese, you don't change the noun (for example, "book" to "books"). Instead, you just indicate the plural with a number. "Three books" in Chinese is "three (measure word) book"—*sān běn shū*. The plural, however, can be signaled with the measure word *xiē* (several), as well. The question *Nǐ wǎnshang dōu zuò xiē shénme?* expects plurality in the answer. The plural signal *xiē* is supported in this question by *dōu* (all), which also indicates that the person asking the question expects several things in a listed answer.

Encounter 4   Discussing weekend activities

8.26 *Getting ready: What do you generally do during weekends and holidays?*

_____

_____

_____

_____

8.27 *Watch and listen to the video segment. Then check the appropriate activities, according to what each person says he or she does.*

	1.	2.	3.	4.	5.
a. shuì lǎnjiào *sleep in*	☐	☐	☐	☐	☐
b. kàn diànyǐng *go to the movies*	☐	☐	☐	☐	☐
c. guàng shāngchǎng *go to the mall*	☐	☐	☐	☐	☐
d. qù sànsanbù *go for a walk*	☐	☐	☐	☐	☐
e. gēn péngyou yìqǐ chūqu wánr *go out with friends*	☐	☐	☐	☐	☐
f. dāizai jiāli *stay at home*	☐	☐	☐	☐	☐
g. zuò jiāwù *do housework*	☐	☐	☐	☐	☐
h. gēcǎo *mow the lawn* *(literally, "cut grass")*	☐	☐	☐	☐	☐
i. dǎgōng *do (part-time) work*	☐	☐	☐	☐	☐
j. zuò gōngkè *do homework*	☐	☐	☐	☐	☐

8.28 *Match the corresponding items in the columns below.*

a. shuì lǎnjiào 睡懒覺   1. 呆在家里
b. kàn diànyǐng 看電影   2. 去散散步
c. guàng shāngchǎng 逛商場   3. 做家务
d. qù sànsanbù 去散散步   4. 跟朋友一起出去玩儿
e. gēn péngyou yìqǐ chūqu wánr 跟朋友一起出去玩兒   5. 打工
f. dāizai jiāli 呆在家裡   6. 睡懒觉
g. zuò jiāwù 做家務   7. 做功课
h. gēcǎo 割草   8. 看电影
i. dǎgōng 打工   9. 逛商场
j. zuò gōngkè 做功課   10. 割草

8.29 *What do you do on weekends and holidays? Fill in the blanks below with choices from the list above, using pinyin.*

a. Wǒ zhōumò xǐhuan _____.

我週末喜歡……／我周末喜欢……

(On) weekends I like to . . .

b. Wǒ zhōumò yě děi _____.

我週末也得……／我周末也得……

(On) weekends I also have to . . .

8.30 *Pair work: Find out your partner's answers to the questions above. Ask:*

Q: Nǐ zhōumò dōu zuò xiē shénme?

你週末都做些甚麼？／你周末都做些什么？

What (all) do you do on weekends?

A: (write your partner's name in the blank on the left)

_____ xǐhuan _____, yě xǐhuan _____ ;

děi _____, yě děi _____.

Encounter 5 Expressing actions that occur before, during, or after other actions

8.31 Getting ready: *What do you do before dinner, during dinner (besides eating), and after dinner?*

_____

_____

8.32 *Watch and listen to the video segment. Then, using pinyin, write what the speaker says she likes to do during the time specified.*

a. before dinner	b. during dinner	c. after dinner
_____	_____	_____

8.33 *Match the corresponding items.*

a. chī wǎnfàn yǐqián   1. 吃晚飯以後   A. 吃晚饭以前

b. chī wǎnfàn de shíhou   2. 吃晚飯以前   B. 吃晚饭以后

c. chī wǎnfàn yǐhòu   3. 吃晚飯的時候   C. 吃晚饭的时候

8.34 *In pinyin, write one thing you like to do before, during, and after dinner.*

a. Chī wǎnfàn yǐqián, wǒ xǐhuan _____.

b. Chī wǎnfàn de shíhou, wǒ xǐhuan _____.

c. Chī wǎnfàn yǐhòu, wǒ xǐhuan _____.

8.35 *Now complete each of the following sentences to state one thing you do before doing homework, while you do it, and after you do it.*

a. Wǒ zuò gōngkè yǐqián _____.

b. Wǒ zuò gōngkè de shíhou_____.

c. Wǒ zuò gōngkè yǐhòu_____.

8.36 *Is there something notable about your daily activities? See the following examples.*

> Wǒ chīfàn yǐhòu děi shuāyá.
>
> Wǒ qǐ chuáng yǐhòu zuò yújiā.
>
> Wǒ bù xǐhuan zuò gōngkè de shíhou kàn diànshì.
>
> Wǒ xǐhuan chīfàn de shíhou kànshū.

Write three sentences about something that is notable about your daily activities. Use the terms yǐqián, yǐhòu, and de shíhou, if appropriate.

_____

_____

_____

8.37 *Pair work: Share your sentences with your partner. Take notes about what your partner tells you.*

_____

_____

_____

8.38 *Mingling: Interview someone in the class. Find out six to ten facts about his or her daily routine. Take notes on your copy of the class roster.*

FYI 供你参考

When are teeth best brushed?

While "breakfast in bed" is a luxury many in the West would welcome, the idea is not appealing to most Chinese. Why? In China, people tend to brush their teeth shortly after getting out of bed, to rid their mouths of the staleness built up overnight. Surely, they feel, the "debris" from the night's sleep should be eliminated before ingesting food. Many Americans, on the other hand, prefer to brush their teeth after breakfast, not before, to follow the habit of brushing after every meal. Small habits such as these tend to be deeply ingrained and hard to change over the course of a lifetime, and people can become quite vehement in defending their choice of habit.

♫ Unit Rap

Go to the **Encounters** *website at www.EncountersChinese.com and listen to the song to review key expressions from Unit 8. Listen again and sing along!*

Encounter 6 **Reading and writing**

▶ Reading familiar sentences in Chinese characters

8.39 *Pair work: Read the following dialogues (written in traditional characters) aloud with a partner, using the English as a guide.*

1 甲：你每天幾點起床？   *(What time do you get up every day?)*

乙：我每天六點就起床了。你呢？   *(I'm up as early as six every day. And you?)*

甲：我七點半才起。你比我起得早。   *(I don't get up until seven thirty. You get up earlier than I do.)*

2 甲：我們明天早上一起去吃早飯，好嗎？   *(Let's go have breakfast together tomorrow morning, OK?)*

乙：好啊。幾點？   *(OK. What time?)*

甲：你幾點起床？   *(What time do you get up?)*

乙：跟你一樣時間。七點，七點半。   *(The same time as you. Seven, seven thirty.)*

甲：那我們八點見，怎麼樣？   *(Then let's meet up at eight, how about it?)*

乙：行。老地方？   *(Fine. The usual place?)*

甲：好。明天八點見。   *(OK. See you at eight tomorrow.)*

乙：好，不見不散！   *(Fine. Let's wait for each other.)*

3 甲：小明！去洗臉刷牙！要吃早飯了！   *(Xiao Ming! Go wash your face and brush your teeth! We're about to have breakfast!)*

乙：知道，知道。   *(I know, I know.)*

甲：別忘了梳頭髮！   *(Don't forget to brush your hair!)*

乙：知道了，知道了。   *(I know, I know.)*

甲：小明！你在做甚麼？   *(Xiao Ming! What are you doing?)*

乙：來了！來了！   *(I'm coming! I'm coming!)*

甲：快點啊！吃飯了！   *(Hurry up! We're eating!)*

乙：知道了。   *(I know, I know.)*

4 甲：你跑步嗎？   *(Do you jog?)*

乙：不，我做瑜珈。   *(No, I do yoga.)*

甲：天天都做嗎？   *(Do you do it every day?)*

乙：不，一週三次。你呢？   *(No, three times a week. And you?)*

甲：我每天都跑步。   *(I jog every day.)*

5 甲：我們家人都是晚上洗澡。你們家人呢？　*(My whole family bathes at night. What about yours?)*

乙：我爸爸媽媽也是晚上洗，可是我喜歡早上洗。我哥哥呢，早上晚上都洗！　*(My father and mother also bathe at night, but I like to shower in the morning. As for my brother, he takes a shower both morning and night!)*

甲：哇，一天洗兩次澡啊！　*(Wow, two baths a day!)*

乙：對。　*(Right.)*

6 甲：你們家誰做晚飯？　*(Who cooks in your family?)*

乙：我爸爸或者我媽媽。看 (kàn) 誰先回家。你們家呢？
(My father or my mother, depending on [kàn] who comes home first. How about in your family?)

甲：我，我姐姐或者我弟弟。看誰在家。　*(Me, my sister, or my brother, depending on who is at home.)*

7 甲：你早上幾點出門？　*(What time do you leave the house in the morning?)*

乙：七點五十分。我跟我妹妹一起走。我上大學去, 妹妹上小學去。　*(Seven fifty. I go with my younger sister. I go to college, and my younger sister goes to grade school.)*

甲：我六點半就出門了。我跟我媽媽走。媽上班, 我上學。
(I'm already out by six thirty. I leave with my mom. Mom goes to work, and I go to school.)

8 甲：爸爸，您明天幾點下班？　*(Dad, what time do you get off work tomorrow?)*

乙：五點半。你為甚麼問這個？　*(Five thirty. Why do you ask?)*

甲：爸，您回來吃晚飯嗎？　*(Are you coming back for dinner, Dad?)*

乙：對，回家吃飯。為甚麼問？　*(Yes, I'm coming home for dinner. Why do you ask?)*

甲：我只是問問。　*(I'm just asking.)*

乙：你幾點放學？　*(What time do you get out of school?)*

甲：四點半。　*(Four thirty.)*

乙：想不想出去吃飯？　*(Want to go out for dinner?)*

甲：想！　*(I do!)*

9 甲：你們大家都在做甚麼？　*(What are you all doing?)*

乙：媽媽在上網，爸爸在看電視，妹妹在做功課。　*(Mom's online, Dad's watching TV, and my younger sister's doing homework.)*

甲：你在做甚麼？　*(What are you doing?)*

乙：没做甚麼。我在聽音樂。為甚麼問呢？　*(Not much. Listening to music. Why do you ask?)*

甲：要不要過來玩電子遊戲？　*(Want to come over and play video games?)*

乙：不了。我還要做功課呢。你過來我們一起做吧。　*(Better not. I still have to do homework. You come over and we'll do it together.)*

甲：好吧。做好功課就玩電子遊戲，行不行？　*(OK. After we're done we can play video games, all right?)*

乙：行！做好功課以後還有時間嗎？你幾點睡覺？　*(Fine. Will we still have time after finishing our homework? What time do you go to sleep?)*

甲：我很晚睡覺。　*(I go to bed really late.)*

乙：我是早睡早起。玩一會兒吧！　*(I go to sleep early and get up early. Let's have some fun for a while, then!)*

⑩ 甲：週末到了！可以睡懶覺了！　*(The weekend's here! We can sleep in!)*

乙：別睡覺了。出去走走吧。　*(Don't sleep. Let's go out!)*

甲：去哪兒？　*(Go where?)*

乙：逛逛商場，看看電影……　*(We could cruise the mall, see a movie . . .)*

甲：做做家務……　*(Do some housework . . .)*

乙：別做家務了！你老想呆在家裡！　*(No more housework! You always want to stay home!)*

甲：家裡有甚麼不好？　*(What's wrong with being at home?)*

乙：老呆在家裡沒意思！　*(Always staying home is boring.)*

甲：好吧好吧。出去吧。　*(OK, OK. Let's go out.)*

乙：我們可以早一點回家，好不好？　*(We can come back early, OK?)*

甲：好好好。　*(Fine, fine, fine.)*

8.40 Pair work: *Read the dialogues aloud with a partner, this time without any English.*

❶ 甲：你每天幾點起床？

乙：我每天六點就起床了。你呢？

甲：我七點半才起。你比我起得早。

❷ 甲：我們明天早上一起去吃早飯，好嗎？

乙：好啊。幾點？

甲：你幾點起床？

乙：跟你一樣時間。七點，七點半。

甲：那我們八點見，怎麼樣？

乙：行。老地方？

甲：好。明天八點見。

乙：好，不見不散！

3 甲：小明！去洗臉刷牙！要吃早飯了！

乙：知道，知道。

甲：別忘了梳頭髮！

乙：知道了，知道了。

甲：小明！你在做甚麼？

乙：來了！來了！

甲：快點啊！吃飯了！

乙：知道了。

4 甲：你跑步嗎？

乙：不，我做瑜珈。

甲：天天都做嗎？

乙：不，一週三次。你呢？

甲：我每天都跑步。

5 甲：我們家人都是晚上洗澡。你們家人呢？

乙：我爸爸媽媽也是晚上洗，可是我喜歡早上洗。我哥哥呢，早上晚上都洗!

甲：哇，一天洗兩次澡啊！

乙：對。

6 甲：你們家誰做晚飯？

乙：我爸爸或者我媽媽。看 (kàn) 誰先回家。你們家呢？

甲：我，我姐姐或者我弟弟。看誰在家。

7 甲：你早上幾點出門？

乙：七點五十分。我跟我妹妹一起走。我上大學去,妹妹上小學去。

甲：我六點半就出門了。我跟我媽媽走。媽上班,我上學。

8 甲：爸爸，您明天幾點下班？

乙：五點半。你為甚麼問這個？

甲：爸，您回來吃晚飯嗎？

乙：對，回家吃飯。為甚麼問？

甲：我只是問問。

乙：你幾點放學？

甲：四點半。

乙：想不想出去吃飯？

甲：想！

9 甲：你們大家都在做甚麼？

乙：媽媽在上網，爸爸在看電視，妹妹在做功課。

甲：你在做甚麼？

乙：没做甚麼。我在聽音樂。為甚麼問呢？

甲：要不要過來玩電子遊戲？

乙：不了。我還要做功課呢。你過來我們一起做吧。

甲：好吧。做好功課就玩電子遊戲，行不行？

乙：行！做好功課以後還有時間嗎？你幾點睡覺？

甲：我很晚睡覺。

乙：我是早睡早起。玩一會兒吧！

10 甲：週末到了！可以睡懶覺了！

乙：別睡覺了。出去走走吧。

甲：去哪兒？

乙：逛逛商場，看看電影……

甲：做做家務……

乙：別做家務了！你老想呆在家裡！

甲：家裡有甚麼不好？

乙：老呆在家裡没意思！

甲：好吧好吧。出去吧。

乙：我們可以早一點回來，好不好？

甲：好好好。

8.41 Pair work: *Now try it once again, this time in simplified characters.*

1 甲：你每天几点起床？

乙：我每天六点就起床了。你呢？

甲：我七点半才起。你比我起得早。

2 甲：我们明天早上一起去吃早饭，好吗？

乙：好啊。几点？

甲：你几点起床？

乙：跟你一样时间。七点，七点半。

甲：那我们八点见，怎么样？

乙：行。老地方？

甲：好。明天八点见。

乙：好，不见不散！

3 甲：小明！去洗脸刷牙！要吃早饭了！
乙：知道，知道。
甲：别忘了梳头发！
乙：知道了，知道了。
甲：小明！你在做什么？
乙：来了！来了！
甲：快点啊！吃饭了！
乙：知道了。

4 甲：你跑步吗？
乙：不，我做瑜珈。
甲：天天都做吗？
乙：不，一周三次。你呢？
甲：我每天都跑步。

5 甲：我们家人都是晚上洗澡。你们家人呢？
乙：我爸爸妈妈也是晚上洗，可是我喜欢早上洗。我哥哥呢，早上晚上都洗！
甲：哇，一天洗两次澡啊！
乙：对。

6 甲：你们家谁做晚饭？
乙：我爸爸或者我妈妈。看 (kàn) 谁先回家。你们家呢？
甲：我，我姐姐或者我弟弟。看谁在家。

7 甲：你早上几点出门？
乙：七点五十分。我跟我妹妹一起走。我上大学去，妹妹上小学去。
甲：我六点半就出门了。我跟我妈妈走。妈上班，我上学。

8 甲：爸爸，您明天几点下班？
乙：五点半。你为什么问这个？
甲：爸，您回来吃晚饭吗？
乙：对，回家吃饭。为什么问？
甲：我只是问问。
乙：你几点放学？
甲：四点半。
乙：想不想出去吃饭？
甲：想！

9 甲：你们大家都在做什么？
  乙：妈妈在上网，爸爸在看电视，妹妹在做功课。
  甲：你在做什么？
  乙：没做什么。我在听音乐。为什么问呢？
  甲：要不要过来玩电子游戏？
  乙：不了。我还要做功课呢。你过来我们一起做吧。
  甲：好吧。做好功课就玩电子游戏，行不行？
  乙：行！做好功课以后还有时间吗？你几点睡觉？
  甲：我很晚睡觉。
  乙：我是早睡早起。玩一会儿吧！

10 甲：周末到了！可以睡懒觉了！
   乙：别睡觉了。出去走走吧。
   甲：去哪儿？
   乙：逛逛商场，看看电影……
   甲：做做家务……
   乙：别做家务了！你老想呆在家里！
   甲：家里有什么不好？
   乙：老呆在家里没意思！
   甲：好吧好吧。出去吧。
   乙：我们可以早一点回来，好不好？
   甲：好好好。

8.42 *Match the corresponding simplified characters, traditional characters, and English.*

a. 洗脸   1. 上大學   A. *wash (one's) face*

b. 梳头发   2. 回家吃飯   B. *go out to eat*

c. 你在做什么   3. 在網上   C. *what are you doing*

d. 一周三次   4. 梳頭髮   D. *cook*

e. 做饭   5. 一週三次   E. *be online*

f. 出门   6. 做飯   F. *return home and eat*

g. 上大学   7. 你在做甚麼   G. *go to college*

h. 放学   8. 出門   H. *comb (one's) hair*

i. 回家吃饭   9. 出去吃飯   I. *three times a week*

j. 出去吃饭   10. 洗臉   J. *leave the house*

k. 在网上   11. 放學   K. *get out of school (for the day)*

8.43 *Match the corresponding simplified characters, traditional characters, and English.*

a. 看电视	1. 週末到了	A. *play video games*
b. 做功课	2. 聽音樂	B. *go to sleep; sleep*
c. 听音乐	3. 睡懶覺	C. *watch a movie*
d. 过来	4. 逛商場	D. *the weekend is here*
e. 玩电子游戏	5. 看電視	E. *do homework*
f. 有时间	6. 做家務	F. *do housework*
g. 睡觉	7. 看電影	G. *sleep in*
h. 周末到了	8. 有時間	H. *listen to music*
i. 睡懒觉	9. 做功課	I. *stroll the shopping center*
j. 逛商场	10. 玩電子游戲	J. *watch TV*
k. 看电影	11. 睡覺	K. *come over*
l. 做家务	12. 過來	L. *have the time*

▶ **Reading real-life texts**

8.44 *Look at the photo.* 吧 ba *is normally used as a particle indicating a suggestion, with a neutral tone. Here it means "bar" and is pronounced* bā. *In the United States, similar establishments tend to use the word "café." Of the three activities below, check the two that you can do in this establishment.*

a. ☐   上網／上网

☐   跑步

☐   吃東西／吃东西

b. How many hours (小時／小时) is this establishment open for business (*yíngyè* 營業／营业)? Answer: _____

8.45 *Look at the photo.* 便利 biànlì *means "convenient," and a* 店 diàn *is a shop or store.*

a. What kind of establishment is this?

_____

b. The last two items on the sign advertise that you can buy cell phone numbers and a rechargeable phone card here: 充 *chōng* "recharge" + 值 *zhí* "value" + 卡 *kǎ* "card." What do the first two items advertise? _____ and

_____

8.46 *Look at the photo. If you go out strolling in Beijing, you might see this sign.*

a. 愛／爱 *ài means "love." What is the name of this store?* _____

b. Look at the logo. How do you think "5i5j" is related to the name of the store?

8.47 *Look at the photo. This is a sign over a sink outside a cafeteria.* 温馨提示 *wēnxīn tíshì means "a friendly reminder." Fill in the blanks below with pinyin and English separately.*

Wèi le _____ _____ jiànkāng

_____ _____ _____ _____ _____ shǒu.

For the sake of your health,

please _____ hands before

_____.

▶ Learning to write characters

8.48 *For stroke order and other useful information about each of the following characters from this unit, go to the* Character Writing Workbook. *Choose either traditional or simplified characters and practice writing them until you can reproduce them on demand.*

每，洗，手，看，電／电，視／视，網／网，玩，睡，覺／觉，
週／周，末，門／门，班，影，以，前，後／后

▶ Writing a note

8.49 *Write a note to a friend, briefly describing a typical day during the week and on the weekend, and suggesting some opportunities when you could get together.*

Cultural Bits 文化点滴

Daily routines

View the video segment "Daily routines" and then discuss the following questions with your classmates.

- What are some differences between the daily routines described here and yours? Name some things the speakers do that you never do.

- What are some things that the speakers do after work or school that you also do?

Recap

▶ Grammar

Commenting on how an action is performed

Use *de* after the verb and follow the verb with a comment.

> Tā shuō de hěn hǎo/kuài/màn/búcuò/bù hǎo. (*He speaks well/fast/slowly/quite well/badly.*)

Expressing similarities and differences

Use *gēn* (with) and *yíyàng* (same) to talk about similarities and differences.

When A and B are the same:

> Wǒ gēn nǐ yíyàng, dōu xǐhuan chīfàn. (*I'm the same as you—we both like to eat.*)

When A and B are different:

> Wǒ gēn nǐ bù yíyàng, nǐ hěn máng, wǒ bù máng. (*I'm different from you; you're busy, I'm not.*)

Use *bǐ* to compare two people, things, etc.

> Duì a! Wǒ bǐ nǐ máng yìdiǎnr. (*Right! I'm a bit busier than you.*)

To negate, use *bù* or *méiyǒu*.

> Wǒ bù bǐ nǐ máng. (*I'm not busier than you.*)
> Wǒ méiyǒu nǐ máng. (*I'm not as busy as you.*)

Counting verbs with *cì*

Use *cì* with a verbal phrase to express how many times an action happens.

> Wǒ měitiān xǐ liǎng cì zǎo. (*I shower twice a day.*)
> Wǒ yào qù sān cì. Jīntiān yí cì. Míngtiān yí cì. Hòutiān yí cì. (*I intend to go three times. Once today, once tomorrow, and once the day after tomorrow.*)
> Wǒ qùguo liǎng cì Fēizhōu. (*I've been to Africa twice.*)

Signaling the plural with *xiē*

Use the measure word *xiē* to signal the plural.

> Nǐ wǎnshang dōu zuò xiē shénme? (*What [all] do you do in the evening?*)
> Zuò gōngkè, tīng yīnyuè, wán diànzǐ yóuxì—wǒ wǎnshang dōu zuò. (*Doing homework, listening to music, playing video games—I do all these things in the evening.*)

▶ Vocabulary

Daily routines

chī zǎofàn/zhōngfàn/wǎnfàn 吃早飯／中飯／晚飯 ‖ 吃早饭／中饭／晚饭 eat breakfast/lunch/dinner

chūmén 出門／出门 leave home

fàngxué 放學／放学 get out of school

guā húzi 刮鬍子／刮胡子 shave (a beard)

huàzhuāng 化妝／化妆 put on makeup

huíjiā 回家 return home

pǎobù 跑步 run, jog

qǐ chuáng 起床 get up (from bed)

shàngbān 上班 go to work/office

shàngxué 上學／上学 go to school

shuāyá 刷牙 brush (one's) teeth

shuìjiào 睡覺／睡觉 sleep; go to bed

shūtóufa 梳頭髮／梳头发 comb (one's) hair

xiàbān 下班 get off work

xǐliǎn 洗臉／洗脸 wash (one's) face

xǐzǎo 洗澡 take a bath/shower

zuò zǎocāo 做早操 do morning calisthenics

zuò zǎofàn/zhōngfàn/wǎnfàn
做早飯／中飯／晚飯 ‖
做早饭／中饭／晚饭
cook breakfast/lunch/dinner

Evening and weekend activities

chūqu wánr 出去玩兒／出去玩儿 go out for some fun

dǎgōng 打工 do part-time work

dāizai jiāli 呆在家裡／呆在家里 stay at home

gēcǎo 割草 cut the grass, mow the lawn

guàng shāngchǎng 逛商場／逛商场 go to the mall

kànbào 看報／看报 read a newspaper

kàn diànshì 看電視／看电视 watch TV

kàn diànyǐng 看電影／看电影 see a movie

kànshū 看書／看书 read, read a book

qù sànsanbù 去散散步 take a walk/stroll

shàngwǎng 上網／上网 go online

shuì lǎnjiào 睡懶覺／睡懒觉 sleep in

tīng yīnyuè 聽音樂／听音乐 listen to music

wán diànzǐ yóuxì 玩電子遊戲／玩电子游戏 play video games

xiě zuòyè 寫作業／写作业 do homework

zuò gōngkè 做功課／做功课 do homework

zuò jiāwù 做家務／做家务 do housework

zuò yújiā 做瑜珈 do yoga

Time expressions

měitiān 每天 every day, daily

tiāntiān 天天 every day, day after day

yì tiān liǎng cì 一天兩次 twice a day

yì zhōu jǐ cì 一周幾次／一周几次 several times a week

Nouns

bào 報／报 newspaper

cǎo 草 grass, lawn

diànshì 電視／电视 television

diànyǐng 電影／电影 movie, film

diànzǐ yóuxì 電子遊戲／电子游戏 video game

gōngkè 功課／功课 homework, schoolwork

húzi 鬍子／胡子 beard

jiāwù 家務／家务 household chores/duties

shāngchǎng 商場／商场 mall, market, bazaar

shíhou 時候／时候 (duration of) time; moment

shíjiān 時間／时间 time; duration

shū 書／书 book

tóufa 頭髮／头发 hair (on human head)

wǎnfàn 晚飯／晚饭 dinner, supper

wǔfàn 午飯／午饭 lunch

yīnyuè 音樂／音乐 music

yújiā 瑜珈 yoga

zǎocān 早餐 breakfast

zǎocāo 早操 morning calisthenics

zǎofàn 早飯／早饭 breakfast

zhōngfàn 中飯／中饭 lunch

zhōngtou 鐘頭／钟头 hour (of time)

More verbs

chá 查 check on, examine

chī 吃 eat

chūqu 出去 go out

dāi (zai) 呆（在）stay (at)

huílai 回来 come back, return

kàn 看 read; see

mǎi 買／买 buy, purchase

nòng 弄 make

qǐ 起 get up (from bed); rise

qù 去 go (to)

tīng 聽／听 listen (to)

wán 玩 play, have fun, amuse oneself

xǐ 洗 wash, bathe, shower

zhīdào 知道 know, realize, be aware of

zuò 做 do; engage in

Stative verbs

ài 愛／爱 love, like

wǎn 晚 late

xǐhuan 喜歡／喜欢 like, prefer

zǎo 早 early

Auxiliary (helping) verbs

děi 得 must, need to

huì 會／会 be sure to, be likely to

kěyǐ 可以 can, may

néng 能 can, be capable of

xǐhuan 喜歡／喜欢 like to (but not "would like to")

yào 要 want to, will

Coverbs

bǐ 比 compared to

gēn 跟 with

zài 在 in, on, at

Adverbs

cái 才 then and only then, not until, until

cónglái bù/méi 從來不／沒 ‖ 从来不／沒 never

yìqǐ 一起 together

Measure words

cì 次 times, occurrences

xiē 些 (for a small amount) several

▶ Checklist of "can do" statements

After completing this unit, you should be able to perform each of the following tasks.

Listening and speaking

☐ Express what you do in the morning to get ready for your day; find out similar information from a friend.

☐ Tell a friend how often and at what time you do a certain activity.

☐ Tell a friend what you generally do after coming home from school or after classes.

☐ Give some details about your evening activities before, during, and after dinner.

☐ Say how you spend a holiday, a day off, or a weekend.

☐ Find out similar information from a friend.

Reading and writing

☐ Read simple statements concerning daily routines.

☐ Read key items on signs advertising services around town.

☐ Write a simple note describing some aspects of your daily routine.

Understanding culture

☐ Name some similarities and differences between your daily routines and those of many young people in China.

"You get what you pay for"

一分價錢一分貨

Yì fēn jiàqian yì fēn huò

Shopping and bargaining

In this unit, you will learn how to:

- handle simple money transactions involved in shopping.
- inquire about the price of an item and bargain for it, if appropriate.
- make simple statements indicating what you wish to buy.
- make simple statements specifying colors and sizes.

- understand key information on signs and promotional material related to products for sale.
- read simple statements about purchases made or planned.
- write simple statements about purchases made or planned.

Encounter 1   **Handling money**

9.1 *View Episode 9 of the dramatic series.*

9.2 *Getting ready: How do you complete simple transactions when shopping, and what questions might you ask?*

_____

_____

9.3 *Watch and listen to the video segment. Write the English translation of* Zhèi ge duōshao qián? 這個多少錢？／这个多少钱？

_____

_____

FYI 供你参考

Dollars and cents in China

Chinese currency is called *Rénmínbì (RMB)* 人民幣／人民币 (the people's currency). The basic monetary unit is the *yuán* 元, more or less equivalent in usage (if not in value) to the U.S. dollar. The term *yuán* is most often used in the written language; its spoken equivalent is *kuài* 塊／块 (piece, lump). *Kuài* is a measure word, so it is preceded by a number and (usually) followed by the noun *qián* (meaning "money"): *liǎng kuài qián* 兩塊錢／两块钱 (two yuán/"dollars"). 1/10 of a *yuán* is a *jiǎo* 角; colloquially, 1/10 of a *kuài* is a *máo* 毛; and 1/10 of a *jiǎo*, or *máo*, is a *fēn* 分. Here's a summary:

written Chinese	**spoken Chinese**
yuán 元 ("*dollar*")	kuài 塊／块 ("*dollar*")
jiǎo 角 ("*dime*")	máo 毛 ("*dime*")
fēn 分 ("*cent*")	fēn 分 ("*cent*")

So, *jiǔshíjiǔ kuài jiǔ máo jiǔ fēn qián* (as spoken) = 九十九元九角九分 (as written) = ¥99.99

Here are some things to keep in mind:

- In speech, the last unit (*máo* 毛 or *fēn* 分) is often unexpressed. Thus:

    liǎng kuài wǔ = "two fifty" or ¥2.50 (The *wǔ* refers to *máo*.)

    liǎng máo wǔ = "twenty-five cents" or ¥0.25 (The *wǔ* refers to *fēn*.)

- The noun *qián* is, by custom, usually used for single-digit sums but is often dropped for double-digit figures and larger. So: *wǔ kuài qián tài shǎo le!* BUT *wǔshí kuài tài duō le!*

- In written Chinese, prices (as well as other numbers) are often given in Arabic numerals, followed by the character 元 or the symbol ¥. So: 9元 or ¥ 9.

9.4 *Fill in the blanks with the correct numbers to express the prices given in both pinyin and characters. Some answers have been provided as examples.*

a. sì kuài qián 四塊錢／四块钱   __ __ 4 . 0 0

b. qī kuài qián 七塊錢／七块钱   __ __ __ . __ __

c. sān máo qián 三毛錢／三毛钱   __ __ __ . 3 0

d. wǔ máo qián 五毛錢／五毛钱   __ __ __ . __ __

e. liù fēn qián 六分錢／六分钱   __ __ __ . 0 6

f. jiǔ fēn qián 九分錢／九分钱   __ __ __ . __ __

g. shíjiǔ kuài jiǔ máo jiǔ 十九塊九毛九／十九块九毛九 __ __ . __ __

h. sì kuài sān máo jiǔ 四塊三毛九／四块三毛九   __ __ . __ __

i. wǔ kuài 五塊／五块   __ __ __ . __ __

j. liù máo yī 六毛一   __ __ __ . __ __

k. yìbǎi kuài 一百塊／一百块   __ __ __ . __ __

9.5 *How do you say, "How much altogether?" Complete the sentence below in pinyin.*

Yígòng _____ qián? 一共多少錢？／一共多少钱？

9.6 *Match the corresponding items below.*

a. *That's right.*	1. Cuò le.	A. 錯了／错了
b. *That's not right.*	2. Duì le.	B. 對了／对了
c. *That's wrong.*	3. Bú duì.	C. 沒錯／没错
d. *There's no mistake.*	4. Méi cuò.	D. 不對／不对

9.7 Pair work: *Work with a partner. Place three items on your desk (for example, a watch, a pen, and a calculator). Write a private note indicating how much each item costs. Now ask your partner how much each of his or her items costs, and then answer your partner's questions in return. Arrange the items in order of most expensive (zuì guì) to least expensive (zuì piányi). Then figure out the total cost of all the items together. Be sure to check each other's calculations and say whether they are right or wrong. Finally, share the total cost of your items with another pair (or with the class).*

9.8 *Watch and listen to the video segment. Then fill in the blanks with the appropriate pinyin.*

a. Měiguórén _____ Měijīn.

美國人用美金。／美国人用美金。

Americans use U.S. dollars.

b. Zhōngguórén _____ Rénmínbì, Táibì, Àomén yuán, háiyǒu Gǎngbì.

中國人用人民幣，台幣，澳門元，還有港幣。／
中国人用人民币，台币，澳门元，还有港币。

Chinese people use RMB, New Taiwan dollars, Macau patacas, and Hong Kong dollars.

9.9 *Match the corresponding items.*

a. *People's Republic of China (RMB)*

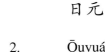

b. *Taiwan (New Taiwan dollar)*

c. *Hong Kong (Hong Kong dollar)*

d. *Macau (pataca)*

e. *United States (U.S. dollar)*

f. *European Union (euro)*

g. *England (pound)*

h. *Japan (yen)*

i. *Australia (Australian dollar)*

j. *Canada (Canadian dollar)*

k. *India (rupee)*

1. _____ Rìyuán
   日元

2. _____ Ōuyuán
   歐元／欧元

3. _____ Jiānádà yuán
   加拿大元

4. _____ Lúbǐ
   盧比／卢比

5. _____ Gǎngbì
   港幣／港币

6. _____ Àomén yuán
   澳門元／澳门元

7. _____ Rénmínbì
   人民幣／人民币

8. _____ Àoyuán
   澳元

9. _____ Táibì
   台幣／台币

10. _____ Měijīn
    美金

11. _____ Yīngbàng
    英鎊／英镑

9.10 *Write the pinyin term for the currency in your home country here:* _____.
*(If the currency of your home country does not appear on p. 218, consult your teacher.)
Then search the Internet for a currency conversion site (e.g., www.xe.com) and complete
the following statements for "your" currency. For convenience, round to the nearest
whole number.*

Yí kuài Měijīn néng (kěyǐ) huàn qī kuài Rénmínbì.

一塊美金能（可以）換七塊人民幣。／
一块美金能（可以）换七块人民币。

(One U.S. dollar converts into seven RMB.)

a. Yí kuài _____ néng (kěyǐ) huàn _____ Rénmínbì.
　　　　　(YOUR CURRENCY)　　　　　　　　　　　(AMOUNT)

b. Yí kuài _____ néng (kěyǐ) huàn _____ Táibì.
　　　　　(YOUR CURRENCY)　　　　　　　　　　　(AMOUNT)

c. Yí kuài _____ néng (kěyǐ) huàn _____ Găngbì.
　　　　　(YOUR CURRENCY)　　　　　　　　　　　(AMOUNT)

d. Yí kuài _____ néng (kěyǐ) huàn _____ Àomén yuán.
　　　　　(YOUR CURRENCY)　　　　　　　　　　　(AMOUNT)

9.11 *Pair work: Take the three items you used in exercise 9.7. Relabel the prices in RMB.
How would you respond if someone were to point at one of the items and ask,* Zhèi ge
Rénmínbì duōshao qián? *Fill in the blank below for your first item.*

_____ kuài Rénmínbì.

Now repeat exercise 9.7 using prices in Rénmínbì.

9.12 *Pair work: Do the exercise again using prices in New Taiwan dollars. The question
would be* Zhèi ge Táibì duōshao qián? *Your answer:* _____ kuài Táibì.

9.13 *Pair work: Do it again using prices in Hong Kong dollars. The question would be*
Zhèi ge Găngbì duōshao qián? *Your answer:* _____ kuài Găngbì.

9.14 *Pair work: Do it one more time using prices in Macau patacas. The question would
be* Zhèi ge Àomén yuán duōshao qián? *Your answer:* _____ kuài Àomén yuán.

Encounter 2 Bargaining

9.15 *Getting ready:* *You can sometimes bargain at a garage sale or flea market. What would you say if you wanted the seller to lower his or her price?*

_____

_____

9.16 *Watch and listen to the video segment. Fill in the blanks to accurately reflect the progression between offer and counter-offer.*

Vendor: ￥50 Customer: _____

Vendor: _____ Customer: _____

Vendor: _____ Customer: _____

Vendor: _____ Customer: _____

Final price: _____

Number of items purchased: _____

9.17 *What do you think each of the following expressions means? Write the English equivalents of each.*

(Note: *mǎi* 買／买 = "buy" and *mài* 賣／卖 = "sell")

a. Nǐ zhèi ge mài duōshao qián? 你這個賣多少錢？／你这个卖多少钱？

_____

b. Tài guì le! 太貴了！／太贵了！ _____

c. Bú guì, bú guì. Hěn piányi. 不貴，不貴。很便宜。／
不贵，不贵。很便宜。

_____

d. Tài duō le! 太多了！ _____

e. Tài shǎo le! 太少了！ _____

f. 30 kuài zěnmeyàng? ３０塊怎麼樣？／３０块怎么样？

_____

g. Xíng le, xíng le. Jiù 30 kuài ba. 行了，行了。就３０塊吧。／就３０块吧。

_____

9.18 *Pair work: Draw an item on an index card and give it a price (make it higher than what you would actually be willing to sell it for). Work with your partner. He or she should "bargain" for your item and try to get it as cheaply as possible; you, of course, would like to keep your price as high as possible. Reverse roles after you have reached an agreement.*

FYI 供你参考

Haggling over price

An astute observer of Chinese culture has remarked that bargaining is an "art form much beloved by the Chinese." However, it's not all about getting a lower price. Of course price is important, but establishing a relationship between buyer and seller that is friendly, not adversarial, is also important. Neither side wants to take advantage of the other; rather, a solution that is pleasing to both is usually the goal of each side. This is entirely within the tradition of seeking harmony, something that lies at the core of Chinese culture. When you're in China, take time to watch how people bargain. If possible, bring a Chinese friend with you when you go shopping, as Alejandro did in the video. You'll have fun, maybe walk away with a bargain, and also have a better opportunity to interact with the vendor who might ask you to come again!

Your bargaining "chips":

- Keep the negotiations good-natured and friendly.
- Know when to bargain and when not to. If you are in doubt, watch Chinese shoppers, or ask a Chinese friend.
- Start by offering less than you are willing to pay and go up slowly.
- If you're getting nowhere by bargaining, consider turning away, feigning disinterest, and then returning later.
- Think of "outside-the-box" bargaining solutions, such as buying multiple items for a lower price, getting a second item thrown in for free or at a significant discount, or getting a service added for free.
- Keep in mind this handy opening line: *Néng bu néng piányi yìdiǎnr?* (Can it be a little bit cheaper?)

Adapted from May-lee and Winberg Chai, *China A to Z: Everything You Need to Know to Understand Chinese Customs and Culture* (New York: Plume/Penguin, 2007), 13.

Encounter 3 Comparing prices

9.19 *Getting ready: What are some items that you most often shop for?*

_____

_____

9.20 *Listen to the audio segment. Then match the traditional and simplified characters.*

a. yì píng shuǐ 一瓶水

1. 一条长裤

b. yì xiē táng 一些糖

2. 一条短裤

c. yì xiē yīfu 一些衣服

3. 一件T-恤衫

d. yì dǐng màozi 一顶帽子

4. 一些衣服

e. yí jiàn T-xù shān 一件 T-恤衫

5. 一瓶水

f. yì tiáo duǎnkù 一條短褲

6. 一顶帽子

g. yì tiáo chángkù 一條長褲

7. 一些糖

9.21 *What is the maximum amount that you would spend for each of the following items? Fill in the blanks below.*

(Note: *kěn* 肯 = "be willing" and *huā* 花 = "spend")

a. Mǎi yì píng shuǐ, wǒ zuì duō kěn huā _____ kuài qián. *(For one bottle of water, I'd be willing to spend at most _____ [units of currency].)*

b. Mǎi yì xiē táng, wǒ zuì duō kěn huā _____ kuài qián.

c. Mǎi yì dǐng màozi, wǒ zuì duō kěn huā _____ kuài qián.

d. Mǎi yí jiàn T-xù shān, wǒ zuì duō kěn huā _____ kuài qián.

e. Mǎi yì tiáo duǎnkù, wǒ zuì duō kěn huā _____ kuài qián.

f. Mǎi yì tiáo chángkù, wǒ zuì duō kěn huā _____ kuài qián.

9.22 *Pair work: Ask your partner,* Mǎi yì píng shuǐ, nǐ zuì duō kěn huā duōshao qián? *Compare his or her answer with your own. Now pretend that each of you bought the item in question for the amount you stated. Whose item would be more expensive?*

- If yours is more expensive, say *Wǒ de bǐ nǐ de guì.* 我的比你的貴。／ 我的比你的贵。 (Mine is more expensive than yours.)

- If your partner's is more expensive, say *Wǒ de méiyǒu nǐ de nàme guì.* 我的没有你的 那麽貴。／我的没有你的那么贵。 (Mine is not as expensive as yours.)

- If your items are the same price, say *Wǒ de gēn nǐ de yíyàng guì.* 我的跟你的一 樣貴。／我的跟你的一样贵。 (Mine is just as expensive as yours.)

9.23 *Mingling: Go around the room and compare your height with each of your classmates'.*

- If you are taller, say *Wǒ bǐ nǐ gāo.* 我比你高。 (I am taller than you.)

- If you are shorter, say *Wǒ méiyǒu nǐ nàme gāo.* 我没有你那麽高。／ 我没有你那么高。 (I am not as tall as you.)

- If you are the same height, say *Wǒ gēn nǐ yíyàng gāo.* 我跟你一樣高。／ 我跟你一样高。 (I am the same height as you.)

Grammar Bits 语法点滴

Another "round" with the comparison pattern

Recall the following patterns from Unit 8:

Wǒ de gēn nǐ de yíyàng guì. *(Mine is just as expensive as yours.)*

Wǒ de bǐ nǐ de guì. *(Mine is more expensive than yours.)*

We can also compare by degrees:

Wǒ de bǐ nǐ de guì yìdiǎnr. *(Mine is a bit more expensive than yours.)*

Wǒ de bǐ nǐ de guì de duō. *(Mine is much more expensive than yours.)*

To express the negative, it's most common to use *méiyǒu . . . nàme.*

Wǒ de méiyǒu nǐ de nàme guì. *(Mine is not as expensive as yours.)*

Note: Never use *hěn* (very) when making comparisons.

Encounter 4 Specifying colors and sizes

9.24 *Getting ready: What are your favorite colors? List four.*

_____   _____

_____   _____

9.25 *Watch and listen to the video segment. What does the following mean? Fill in the blank with the appropriate English equivalent.*

Shénme yánsè? 甚麼顏色?／什么颜色? _____

Grammar Bits 语法点滴

Making your Chinese "colorful"

The Chinese word for "color" is *yánsè*, or just *sè* when used in combinations; thus, "the color red" is *hóng yánsè*, or *hóngsè* for short. You can say either *Wǒ xǐhuan hóng yánsè* or *Wǒ xǐhuan hóngsè* to mean "I like the color red." Similarly, you can say *Wǒ xǐhuan T-xù shān*, which means "I like T-shirts." If you want to say "I like red T-shirts," you can do so in several ways. You could say *Wǒ xǐhuan hóng T-xù shān* (I like red T-shirts), *Wǒ xǐhuan hóngsè de T-xù shān* (I like T-shirts that are the color red), or *Wǒ xǐhuan hóng yánsè de T-xù shān* (I like T-shirts that are the color red).

The particle *de* is sandwiched between a noun *(T-xù shān)* and the word or phrase that describes it. If the descriptive element consists of a single syllable *(hóng)*, *de* is often omitted *(hóng T-xù shān)*. However, if the descriptive element consists of more than one syllable *(hóngsè)*, *de* is almost always included *(hóngsè de T-xù shān)*.

If the topic is known—in this case, "T-shirts"—you can drop the noun. Thus, *Wǒ xǐhuan hóng de*, *Wǒ xǐhuan hóngsè de*, and *Wǒ xǐhuan hóng yánsè de* all mean "I like red ones."

9.26 *Match the corresponding items.*

a.	black	1. hóngsè 红色	A. 金色
b.	red	2. jīnsè 金色	B. 银色
c.	blue	3. hēisè 黑色	C. 红色
d.	green	4. júhóngsè 橘红色	D. 咖啡色
e.	yellow	5. mǐsè 米色	E. 黄色
f.	orange	6. lánsè 藍色	F. 绿色
g.	brown	7. zǐsè 紫色	G. 米色
h.	purple	8. huángsè 黄色	H. 黑色
i.	white	9. huīsè 灰色	I. 紫色
j.	beige	10. lǜsè 綠色	J. 橘红色
k.	pink	11. yínsè 銀色	K. 灰色
l.	gold	12. kāfēisè 咖啡色	L. 蓝色
m.	silver	13. fěnhóngsè 粉红色	M. 白色
n.	gray	14. báisè 白色	N. 粉红色

Note: "Orange" can be said one of several ways:

- júhóngsè 橘红色 *(the red of the tangerine)*

- júsè 橘色 *(the color of the tangerine)*

- chéngsè 橙色 *(the color of the orange)*

Similarly, "brown" can be expressed as follows:

- kāfēisè 咖啡色 *(the color of coffee)*

- chásè 茶色 *(the color of tea)*

- zōngsè 棕色 *(the color of bark)*

9.27 Pair work: *Work with a partner. You'll need a set of pens, pencils, or crayons for each of the 14 colors on the preceding page. Fill in each of the boxes below with a color of your choice. Use a different color for each box.*

Note: Ordinal numbers are as follows: *dì-yī* 第一, *dì-èr* 第二, *dì-sān* 第三, *dì-sì* 第四, etc. A "box" (on a form, such as an application, or in an activity, as above) is a *gézi* 格子. So, *dì-qī ge gézi* means "the seventh box."

Sit back to back with your partner so that you can't see each other's books, and tell how you've colored your boxes. Then, following your partner's descriptions, duplicate his or her row below.

For example, say Dì-yī ge gézi shì hóng de. Dì-èr ge gézi shì hēi de.

Practice asking questions such as Dì-wǔ ge gézi shì shénme yánsè? Dì-qī ge gézi shì lán de ma?

When you're done, compare your rows. If you did the exercise correctly, your second row should match your partner's first row, and vice versa.

9.28 Pair work: *Work with a partner. Identify the color of each clothing item you and your partner are wearing. Use the following pattern. Then reverse roles.*

Q *(tugging at an article of your clothing, ask)*: Zhè shì shénme yánsè?

A: Nà shì hóngsè de.

9.29 *Watch and listen to the video segment. Then match the corresponding items below.*

a. **XS**   1. dàhào 大號   A. 中号

b. **S**   2. zhōnghào 中號   B. 加大号

c. **M**   3. xiǎohào 小號   C. 大号

d. **L**   4. jiādàhào 加大號   D. 加小号

e. **XL**   5. jiāxiǎohào 加小號   E. 小号

Note: In Taiwan, XL is *tèdàhào* 特大号 (especially large size) and XS is *tèxiǎohào* 特小号 (especially small size).

9.30 *Mingling:* *This exercise works perfectly if you and your classmates are wearing T-shirts. If you are not, pretend that you are. What size do you wear? Walk around and engage in a dialogue similar to the one below, but adjust the details to match your specific situation.*

A: Nǐ chuān jǐ hào de T-xù shān? (*chuān* = wear)

B: Wǒ chuān zhōnghào de. Nǐ ne?

A: Wǒ chuān dàhào de.

B: Nǐ de bǐ wǒ de dà.

A: Nǐ de bǐ wǒ de xiǎo.

B: Nǐ de duōshao qián?

A: Shíwǔ kuài. Nǐ de ne?

B: Bǐ nǐ de guì yìdiǎnr. / Bǐ nǐ de guì de duō. *OR* Gēn nǐ de yíyàng guì. *OR* Méiyǒu nǐ de nàme guì.

9.31 *Mingling:* *Draw a T-shirt in one of the colors introduced in this unit. Write a size on the front of the shirt. This is the T-shirt you have available "for sale." On the back of the paper, write a different size and list two different colors. These are sizes and colors that are "also available." Decide which T-shirt you wish to "buy," and then write its size and two possible colors below.*

_____   _____   _____

Now walk around the classroom. How many of your classmates are "selling" the exact shirt you want? You might use dialogue such as the following to determine if someone has the shirt you want.

A: Zhèi jiàn T-xù shān yǒu xiǎohào de ma?

B: Duìbuqǐ, méiyǒu. Kěshì lán de yǒu xiǎohào de. Yào ma?

A: Duìbuqǐ, bú yào. Wǒ bú yào lán de. Yǒu bái de ma?

B: Yǒu!

A: Yǒu xiǎohào de ma?

B: Yǒu! Báisè de xiǎohào.

A: Tài hǎo le!

❙ Putting it all together

9.32 *Work in pairs or small groups of three to four people. Write a one-minute script about shopping, using language you've learned in this unit. Practice performing the script (make sure each person gets approximately equal talking time), and then perform it for your class.*

🎵 Unit Rap

Go to the **Encounters** *website at www.EncountersChinese.com and listen to the song to review key expressions from Unit 9. Listen again and sing along!*

Encounter 5 Reading and writing

❙ Reading familiar sentences in Chinese characters

9.33 *Pair work: Read the following dialogues (written in traditional characters) aloud with a partner, using the English as a guide.*

1 甲：老闆(lǎobǎn)，這個多少錢？ *(Owner, how much is this?)*

乙：我看看⋯⋯那個十塊錢。 *(Let me see . . . that's ten "dollars.")*

甲：這個呢？ *(How about this one?)*

乙：五塊五。 *(Five "dollars" and fifty "cents.")*

甲：這個呢？ *(How about this one?)*

乙：九毛五。 *(Ninety-five "cents.")*

甲：好。我都要。一共多少錢？ *(Fine. I'll take them all. How much altogether?)*

乙：一共十六塊九毛五分錢。 *(Altogether, that's sixteen "dollars" and ninety-five "cents.")*

甲：不對吧⋯⋯ *(I don't think that's right . . .)*

乙：哦，錯了。是十六塊四毛五。對不起！ *(Oh, that's wrong. It's sixteen "dollars" and forty-five "cents." Sorry!)*

2 甲：一塊美金能換六塊人民幣，對不對？ *(One U.S. dollar can convert into six RMB, is that right?)*

乙：差不多。 *(Approximately.)*

甲：一塊歐元呢？ *(How about one euro?)*

乙：對不起，我不知道。 *(Sorry, I don't know.)*

3 甲：英國用的是甚麼錢？　*(What currency does England use?)*

乙：英鎊。　*(The pound.)*

甲：加拿大呢？　*(How about Canada?)*

乙：加拿大元。　*(Canadian dollars.)*

甲：澳大利亞呢？　*(And Australia?)*

乙：澳元。你為甚麼問這些？　*(Australian dollars. Why are you asking all this?)*

甲：沒甚麼。只是問問。　*(No reason. I'm just asking.)*

4 甲：我要去歐洲。得去換些歐元。　*(I have to go to Europe. I have to exchange some "dollars" for euros.)*

乙：你想換多少歐元？　*(How many euros are you thinking of getting?)*

甲：七百塊夠不夠？　*(Is seven hundred enough?)*

乙：你去幾天？　*(How many days are you going for?)*

甲：一個星期。　*(A week.)*

乙：差不多。夠了吧。　*(That's about right. [That] should be enough.)*

5 甲：這是甚麼錢啊？　*(What kind of money is this?)*

乙：是盧比嗎？　*(Are these rupees?)*

甲：不是吧。　*(I don't think so.)*

乙：哦，我知道了，是日元。　*(Oh, I know. These are Japanese yen.)*

甲：是嗎？不對吧。　*(Are they? I don't think that's right.)*

乙：是不是港幣？　*(Are they Hong Kong dollars?)*

甲：對了，對了。是港幣。　*(Right, right. They're Hong Kong dollars.)*

6 甲：老闆，你這個賣多少錢？　*(Owner, how much are you selling this for?)*

乙：兩百塊。　*(Two hundred "dollars.")*

甲：兩百塊太貴了！怎麼那麼貴？　*(Two hundred is too expensive. How come it's so expensive?)*

乙：不貴！這是好東西啊！　*(It's not expensive! This is really good stuff!)*

甲：一百塊行嗎？　*(Is one hundred OK?)*

乙：一百塊太少了！你看看，多好的東西。　*(One hundred is too little! Look! Such fine stuff!)*

甲：你賣得太貴了。不買不買。　*(You sell things at too high a price. I'm not buying.)*

7 甲：我要買一些衣服。　*(I want to buy some clothes.)*

乙：甚麼衣服？　*(What clothes?)*

甲：想買一條長褲，一條短褲，還想買件T-恤衫。　*(I'd like to buy a pair of pants, a pair of shorts, and I'd also like to buy a T-shirt.)*

乙：哦，好。我跟你一起去買。走吧。　*(Oh, OK. I'll go shopping with you. Let's go.)*

8 甲：有沒有紅帽子？ *(Do you have red hats?)*

乙：對不起，沒有紅的。黑的或白的行不行？也有灰色的和米色的。　*(Sorry, we don't have red. Is black or white OK? We also have gray or beige.)*

甲：有藍的嗎？ *(Do you have blue?)*

乙：對不起，藍的也沒有。 *(Sorry, we don't have blue either.)*

甲：那我就要那頂米色的吧。有大號的嗎？ *(Then I'll take that beige one. Do you have it in large?)*

乙：有有有。這是大號的。這是加大號的。 *(Yes, yes, yes. This is large, and this is extra large.)*

甲：好，我買一頂大號的。 *(Good. I'll take the large.)*

9 甲：我有三塊糖：一塊橘紅色的、一塊咖啡色的、一塊黃色的。給你一塊。你要哪塊？　*(I have three pieces of candy: an orange-colored one, a brown one, and a yellow one. I'll give you one. Which one do you want?)*

乙：我要第一塊。　*(I'll take the first one.)*

甲：第一塊是橘紅色的。好，給你。　*(The first one is the orange-colored one. OK, here.)*

10 甲：這兩瓶水，怎麼大的便宜，小的貴？　*(These two bottles of water—how come the big one is cheaper and the small one is more expensive?)*

乙：對啊！小瓶比大瓶貴。我也不知道為甚麼。　*(Right, the small one is more expensive than the big one. I don't know why either.)*

甲：那我們去問問老闆吧！ *(Let's go ask the owner!)*

乙：好啊。 *(Fine.)*

9.34 *Pair work: Read the dialogues aloud with a partner, this time without any English.*

1 甲：老闆(lǎobǎn)，這個多少錢？

乙：我看看……那個十塊錢。

甲：這個呢？

乙：五塊五。

甲：這個呢？

乙：九毛五。

甲：好。我都要。一共多少錢？

乙：一共十六塊九毛五分錢。

甲：不對吧……

乙：哦，錯了。是十六塊四毛五。對不起！

2 甲：一塊美金能換六塊人民幣，對不對？

乙：差不多。

甲：一塊歐元呢？

乙：對不起，我不知道。

3 甲：英國用的是甚麼錢？

乙：英鎊。

甲：加拿大呢？

乙：加拿大元。

甲：澳大利亞呢？

乙：澳元。你為甚麼問這些？

甲：沒甚麼。只是問問。

4 甲：我要去歐洲。得去換些歐元。

乙：你想換多少歐元？

甲：七百塊夠不夠？

乙：你去幾天？

甲：一個星期。

乙：差不多。夠了吧。

5 甲：這是甚麼錢啊？

乙：是盧比嗎？

甲：不是吧。

乙：哦，我知道了，是日元。

甲：是嗎？不對吧。

乙：是不是港幣？

甲：對了，對了。是港幣。

6 甲：老闆，你這個賣多少錢？

乙：兩百塊。

甲：兩百塊太貴了！怎麼那麼貴？

乙：不貴！這是好東西啊！

甲：一百塊行嗎？

乙：一百塊太少了！你看看，多好的東西。

甲：你賣得太貴了。不買不買。

7 甲：我要買一些衣服。

乙：甚麼衣服？

甲：想買一條長褲，一條短褲，還想買件T-恤衫。

乙：哦，好。我跟你一起去買。走吧。

8 甲：有沒有紅帽子？

乙：對不起，沒有紅的。黑的或白的行不行？也有灰色的和米色的。

甲：有藍的嗎？

乙：對不起，藍的也沒有。

甲：那我就要那頂米色的吧。有大號的嗎？

乙：有有有。這是大號的。這是加大號的。

甲：好，我買一頂大號的。

9 甲：我有三塊糖：一塊橘紅色的、一塊咖啡色的、一塊黃色的。給你一塊。你要哪塊？

乙：我要第一塊。

甲：第一塊是橘紅色的。好，給你。

10 甲：這兩瓶水，怎麼大的便宜，小的貴？

乙：對啊！小瓶比大瓶貴。我也不知道為甚麼。

甲：那我們去問問老闆吧！

乙：好啊

9.35 *Pair work: Now try it once again, this time in simplified characters.*

1 甲：老板(lǎobǎn)，这个多少钱？

乙：我看看……那个十块钱。

甲：这个呢？

乙：五块五。

甲：这个呢？

乙：九毛五。

甲：好。我都要。一共多少钱？

乙：一共十六块九毛五分钱。

甲：不对吧……

乙：哦，错了。是十六块四毛五。对不起！

2 甲：一块美金能换六块人民币，对不对？

乙：差不多。

甲：一块欧元呢？

乙：对不起，我不知道。

3 甲：英国用的是什么钱？

乙：英镑。

甲：加拿大呢？

乙：加拿大元。

甲：澳大利亚呢？

乙：澳元。你为什么问这些？

甲：没什么。只是问问。

4 甲：我要去欧洲。得去换些欧元。

乙：你想换多少欧元？

甲：七百块够不够？

乙：你去几天？

甲：一个星期。

乙：差不多。够了吧。

5 甲：这是什么钱啊？

乙：是卢比吗？

甲：不是吧。

乙：哦，我知道了，是日元。

甲：是吗？不对吧。

乙：是不是港币？

甲：对了，对了。是港币。

6 甲：老板，你这个卖多少钱？

乙：两百块。

甲：两百块太贵了！怎么那么贵？

乙：不贵！这是好东西啊！

甲：一百块行吗？

乙：一百块太少了！你看看，多好的东西。

甲：你卖得太贵了。不买不买。

7 甲：我要买一些衣服。

乙：什么衣服？

甲：想买一条长裤，一条短裤，还想买件T-恤衫。

乙：哦，好。我跟你一起去买。走吧。

8 甲：有没有红帽子？

乙：对不起，没有红的。黑的或白的行不行？
也有灰色的和米色的。

甲：有蓝的吗？

乙：对不起，蓝的也没有。

甲：那我就要那顶米色的吧。有大号的吗？

乙：有有有。 这是大号的。这是加大号的。

甲：好，我买一顶大号的。

9 甲：我有三块糖：一块橘红色的、一块咖啡色的、
一块黄色的。给你一块。你要哪块？

乙：我要第一块。

甲：第一块是橘红色的。好，给你。

10 甲：这两瓶水，怎么大的便宜，小的贵？

乙：对啊！小瓶比大瓶贵。我也不知道为什么。

甲：那我们去问问老板吧！

乙：好啊。

9.36 *Match the corresponding simplified characters, traditional characters, and English.*

a. 多少钱	1. 不對	A. *how much (money)*
b. 两百一十块	2. 台幣	B. *RMB*
c. 不对	3. 澳大利亞元	C. *Hong Kong dollar*
d. 对吗	4. 港幣	D. *British pound*
e. 错了	5. 錯了	E. *euro*
f. 澳门元	6. 盧比	F. *Australian dollar*
g. 人民币	7. 英鎊	G. *Macau pataca*
h. 欧元	8. 對嗎	H. *rupee*
i. 英镑	9. 歐元	I. *It's wrong.*
j. 澳大利亚元	10. 兩百一十塊	J. *210 "dollars" [yuan]*
k. 卢比	11. 澳門元	K. *not right*
l. 台币	12. 人民幣	L. *Is that right?*
m. 港币	13. 多少錢	M. *New Taiwan dollar*

9.37 *Match the corresponding simplified characters, traditional characters, and English.*

a. 买	1. 買	A. *long pants*
b. 卖	2. 短褲	B. *the color blue*
c. 贵	3. 長褲	C. *give*
d. 长裤	4. 貴	D. *large size*
e. 短裤	5. 紅色	E. *extra-small size*
f. 一顶帽子	6. 大號	F. *sell*
g. 红色	7. 一頂帽子	G. *buy*
h. 蓝色	8. 給	H. *shorts*
i. 大号	9. 加小號	I. *the color red*
j. 加小号	10. 藍色	J. *expensive*
k. 给	11. 賣	K. *a hat/cap*

▶ Reading real-life texts

9.38 *Look at the photos. What does each sign mean? Write the letter on the line.*

a.   b.

_____ Closed (literally "Resting")

_____ Open for business

9.39 *Look at the photos. Match the signs with their pinyin.*

a.   b.   c.

_____ Chángtú líng diǎn èr yuán fēn zhōng

_____ Yuán tǒng bīngqílín sān yuán

_____ Xǐ jiǎn chuī shí yuán, jiē fà liù bǎi yuán

Now fill in the blanks to complete the English translation of the signs.

d. Ice cream cone: ¥ _____

e. _____, cut, and blow-dry: _____ 10; _____ extensions: _____ 600

f. Long-distance calls: _____ per _____

9.40 *Look at the photo. What does the sign say about the price of the product? Fill in the blanks.*

Chāo dī tèjià 78 yuán/píng

Extra low special price _____

per _____

9.41 *Look at the photo. The Chinese word for "club" is* jùlèbù 俱樂部／俱乐部. *Circle the characters for "five color," which also means "multicolored."*

▶ Learning to write characters

9.42 *For stroke order and other useful information about each of the following characters from this unit, go to the* Character Writing Workbook. *Choose either traditional or simplified characters and practice writing them until you can reproduce them on demand.*

買／买，賣／卖，黑，紅／红，白，金，銀／银，少，元，太，
貴／贵，便，宜，夠／够，能，比，跟，給／给

▶ Writing a note

9.43 *Write a few sentences to a friend, telling him or her about some recent purchases you made; include details such as price, color, and size.*

Cultural Bits 文化点滴

Shopping and handling money

View the video segment "Shopping and handling money" and then discuss the following questions with your classmates.

- *Zuì dī jiàgé* 最低價格／最低价格 means "the lowest price." How would you use this phrase in bargaining?
- Discuss different situations in which you might or might not bargain.
- Make a list of everything you might say while bargaining.

Recap

Grammar

Money measure words

Here are some examples of money measure words. Pinyin words in parentheses may be omitted in speech.

wǔ kuài (qián) (*five "dollars," ¥5.00*)
wǔ kuài wǔ (máo qián) (*five "dollars" and fifty "cents," ¥5.50*)
wǔ kuài wǔ máo wǔ (fēn qián) (*five "dollars" and fifty-five "cents," ¥5.55*)

In the written language—on signs indicating prices, receipts, etc.—the word *yuán* is used in place of *kuài*, and the word *jiǎo* is used in place of *máo*.

三元三角三分 OR 3.33元

Comparison: Review and expansion

Use *bǐ* + *yìdiǎnr* or *de duō* to compare two things.

Zhèige bǐ nèige dà yìdiǎnr. (*This one is a bit bigger than that one.*)
Zhèige bǐ nèige dà de duō. (*This one is much bigger than that one.*)

Use *gēn . . . yíyàng* to say that two things are the same or similar.

Zhèige gēn nèige yíyàng dà. (*This one and that one are the same size.*)

To express the negative, it's most common to use *méiyǒu . . . nàme*.

Zhèige méiyǒu nèige nàme dà. (*This one is not as big as that one.*)

Remember, don't use *hěn* when making comparisons.

~~Zhèige bǐ nèige hěn dà.~~

More "colorful" grammar

Note the various ways of expressing colors.

báisè (*the color white*)
bái yánsè (*the color white*)
bái de (*white [ones]*)

Remember that if a color is used to describe a noun, add the modifying particle *de* before the noun if the color term is more than one syllable. Thus, "a black cap/hat" can be:

hēi màozi
hēisè de màozi
hēi yánsè de màozi

Vocabulary (Starred items are for review.)

Money

fēn 分 a measure word for 1/100 of the primary monetary unit; "cent"

jiǎo 角 written form of the measure word for 1/10 of the primary monetary unit; "dime"

kuài 塊／块 spoken form of the measure word for the primary monetary unit; "dollar"

máo 毛 spoken form of the measure word for 1/10 of the primary monetary unit; "dime"

qián 錢／钱 money

yuán 元 written form of the measure word for the primary monetary unit; "dollar"

Currencies

Àomén yuán 澳門元／澳门元 Macau pataca

Àoyuán 澳元 Australian dollar

Gǎngbì 港幣／港币 Hong Kong dollar

Jiānádà yuán 加拿大元 Canadian dollar

Lúbǐ 盧比／卢比 rupee (India and Pakistan)

Měijīn 美金 U.S. dollar

Ōuyuán 歐元／欧元 euro

Rénmínbì 人民幣／人民币 People's money (People's Republic of China)

Rìyuán 日元 Japanese yen

Táibì 台幣／台币 New Taiwan dollar

Yīngbàng 英鎊／英镑 British pound

Consumer items (with measure words)

chángkù (tiáo) 長褲／长裤 (條／条) pants, trousers

duǎnkù (tiáo) 短褲／短裤 (條／条) shorts

màozi (dǐng) 帽子 (頂／顶) hat/cap

shuǐ (píng, bēi) 水 (瓶，杯) water (bottle, glass)

táng (xiē, kuài) 糖 (些，塊／块) candy (some, piece)

T-xù shān (jiàn) T-恤衫 (件) T-shirt

yīfu (jiàn) 衣服 (件) clothing

Colors

báisè 白色 white

fěnhóngsè 粉紅色／粉红色 pink

hēisè 黑色 black

hóngsè 紅色／红色 red

huángsè 黃色 yellow

huīsè 灰色 gray

jīnsè 金色 gold

júhóngsè 橘紅色／橘红色 orange

kāfēisè 咖啡色 brown, coffee color

lánsè 藍色／蓝色 blue

lǜsè 綠色／绿色 green

mǐsè 米色 beige

yínsè 銀色／银色 silver

zǐsè 紫色 purple

Sizes

dàhào 大號／大号 large

jiādàhào 加大號／加大号 extra large

jiāxiǎohào 加小號／加小号 extra small

xiǎohào 小號／小号 small

zhōnghào 中號／中号 medium

Question words

duōshao* 多少 how many, how much (usually more than ten)

jǐ* 幾／几 how many (usually fewer than ten)

zěnme* 怎麼／怎么 how, how could

zěnmeyàng* 怎麼樣／怎么样 how, how does that sound to you (after a proposal or suggestion)

Stative verbs (adjectives)

duō 多 many, much

gāo* 高 tall, high

guì 貴／贵 expensive

piányi 便宜 inexpensive, cheap

shǎo 少 few

xíng* 行 OK, all right, acceptable

yíyàng* 一樣／一样 same, identical, alike

Verbs

chuān 穿 wear, put on, dress

gěi 給／给 give to

huā 花 spend

huàn 換／换 exchange, change

mǎi 買／买 buy

mài 賣／卖 sell

Coverbs

bǐ* 比 compare to (used to compare)

gēn* 跟 with, and (used to compare)

Adverbs

jiù 就 only

tài . . . (le) 太……(了) too, overly, extremely

yígòng 一共 altogether, in all, in total

Auxiliary (helping) verbs

děi* 得 must, have to

huì* 會／会 can (do a learned activity); will, might

kěn 肯 willing to

kěyǐ* 可以 may, permit to

néng* 能 able to, can (if circumstances permit)

xiǎng* 想 would like to

yào* 要 going to, will, want to

Pronouns

nèige* 那個／那个 that, that one

zhèige* 這個／这个 this, this one

Prefixes

dì 第 (for ordinal numbers)

▶ Checklist of "can do" statements

After completing this unit, you should be able to perform each of the following tasks.

Listening and speaking

☐ Indicate your interest in a particular item for sale.

☐ Ask the price of an item.

☐ Understand prices that are given to you.

☐ Express your desire, or lack of desire, to purchase an item.

☐ Indicate specific characteristics (color, size, etc.) of your desired purchase.

☐ Ask the total price of several items.

☐ Say how much you are paying in a transaction.

☐ Close a transaction appropriately.

☐ Understand various terms for currency.

☐ Use appropriate bargaining expressions.

Reading and writing

☐ Understand simple declarative sentences related to money and shopping.

☐ Understand key information on signs related to products for sale.

☐ Write a brief note listing purchases that were made or are planned.

Understanding culture

☐ Visit a local Chinese grocery store or shop and buy something using your Chinese.

"Good quality at a low price"

價廉物美

Jiàliánwùměi

Getting around town to shop

In this unit, you will learn how to:

- state where you go to shop for certain things.
- ask for and interpret directions to stores and within stores.
- provide simple directions as requested.
- understand and follow directions as given.

- handle basic shopping transactions.
- understand key information on signs related to shopping.
- discuss modes of transportation.
- read and write simple sentences regarding purchases.

Encounter 1 Picking a store

 10.1 *View Episode 10 of the dramatic series.*

10.2 *Getting ready: What do you most often shop for, and where do you go to shop?*

_____

 10.3 *Watch and listen to the video segment. What do you think is the meaning of* Zuìhǎo dào nǎr qù mǎi yīfu? 最好到哪兒去買衣服？／最好到哪儿去买衣服？ *Write the English translation below.*

_____

10.4 *Match the corresponding items.*

a. gòuwù zhōngxīn   1. 商店   A. *store*

b. shāngdiàn   2. 百貨商店／百货商店   B. *shopping center*

c. bǎihuò shāngdiàn   3. 購物中心／购物中心   C. *department store*

Note: A group of *shāngdiàn* 商店 clustered together is called a *shāngchǎng* 商場／商场—a shopping mall. A larger shopping mall becomes a *bǎihuò shāngchǎng* 百貨商場／百货商场, which is similar to a *gòuwù zhōngxīn* 購物中心／购物中心.

FYI 供你参考

Shopping in China: Then and now

Gone are the days when travelers visiting China from abroad were advised to shop in what were known as Friendship Stores. Called *Yǒuyì Shāngdiàn* 友誼商店／友谊商店, these stores were for foreigners only; they are now only a faint reminder of the socialist China that existed before the country became a shopper's paradise. With the rapid economic growth China has experienced during the past generation, both overseas visitors and Chinese citizens can now afford to shop for almost anything imaginable. The country has witnessed a veritable explosion of Chinese department stores, malls, and markets, as well as a wide variety of foreign stores, ranging from Walmart all the way up to Christie's and Sotheby's.

Gone also is the special currency (*wàihuìjuàn* 外匯卷／外汇卷) issued by the government for use by foreigners; it's now *Rénmínbì* 人民幣／人民币 for all. The change in currency regulations that permitted visitors free access to buy anything anywhere sounded the closing bell for most of China's Friendship Stores. Indeed, Beijing's Friendship Store has since given way to a modern luxury hotel.

So where should one shop? The most interesting places are the bustling local markets and shopping alleys. They are also where you can find the best prices. Great deals and wonderful treasures are usually only as far away as the next pushcart, hastily set up stall, or tattered blanket laid on the ground. Visit these local places, use your Chinese, and bargain for the best price. You'll be rewarded, not only with a cheaper price but also with an invaluable learning experience. Buy Chinese and learn Chinese!

Alternatively, you may choose to explore a local department store or convenience store. These are likely to be full of both familiar and unfamiliar goods. Many Western and Japanese products are available to Chinese consumers. You'll notice that no one bargains at these places. These stores are staffed by employees earning a monthly salary who have no authority to set or adjust prices. If you ask for a price reduction, you'll quickly be refused.

Some shopping tips:

- Don't be surprised if fellow shoppers take a good deal of interest in you, especially in smaller towns or in the countryside. Appreciate their interest and try out a bit of your Chinese. You may occasionally feel as if your personal space is being invaded, but do your best to remain calm and accommodating. Enjoy the experience!

- If possible, shop in the company of local friends. They can give you a sense of where to shop, how much things should cost, what to look for in quality, and how and where to bargain.

- If you spot something you really want in a local market, buy it immediately; you may not be able to find it again later. You can ship it home, if necessary.

- You can use your credit card (*xìnyòngkǎ* 信用卡) and swipe your card (*shuākǎ* 刷卡) at most major stores.

- If you shop in hotel gift shops and upscale department stores for comfort and convenience, bear in mind that prices will probably be inflated.

- Wherever and whenever you shop, remember that a smile will buy you more good-will than any amount of *Rénmínbì*, *Gǎngbì*, or *Táibì* ever can.

 10.5 *Listen to the audio segment. Then match the traditional and simplified characters.*

a. chènshān 襯衫   1. 运动服

b. jiákè 夾克   2. 外套

c. yùndòngfú 運動服   3. 衬衫

d. qúnzi 裙子   4. 毛衣

e. máoyī 毛衣   5. 夹克

f. wàitào 外套   6. 裙子

10.6 *Where do you like to shop for shirts? Fill in the blanks below, in English, with the name of your favorite store.*

Wǒ xǐhuan dào _____ qù mǎi chènshān.

我喜歡到_____去買襯衫。／

我喜欢到_____去买衬衫。

Following the pattern above, list places where you like to shop for different clothing items. If you like to shop online, use a variation of the following:

Wǒ xǐhuan shàngwǎng mǎi jiákè.

我喜歡上網買夾克。／我喜欢上网买夹克。

_____

_____

_____

_____

Grammar Bits 语法点滴

Readying the action: Using coverbs

Although "going places" can be expressed quite simply in Chinese in a **subject + qù + place** format (e.g., *Wǒ qù shāngdiàn.* = "I'm going to the store."), a coverb is just as often used, particularly in more complex sentences involving purpose or follow-up activities.

Coverbs precede the main verb in a sentence. There are many coverbs in Chinese, and they can all be translated by English prepositions such as "to," "from," "on," "at," etc.

To express motion to an intended place, use the coverb *dào* (to) plus the destination with the verbs *qù* (go) or *lái* (come).

Thus: **Subject + *dào* + place + *qù*/*lái* + purpose**

Examples:

Tā dào shāngdiàn qù mǎi yīfu. (*She is going to the store to buy some clothes.*)

Tā dào xuéxiào lái kàn wǒmen. (*She is coming to school to see us.*)

If you're not "going there," add the negative *bù* to the coverb.

Tā búdào shāngdiàn qu. (*She is not going to the store.*)

Other adverbs and auxiliary verbs can also appear directly before the coverb.

Tā yào dào Zhōngguó qù kàn qīnqi. (*She wants/intends/will go to China to see her relatives.*)

Tā bù xiǎng dào Zhōngguó qù gōngzuò. (*She doesn't feel like going to China to work.*)

Usually when you "go" or "come," your action is purposeful. The position of the purpose in the Chinese sentence reflects something important about Chinese grammar: sentences are usually arranged in chronological order. In other words, you have to arrive at a place before you can achieve your purpose; thus, the "purpose" follows the action of going or coming.

Note that the verbs *lai* and *qu* are usually toneless when used at the end of a sentence. Additional coverbs will be introduced later in this unit.

10.7 Pair work: *Ask your partner,* Nǐ xǐhuan dào nǎr qù mǎi yīfu? 你喜歡到哪兒去買衣服？／你喜欢到哪儿去买衣服？ *Take notes on his or her response.*

_____

_____

_____

Compare your partner's answers with your own. Together, pick two stores where both of you have shopped for clothes, and list them below (you can write the names in English). Your answers should match your partner's.

A: _____　　B: _____

Think about your experiences at these stores, and pick the most appropriate choice below.

☐ Wǒ juéde (A) bǐ (B) hǎo.
　　我觉得A比B好。／
　　我覺得A比B好 。

☐ Wǒ juéde (A) méiyǒu (B) hǎo.
　　我覺得A沒有B好。／
　　我觉得A没有B好。

☐ Wǒ juéde (A) gēn (B) yíyàng hǎo.
　　我覺得A跟B一樣好。／
　　我觉得A跟B一样好。

Check to see which sentence your partner picked. Report your conclusions to another pair or to the class. Try to give a reason for your conclusion (for example, A de dōngxi duō. B de dōngxi piányi).

10.8 *Listen to the audio segment. Match the corresponding items below.*

a.   *athletic shoes*   1. liángxié 涼鞋   A. 高跟鞋

b.   *leather [dress] shoes*   2. gāogēnxié 高跟鞋   B. 皮鞋

c.   *high-heeled shoes*   3. yùndòngxié 運動鞋   C. 拖鞋

d.   *sandals*   4. tuōxié 拖鞋   D. 运动鞋

e.   *slippers*   5. píxié 皮鞋   E. 涼鞋

10.9 Nǐ xǐhuan dào nǎr qù mǎi xié? 你喜歡到哪兒去買鞋？／你喜欢到哪儿去买鞋？ *Fill in the blanks below, in English, with your favorite stores.*

Wǒ xǐhuan dào _____ qù mǎi liángxié, gāogēnxié, hé píxié. (hé = *and*)

我喜歡到_____去買涼鞋、高跟鞋和皮鞋。／

我喜欢到_____去买涼鞋、高跟鞋和皮鞋。

Wǒ xǐhuan dào _____ qù mǎi yùndòngxié.

我喜歡到_____去買運動鞋。／

我喜欢到_____去买运动鞋。

Wǒ xǐhuan dào _____ qù mǎi tuōxié.

我喜歡到_____去買拖鞋。／

我喜欢到_____去买拖鞋。

FYI 供你参考

Chinese taste in clothing: Then and now

Over the past couple decades, the pace of cultural change in China has been dizzying. Perhaps the most obvious change has been in the way Chinese people dress. In the 1960s and 1970s, practically everyone wore the so-called Mao suit, a combination of a close-fitting, high-collared jacket and baggy pants, usually gray, green, or blue. Called *Zhōngshān zhuāng*, curiously named after Sun Yat-Sen (*Sūn Zhōngshān*), "father" of the 1911 revolution that overthrew the imperial system, this outfit was intended to promote egalitarianism. After Mao passed away in 1976, China "opened" to the West, bringing rapid economic growth, an expansion of the middle class, and the end of the Mao suit. Nowadays, Chinese are just as fashionable, chic, and hip as any other citizens of the world. Generally speaking, however, Chinese dress more formally than people in the West. Men favor slacks and button-down shirts, while women prefer skirts, blouses, and dresses. However, as in the rest of the world, jeans are everywhere. Shorts, on both women and men, are becoming more visible, but it is still a good idea not to show too much skin in China. A short stroll down Beijing's most famous shopping street, Wangfujing Avenue, will give you a good idea of what's appropriate and what's not.

10.10 *Pair work: Ask your partner,* 你喜歡到哪兒去買鞋？／你喜欢到哪儿去买鞋？*Take notes on his or her answers and then compare them with your own.*

_____

_____

_____

Based on your partner's answers, follow up by saying that your favorite stores are better, by agreeing that your partner's stores are better, or by recognizing that the stores are equal in quality. Give a reason or two to support your response. (For example, you can suggest that a particular store's shoes are better [hǎo 好], cheaper [piányi 便宜], or more numerous [duō 多].)

10.11 *Listen to the audio segment. Then match the traditional and simplified characters.*

a. féizào 肥皂   1. 卫生纸

b. yáshuā 牙刷   2. 牙膏

c. xǐfàshuǐ 洗髮水   3. 牙线

d. wèishēngzhǐ 衛生紙   4. 牙刷

e. hùfàsù 護髮素   5. 梳子

f. shūzi 梳子   6. 洗发水

g. yáxiàn 牙線   7. 护发素

h. yágāo 牙膏   8. 毛巾

i. máojīn 毛巾   9. 肥皂

10.12 *What do you think is the meaning of* Nǐ tōngcháng zài nǎr mǎi rìyòngpǐn? 你通常在哪兒買日用品？／你通常在哪儿买日用品？ *Complete the following English translation.*

Where do you generally _____?

Fill in the blank below with the English name of a store where you usually shop.

Wǒ tōngcháng zài _____ mǎi yágāo.
我通常在_____買牙膏。／我通常在_____买牙膏。

Based on the model above, write three more sentences about where you might shop for various items for everyday use (assuming you wouldn't shop for everything at the same store).

_____

_____

_____

10.13 *Pair work: Ask your partner,* 你通常在哪兒買日用品？／你通常在哪儿买日用品？ *Compare his or her answer with your own.*

_____

_____

_____

Based on your partner's answer, say that your favorite store is better, agree that his or her favorite store is better, or say that the two stores are the same. Then give a reason or two to support your response. If you shop at the same store, be sure to indicate this by saying Wǒmen zài tóngyàng de dìfang mǎi rìyòngpǐn.

10.14 *Listen to the audio segment. Then match the traditional and simplified characters.*

a.   bǐjìběn 筆記本   1. 电脑

b.   zhǐ 紙   2. 笔记本

c.   bǐ 筆   3. 纸

d.   míngxìnpiàn 明信片   4. 笔

e.   diànnǎo 電腦   5. 明信片

f.   jìniànpǐn 紀念品   6. 纪念品

10.15 Nǐ tōngcháng dào nǎr qù mǎi diànnǎo, wénjù hé jìniànpǐn? 你通常到哪兒去買電腦、文具和紀念品？／你通常到哪儿去买电脑、文具和纪念品？ *Fill in the blanks below with the names, in English, of your favorite stores for these items. Note:* Qítā 其他 *means "other."* Wénjù 文具 *means "stationery."*

Wǒ tōngcháng dào _____ qù mǎi bǐjìběn, zhǐ, bǐ hé qítā wénjù.

我通常到_____去買筆記本、紙、筆和其他文具。／

我通常到_____去买笔记本、纸、笔和其他文具。

Wǒ tōngcháng dào _____ qù mǎi diànnǎo.

我通常到_____去買電腦。／

我通常到_____去买电脑。

Wǒ tōngcháng dào _____ qù mǎi míngxìnpiàn hé qítā jìniànpǐn.

我通常到_____去買明信片和其他紀念品。／

我通常到_____去买明信片和其他纪念品。

10.16 *Pair work:* Ask your partner, 你通常到哪兒去買電腦、文具和紀念品？／你通常到哪儿去买电脑、文具和纪念品？ *Compare his or her answers with your own from the previous exercise.*

Based on these answers, you may want to follow up by saying that your favorite stores are better, by agreeing that your partner's stores are better, or by saying that they are the same. Then give a reason or two to support your response.

Grammar Bits 语法点滴

The measure of the thing

You already know measure words such as *ge* 個／个 (general use), *tiáo* 條／条 (used for long, thin things like pants), *jiàn* 件 (used for general clothing), and *dǐng* 頂／顶 (used for hats). For all the objects introduced in this Encounter, the standard rule applies: if you don't know the specific measure word, use *ge* 個／个, but if you can manage, learn the specific measure word and use it in conjunction with the noun. The following are some more specific measure words you will find useful as your vocabulary develops.

All the clothing items in this Encounter use *jiàn* 件, except *qúnzi* (skirt) and *kùzi* (pants), which use *tiáo* 條／条. Since shoes come in pairs, they take the measure word *shuāng* 雙／双 (pair), unless you are specifically talking about only one shoe (i.e., "Where's my left shoe? I've lost a shoe!"), in which case you would use *zhī* 隻／只. (Note that the traditional character is half of the traditional character for "pair.")

Personal grooming items are more complex. Toothbrushes and toothpaste (like pencils and pens) are stick-like objects and take the measure word *zhī* 支 (twig). Shampoo and conditioner come in bottles and take the measure word *píng* 瓶 (bottle). Soap (like candy and metal coins) is made in a big vat, hardened, and then processed into usable pieces, and therefore is matched with the measure word *kuài* 塊／块 (piece). Toilet paper comes in a roll and therefore takes the measure word *juǎn* 卷 (roll). A comb (as well as an umbrella and the Olympic torch) is held in your fist, and is measured with *bǎ* 把 (to grab). Most Chinese towels are narrow and long and, like pants, are matched with *tiáo* 條／条. As for dental floss, the measure word depends on how the floss is sold: if it's in a hard, box-like container as in the United States, the measure word is *hé* 盒 (box); if it's in a plastic bag as in China, the measure word is *bāo* 包 (packet). However, if you are talking about a length of floss you have broken off and are holding in your hands, you have a *gēn* 根 (root) of floss.

Office supplies, paper, and name cards (as well as photographs and pictures) are flat sheets and measured with *zhāng* 張／张. A notebook, like a book, is measured with *běn* 本, and computers are measured with *tái* 台.

These measure words are a lot to remember, but give yourself time. If you get them wrong, don't worry; you'll still be comprehensible, but you might sound funny, as if you were talking about a "flock of children feeding a group of chickens" or a "herd of soldiers walking by a platoon of cattle."

Encounter 2 Giving and following directions

10.17 *Getting ready:* *How do you give someone directions to somewhere?*

_____

_____

 10.18 *Watch and listen to the video segment. Then match the corresponding items.*

a. *turn left*

b. *turn right*

c. *go straight ahead*

d. *go two blocks*

e. *It's not far from here.*

f. *It's very close to here.*

g. *It's one mile (away).*

h. *the third traffic light*

i. *two blocks away*

1. wǎng zuǒ guǎi 往左拐

2. wǎng qián zǒu 往前走

3. dì sān ge hónglǜdēng 第三個紅綠燈

4. lí zhèr yì lǐ lù 離這兒一里路

5. lí zhèr hěn jìn 離這兒很近

6. wǎng yòu guǎi 往右拐

7. lí zhèr bù yuǎn 離這兒不遠

8. guò liǎng tiáo jiē 過兩條街

9. lí zhèr liǎng tiáo jiē 離這兒兩條街

A. 离这儿不远

B. 离这儿很近

C. 往左拐

D. 往前走

E. 往右拐

F. 过两条街

G. 离这儿两条街

H. 第三个红绿灯

I. 离这儿一里路

Note: *lǐ* 里 (Chinese mile) is about 1/3 of an English mile.

Grammar Bits 语法点滴

More about coverbs and the locative verb *zài*

Use the coverb *wǎng*, meaning "toward," with verbs such as *zǒu* (go) and *guǎi* (turn) to indicate motion in the direction of a place that is not one's final destination.

> Wǎng zuǒ/yòu zǒu. (*Go to the left/right.*)
>
> Wǎng zuǒ/yòu guǎi. (*Turn to the left/right.*)

Use *cóng*, meaning "from," to indicate from where an action originates.

> Cóng zhèr wǎng qián zǒu. (*Go straight from here.*)
>
> Cóng shūdiàn wǎng zuǒ guǎi. (*Turn left from/at the bookstore.*)

Use the verb *zài*, meaning "at, in, on," to express location at a place, following this pattern:

> **Subject + *zài* + place**
>
> **"The subject is at the place."**
>
> Shāngdiàn zài zhèr. (*The store is here.*)
>
> Tā bú zài nàr. (*She's not over there.*)
>
> Nǐ zài nǎr? (*Where are you?*)

Use the coverb *lí*, meaning "separated/distant from," to separate one place from another, following this pattern:

> **Place 1 + *lí* + place 2 + *yuǎn* / *jìn* / (number) *lǐ lù***
>
> **"Place 1 is far from Place 2." /**
>
> **"Place 1 is near Place 2." /**
>
> **"Place 1 is (number) miles from Place 2."**
>
> Caution: Qualifying adverbs (*hěn, bù,* etc.) are placed before the stative verb (*yuǎn, jìn*).

> Wǒ jiā lí shāngchǎng bù yuǎn. (*My home is not far from the mall.*)
>
> Běijīng lí Huáshèngdùn hěn yuǎn. (*Beijing is very far away from Washington, D.C.*)
>
> Wǒ jiā lí gòuwù zhōngxīn yì lǐ lù. (*My house is a mile from the shopping center.*)

10.19 *Pair work:* *Work with a partner. Look at the map, pick a destination, and write it here:*

_____

Give your partner directions to this destination without naming it. If your partner follows your directions and arrives at the destination you intended, then you both did well! If not, go over your directions together and see where you went wrong. Then reverse roles and repeat the process.

1. Dì-wǔ Xiǎoxué
第五小學／第五小学
(*No. 5 Elementary School*)

2. Dì-yī Zhōngxué
第一中學／第一中学
(*No. 1 High School*)

3. Hépíng Gòuwù Zhōngxīn
和平購物中心／和平购物中心
(*Peace Shopping Center*)

4. Rénrén Biànlìdiàn
人人便利店
(*Everyone's Convenience Store*)

5. Sānxīng Chāoshì
三星超市
(*Three Stars Supermarket*)

6. Yǒuyì Shāngdiàn
友誼商店／友谊商店
(*Friendship Store*)

7. Yuǎndōng Bǎihuò Shāngchǎng
遠東百貨商場／远东百货商场
(*Far East Shopping Mall*)

8. Zhōngguó Yínháng
中國銀行／中国银行
(*Bank of China*)

9. Zhōng-Měi Fúzhuāng Gōngsī
中美服裝公司
(*China-U.S. Apparel Company*)

Bonus: What do you think is the meaning of wǎng húi zǒu 往回走*?*

Answer: _____

Encounter 3 Managing directions

 10.20 *Watch and listen to the video segment. Then match the corresponding items.*

1. dōngběi 東北   A. 东

2. nán 南   B. 西

3. běi 北   C. 西南

4. dōng 東   D. 东南

5. dōngnán 東南   E. 南

6. xī 西   F. 北

7. xīběi 西北   G. 东北

8. xīnán 西南   H. 西北

10.21 *Write the English meaning of* Qǐng gàosu wǒ zěnme zǒu 请告诉我怎麽走／请告诉我怎么走。

10.22 *Pair work:* Work with a partner. Choose one of the destinations shown below. Have your partner start at the X, and then give him or her directions to the destination. Your partner will first ask Zěnme zǒu? and you should reply with Wǎng [direction] zǒu. Your partner should then answer with Dào [place] le. If this is right, say Duì le, and then switch roles. If this is wrong, start over. Repeat the activity several times.

(Note: Don't try to memorize the names of the destinations now. These terms are the subject of a later lesson.)

diànyǐngyuàn

yīyuàn

xuéxiào

gōngyuán

X

fànguǎn

huǒchēzhàn

jiāyóuzhàn

chāojí shìchǎng

Encounter 4   Discussing modes of transportation

10.23 *Getting ready:* How do you move around town? Make a list of a few modes of transportation.

_____

_____

_____

_____

10.24 *Watch and listen to the video segment. Then match the corresponding items.*

a.

1. zuò gōnggòngqìchē 坐公共汽車

A.开车

b.

2. kāichē 開車

B.走路

c.

3. zǒulù 走路

C.打的

d.

4. qí zìxíngchē 騎自行車

D.坐火车

e.

5. qí mótuōchē 騎摩托車

E.坐地铁

f.

6. zuò dìtiě 坐地鐵

F.骑自行车

g.

7. dǎdī 打的

G.坐公共汽车

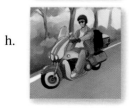

h.

8. zuò huǒchē 坐火車

H.骑摩托车

FYI供你参考

Modes of transportation

Gōnggòngqìchē 公共汽車／公共汽车 (public bus) is often shortened to *gōngchē* 公車／公车. The term *dǎdī* 打的 (take a cab) comes into Mandarin from Cantonese, in which "*diksī*" 的士 (pronounced like the English word "Dixie") is the transliteration of "taxi." The Cantonese "*dik*" 的 is in this case pronounced *dī* in Mandarin. As you know, it is usually pronounced *de*, as in *wǒ de* 我的. *Dǎ* 打 (literally, "to hit") is the equivalent of the English verb "to catch." The more formal term for "take a taxi" is different in the PRC and Taiwan. In the PRC, the formal term for "taxicab" is *chūzūqìchē* 出租汽車／出租汽车 (literally, "car for rent"), whereas in Taiwan it is *jìchéngchē* 計程車／计程车 (literally, "the car [in which the fare] is calculated based on distance"). "To take" is *zuò* 坐 (literally, "to sit"), but *dǎdī* is far easier and more hip, so this term has become much more popular than either *zuò chūzūqìchē* or *zuò jìchéngchē*.

Also, in the PRC a bicycle is known as a *zìxíngchē* 自行車／自行车—a "self-propelled vehicle"—whereas in Taiwan it is a *jiǎotàchē* 脚踏車／脚踏车—a "foot-pedaled vehicle." Same animal, different coat!

Grammar Bits 语法点滴

Taking a ride with more coverbs—*zuò, dā, qí*

Most of the time when you travel, you travel with the coverb *zuò* 坐 (to ride in a conveyance). Since *zuò*, as a verb (rather than a coverb), means "to sit," it is used with many nouns linked to travel, although in some instances you may not be literally sitting down. Like other coverbs, it is used along with main verbs, such as *qù* (go).

　　zuò diàntī *(take an elevator)*
　　zuò huǒchē *(take the train)*
　　zuò gōngchē qù *(go by bus)*
　　zuò dìtiě qù *(go by subway)*

For mass transit, the coverb *dā* 搭 (ride) is used interchangably with *zuò*.

　　dā gōngchē *(ride the bus)*
　　dā dìtiě *(ride the subway)*

When you ride a bicycle, motorcycle, or horse, you ride astraddle with *qí* 騎／骑.

　　qí zìxíngchē *(ride a bike)*

When *zuò* is used with *dào* (to), elements of the sentence are lined up in chronological order.

　　Wǒ xiǎng zuò gōnggòngqìchē dào shāngdiàn qù mǎi dōngxi. *(I'd like to take the bus to the store to buy some stuff.)*

10.25 *What do you think is the meaning of* zǒulù yào yí ge zhōngtóu? *Complete the English translation below.*

a. _____ takes an hour.

b. *Now write the English for the following:* Kāichē zhǐ yào shí fēn zhōng.

     _____

c. *Write the term for "one hour" in pinyin.* _____

d. *Write the term for "one minute" in pinyin.* _____

10.26 *Pair work: How often do you use each of the following modes of transportation? Check the appropriate boxes in the chart below.*

	每天	每個星期／ 每个星期	每個月／ 每个月	從來不／ 从来不
a. 坐公共汽車／ 坐公共汽车	☐	☐	☐	☐
b. 開車／开车	☐	☐	☐	☐
c. 走路	☐	☐	☐	☐
d. 騎自行車／ 骑自行车	☐	☐	☐	☐
e. 騎摩托車／ 骑摩托车	☐	☐	☐	☐
f. 打的	☐	☐	☐	☐
g. 坐地鐵／ 坐地铁	☐	☐	☐	☐
h. 坐火車／ 坐火车	☐	☐	☐	☐

10.27 *Pair work: Ask your partner how often he or she uses certain modes of transportation. Note his or her answers below.*

_____

_____

_____

_____

_____

10.28 *Group work: Work in groups of three or four. Make an appointment to go shopping. Decide on specifics about: (1) date and time; (2) three items you will shop for; (3) where you are going; (4) how far away your destination is (how many miles); and (5) how you are going to get there. Take notes about your appointments below. Be prepared to report to your group or to the class.*

Date and time: _____

Items to shop for: _____ _____ _____

Where: _____

How far: _____

How to get there: _____

FYI 供你参考

From bicycle-to-bicycle to bumper-to-bumper

It wasn't too long ago that China was known as the *Zìxíngchē Wángguó* 自行車王國／自行车王国, or the "Kingdom of Bicycles." An entire family riding a single bicycle down the street; someone moving house with seemingly his or her entire life's possessions balanced precariously on board; a farmer pedaling an ancient bicycle to tug a cart loaded down with live chickens from the countryside—all were common sights on the bicycle-crowded streets of Beijing. People from all walks of life in China relied on the humble bicycle, now extolled, at least in the United States, as a "green solution" to sky-high gas prices and environmental pollution, as well as a sure road to fitness and good health. However, in China's capital today, the streets are crowded with another sort of vehicle: the automobile. As the rapidly emerging Chinese middle class embraces four wheels instead of two, China is signaling the beginning of the end of its status as the bicycle kingdom. In Beijing alone, some ten million bicycles now compete with two million cars. China is the fastest-growing market for cars in the world. Gridlock—*sāichē* 塞車／塞车—has officially become part of the Chinese vocabulary, reflecting changes in Chinese life and culture. A word of advice: traveling by bicycle is still the best way to see and experience China, but watch out for other vehicles vying for your space.

Encounter 5 Moving around within a department store

10.29 *Watch and listen to the video segment. Match the corresponding items below.*

a. *in front*	1. zuǒbian 左邊	A. 前面
b. *in back*	2. qiánmian 前面	B. 中间
c. *in the center*	3. yòubian 右邊	C. 后面
d. *to the left*	4. zhōngjiān 中間	D. 左边
e. *to the right*	5. hòumian 後面	E. 右边

10.30 *Pair work: Work with a partner. Take five blocks (or squares of colored paper) in five different colors, and sit back-to-back with your partner. Position four blocks on each side of the fifth, central block, like this:*

$$X$$
$$X \quad X \quad X$$
$$X$$

Describe your color pattern for your partner, so that he or she can re-create it with his or her blocks. For example, say Hóng de zài zhōngjiān, huáng de zài zuǒbian, bái de zài qiánmian. *If your partner is successful in re-creating your pattern, reverse roles. If your patterns aren't identical, do the exercise over!*

10.31 *Can you guess what the following terms mean? Write the English.*

a. shàngmian 上面 _____

b. xiàmian 下面 _____

10.32 *Match the corresponding items below.*

a. *fifth floor*   1. wǔ céng 五層   A. 五楼

b. *five floors*   2. wǔ lóu 五樓   B. 五层

Fill in the blanks using numerals, and then write the English meanings of the sentences.

c. Wǒ sùshè (dorm) yǒu _____ céng. Wǒ zhù _____ lóu.

_____

d. Wǒmen de jiàoxuélóu (classroom building) yǒu _____ céng. Wǒ zài _____ lóu shàngkè.

_____

Note: Don't be confused. *Sān lóu* 三樓／三楼 means "the third floor," even without the ordinal prefix *dì* 第. (Remember *dì sān cì* 第三次"the third time"?) Example: "Go to the third floor" 到三樓去／到三楼去.

10.33 *Pair work: Ask your partner,* Nǐ jiā yǒu jǐ céng? Nǐ zhù jǐ lóu? 你家有幾層？你住幾樓？／你家有几层？你住几楼？ *Then compare your answers. If there's time, repeat with other people in your class. Take notes on everyone's answers.*

10.34 *Watch and listen to the video segment from exercise 10.29 again. Figure out the sales, and match the corresponding items.*

a. *big sale*   1. dà jiǎnjià 大減價   A. 打六折

b. *40 percent off*   2. dǎ liù zhé 打六折   B. 大减价

Note: You might have noticed that, in Chinese, the amount of a discount is expressed in reverse ratio to the English. Thus, *bā zhé* 八折 means "20 percent off," and *èr zhé* 二折 means "80 percent off."

10.35 *Look at the clothes you are wearing and other items in your possession. Think of three items that you bought on sale and try to remember how much the sale price was discounted. Complete the chart below. Write in English if you don't know how to say the items in Chinese. Fill in the discounted amount according to the "Chinese style" by writing a figure in the blank between the Chinese characters.*

Item   **Discount**

_____   打 _____ 折

_____   打 _____ 折

_____   打 _____ 折

10.36 *Pair work: Tell your partner about your three items. For example, you might say Zhèi ge dǎ qī-wǔ zhé (This was 25 percent off) or Zhèi ge dǎ jiǔ zhé (This was 10 percent off). Take notes about your partner's items below.*

_____

Compare your answers to see who obtained the biggest discount.

10.37 *Figure out payments. Match the corresponding items below.*

a. *pay*   1. xìnyòngkǎ 信用卡   A. 现金

b. *cash*   2. xiànjīn 现金   B. 付现金

c. *pay in cash*   3. fùqián 付錢   C. 刷卡

d. *credit card*   4. fù xiànjīn 付现金   D. 信用卡

e. *pay with a credit card* 5. shuākǎ 刷卡   E. 付钱

10.38 *Write three sentences (in pinyin) about your preferred method of payment. For example:* Wǒ hěn shǎo shuākǎ.

_____

_____

_____

10.39 *Pair work: Share your sentences with your partner. Write your partner's sentences below.*

_____

_____

_____

🎵 **Unit Rap**

Go to the **Encounters** *website at www.EncountersChinese.com and listen to the song to review key expressions from Unit 10. Listen again and sing along!*

Encounter 6 Reading and writing

▶ **Reading familiar sentences in Chinese characters**

10.40 *Pair work: Read the following dialogues (written in traditional characters) aloud with a partner, using the English as a guide.*

1 甲：我想去買些衣服。你說到哪兒去買最好？ *(I'd like to go shopping for clothes. Where do you say is the best place to go?)*

乙：甚麼樣的衣服？ *(What kind of clothes?)*

甲：我要一條短褲，一件T-恤衫。 *(I want a pair of shorts and a T-shirt.)*

乙：你T-恤衫不是很多嗎？為甚麼還要買？ *(Don't you have a lot of T-shirts? Why do you want to buy more?)*

甲：不夠，不夠…… *(Not enough, not enough . . .)*

乙：那我跟你一起去吧。走！我們去遠東百貨商店。 *(Then I'll go with you. Let's go! We'll go to the Far East Department Store.)*

2 甲：你覺得這件外套好看嗎？ *(Do you like how this coat looks?)*

乙：還可以。 *(It's OK.)*

甲：這件呢？ *(How about this one?)*

乙：嗯。這件比剛才那件好看。 *(Uh-huh. This one is better than the one just now.)*

甲：那這件呢？ *(How about this one, then?)*

乙：那件沒有第二件好看。 *(It doesn't look as nice as the second one.)*

甲：可是第二件最貴…… *(But the second one is the most expensive . . .)*

乙：價錢 (jiàqian) 貴一點，可是東西好多了。一分價錢一分貨。 *(It's a little more in price, but it's a much better item. You get what you pay for. [Literally: Pay a penny and get a penny's worth of goods.])*

3 甲：你要買甚麼樣的鞋？ *(What kinds of shoes do you want to buy?)*

乙：運動鞋。你呢？ *(Athletic shoes. And you?)*

甲：高跟涼鞋。 *(High-heeled sandals.)*

乙：涼鞋也有高跟的嗎？   *(Are there sandals with high heels?)*

甲：有啊！高跟才好看。   *(There are! They only look good if they have high heels!)*

乙：好吧！你去買你的高跟涼鞋，我去找 (zhǎo) 運動鞋！   *(Well then! You go buy your high-heeled sandals, and I'll go look for athletic shoes!)*

4 甲：先生，請問，日用品是在三樓嗎？   *(Sir, may I ask, are the personal grooming products [items for daily use] on the third floor?)*

乙：對，三樓。可以坐 扶手電梯 (fúshǒu diàntī) 上去。   *(Right, the third floor. You can take the escalator up.)*

甲：扶手電梯在哪兒呢？   *(Where is the escalator?)*

乙：在後面。你從 這兒往右走，就在那兒。   *(In the back. Turn right here, and it's over there.)*

甲：三樓賣牙膏，牙刷，肥皂，洗髮水嗎？   *(On the third floor, do they sell toothpaste, toothbrushes, soap, and shampoo?)*

乙：都有，都有。   *(Yes, yes, they have all that.)*

5 甲：哪兒有電腦賣？   *(Where are there computers for sale?)*

乙：離這兒不遠有一家商店賣電腦的。不到一里路。   *(Not too far from here is a store that sells computers. Less than a mile away.)*

甲：怎麼走？   *(How do I get there?)*

乙：往前走，前面那兒往左拐，就看到了。很近。叫美德電腦商店。   *(Go straight, and up ahead turn left, and you'll see it. It's really close. It's called the Meide Computer Store.)*

甲：好，謝謝。我等一會兒就去。   *(OK, thanks. I'll go in just a little while.)*

6 甲：你家離這兒還有多遠？   *(How much farther is your home from here?)*

乙：很近。再走兩里路就到了。   *(It's close. Another two miles and we'll be there.)*

甲：我們現在往西走，對嗎？   *(We're going west now, right?)*

乙：不，我們是往南走。我家在北京南邊兒。   *(No, we're going south. My home is in south Beijing.)*

甲：哦。   *(Oh.)*

7 甲：我們今天晚上怎麼去小王家？   *(How are we getting to Xiao Wang's home tonight?)*

乙：坐公共汽車？   *(By bus?)*

甲：太慢了。打的吧。   *(That's too slow. Let's take a cab.)*

乙：打的好貴啊！　*(It's really expensive to take a cab!)*

甲：可是比坐公共汽車快多了！　*(But it's a lot faster than taking a bus!)*

乙：那這樣：我們騎自行車，好不好？　*(Then let's do this: we'll ride bikes, OK?)*

甲：騎自行車跟坐公共汽車一樣慢。没關係，我們早一點兒出門吧！　*(Riding bikes is just as slow as taking the bus. No matter, let's leave a little earlier!)*

8 甲：你喜歡坐地鐵嗎？　*(Do you like to ride the subway?)*

乙：我從來不坐地鐵。我愛走路。從這兒走路回家只要半個鐘頭。　*(I never ride the subway. I like to walk. It only takes a half hour to walk home from here.)*

甲：哇，你每天都走路回家嗎？　*(Wow, do you walk home every day?)*

乙：對啊！你呢？你怎麼回家？　*(That's right! And you? How do you get home?)*

甲：我跟我姐姐一起回家。她開車。　*(I go home with my sister. She drives.)*

9 甲：我坐左邊，小王坐右邊，你坐中間，好不好？　*(I'll sit on the left, Young Wang will sit on the right, and you sit in the middle, OK?)*

乙：為甚麼？　*(Why?)*

甲：因為我們兩個人都想跟你説話！　*(Because we both want to talk to you!)*

10 甲：我們去購物中心吧。今天衣服大減價。　*(Let's go to the shopping center. There's a big sale on clothing today.)*

乙：是嗎？毛衣也減價嗎？　*(Really? Are sweaters on sale too?)*

甲：有些毛衣打五折呢！　*(Some sweaters are 50 percent off!)*

乙：那走吧！去看看。別忘了帶信用卡。　*(Let's go then! Let's take a look. Don't forget to bring your credit card.)*

甲：我没有信用卡。我都是付現金。　*(I don't have a credit card. I always pay cash.)*

乙：真的？我只刷卡。　*(Really? I only charge.)*

11 甲：你看！我今天在日月商場買了很多好東西，都很便宜。一條褲子，兩條裙子，一雙拖鞋和一雙皮鞋，三條毛巾，兩本筆記本，一包白紙，還有一些筆：紅的，黑的，還有藍的。　*(Look! I bought a lot of nice things at Sun-Moon Mall today, all very inexpensive. A pair of pants, two skirts, a pair of slippers and a pair of leather shoes, three towels, two notebooks, a ream of white paper, and some pens: red ones, black ones, and blue ones.)*

乙：你買了多少錢啊？　*(How much did it cost to buy all of this?)*

甲：不多，不多。都是減價的東西。　*(Not much, not much. It was all stuff on sale.)*

10.41 *Pair work: Read the dialogues aloud with a partner, this time without any English.*

1 甲：我想去買些衣服。你說到哪兒去買最好？

乙：甚麼樣的衣服？

甲：我要一條短褲，一件T-恤衫。

乙：你T-恤衫不是很多嗎？為甚麼還要買？

甲：不夠，不夠……

乙：那我跟你一起去吧。走！我們去遠東百貨商店。

2 甲：你覺得這件外套好看嗎？

乙：還可以。

甲：這件呢？

乙：嗯。這件比剛才那件好看。

甲：那這件呢？

乙：那件沒有第二件好看。

甲：可是第二件最貴……

乙：價錢 (jiàqian) 貴一點，可是東西好多了。一分價錢一分貨。

3 甲：你要買甚麼樣的鞋？

乙：運動鞋。你呢？

甲：高跟涼鞋。

乙：涼鞋也有高跟的嗎？

甲：有啊！高跟才好看。

乙：好吧！你去買你的高跟涼鞋，我去找 (zhǎo) 運動鞋！

4 甲：先生，請問，日用品是在三樓嗎？

乙：對，三樓。可以坐 扶手電梯(fúshǒu diàntī)上去。

甲：扶手電梯在哪兒呢？

乙：在後面。你從 這兒往右走，就在那兒。

甲：三樓賣牙膏，牙刷，肥皂，洗髮水嗎？

乙：都有，都有。

5 甲：哪兒有電腦賣？
乙：離這兒不遠有一家商店賣電腦的。不到一里路。
甲：怎麼走？
乙：往前走，前面那兒往左拐，就看到了。很近。叫美德電腦商店。
甲：好，謝謝。我等一會兒就去。

6 甲：你家離這兒還有多遠？
乙：很近。再走兩里路就到了。
甲：我們現在往西走，對嗎？
乙：不，我們是往南走。我家在北京南邊兒。
甲：哦。

7 甲：我們今天晚上怎麼去小王家？
乙：坐公共汽車？
甲：太慢了。打的吧。
乙：打的好貴啊！
甲：可是比坐公共汽車快多了！
乙：那這樣：我們騎自行車，好不好？
甲：騎自行車跟坐公共汽車一樣慢。沒關係，我們早一點兒出門吧！

8 甲：你喜歡坐地鐵嗎？
乙：我從來不坐地鐵。我愛走路。從這兒走路回家只要半個鐘頭。
甲：哇，你每天都走路回家嗎？
乙：對啊！你呢？你怎麼回家？
甲：我跟我姐姐一起回家。她開車。

9 甲：我坐左邊，小王坐右邊，你坐中間，好不好？
乙：為甚麼？
甲：因為我們兩個人都想跟你說話！

10 甲：我們去購物中心吧。今天衣服大減價。
乙：是嗎？毛衣也減價嗎？
甲：有些毛衣打五折呢！
乙：那走吧！去看看。別忘了帶信用卡。

甲：我沒有信用卡。我都是付現金。

乙：真的？我只刷卡。

11 甲：你看！我今天在日月商場買了很多好東西，都很便宜。一條褲子，兩條裙子，一雙拖鞋和一雙皮鞋，三條毛巾，兩本筆記本，一包白紙，還有一些筆：紅的，黑的，還有藍的。

乙：你買了多少錢啊？

甲：不多，不多。都是減價的東西。

10.42 Pair work: *Read the dialogues aloud with a partner, this time in simplified characters.*

1 甲：我想去买些衣服。你说到哪儿去买最好？

乙：什么样的衣服？

甲：我要一条短裤，一件T-恤衫。

乙：你T-恤衫不是很多吗？为什么还要买？

甲：不够，不够……

乙：那我跟你一起去吧。走！我们去远东百货商店。

2 甲：你觉得这件外套好看吗？

乙：还可以。

甲：这件呢？

乙：嗯。这件比刚才那件好看。

甲：那这件呢？

乙：那件没有第二件好看。

甲：可是第二件最贵……

乙：价钱 (jiàqian) 贵一点，可是东西好多了。一分价钱一分货。

3 甲：你要买什么样的鞋？

乙：运动鞋。你呢？

甲：高根凉鞋。

乙：凉鞋也有高根的吗？

甲：有啊！高根才好看。

乙：好吧！你去买你的高跟凉鞋，我去找 (zhǎo) 运动鞋！

4 甲：先生，请问，日用品是在三楼吗？

乙：对，三楼。可以坐扶手电梯 (fúshǒu diàntī) 上去。

甲：扶手电梯在哪儿呢？

乙：在后面。你从 这儿往右走，就在那儿。

甲：三楼卖牙膏，牙刷，肥皂，洗发水吗？

乙：都有，都有。

5 甲：哪儿有电脑卖？

乙：离这儿不远有一家商店卖电脑的。不到一里路。

甲：怎么走？

乙：往前走，前面那儿往左拐，就看到了。很近。叫美德电脑商店。

甲：好，谢谢。我等一会儿就去。

6 甲：你家离这儿还有多远？

乙：很近。再走两里路就到了。

甲：我们现在往西走，对吗？

乙：不，我们是往南走。我家在北京南边儿。

甲：哦。

7 甲：我们今天晚上怎么去小王家？

乙：坐公共汽车？

甲：太慢了。打的吧。

乙：打的好贵啊！

甲：可是比坐公共汽车快多了！

乙：那这样：我们骑自行车，好不好？

甲：骑自行车跟坐公共汽车一样慢。没关系，我们早一点儿出门吧！

8 甲：你喜欢坐地铁吗？

乙：我从来不坐地铁。我爱走路。从这儿走路回家只要半个钟头。

甲：哇，你每天都走路回家吗？

乙：对啊！你呢？你怎么回家？

甲：我跟我姐姐一起回家。她开车。

9 甲：我坐左边，小王坐右边，你坐中间，好不好？

乙：为什么？

甲：因为我们两个人都想跟你说话！

10 甲：我们去购物中心吧。今天衣服大减价。

乙：是吗？毛衣也减价吗？

甲：有些毛衣打五折呢！

乙：那走吧！去看看。别忘了带信用卡。

甲：我没有信用卡。我都是付现金。

乙：真的？我只刷卡。

11 甲：你看！我今天在日月商场买了很多好东西，都很便宜。一条裤子，两条裙子，一双拖鞋和一双皮鞋，三条毛巾，两本笔记本，一包白纸，还有一些笔：红的，黑的，还有蓝的。

乙：你买了多少钱啊！

甲：不多，不多。都是减价的东西。

10.43 *Match the corresponding simplified characters, traditional characters, and English.*

a. 购物中心	1. 涼鞋	A. *shopping center*
b. 买东西	2. 運動鞋	B. *the most expensive*
c. 卖东西	3. 電梯	C. *third floor*
d. 一条短裤	4. 洗髮水	D. *buy things, shop*
e. 最贵	5. 買東西	E. *three floors*
f. 运动鞋	6. 後面	F. *shampoo*
g. 凉鞋	7. 三層樓	G. *sandals*
h. 三楼	8. 購物中心	H. *notebook*
i. 三层楼	9. 最貴	I. *a pair of shorts*
j. 电梯	10. 三樓	J. *elevator*
k. 后面	11. 電腦	K. *athletic shoes*
l. 洗发水	12. 一條短褲	L. *computer*
m. 电脑	13. 賣東西	M. *sell things*
n. 笔记本	14. 筆記本	N. *in the back, behind*

10.44 *Match the corresponding simplified characters, traditional characters, and English.*

a. 白纸	1. 一樣慢	A. *far from here*
b. 黑笔	2. 付現金	B. *black pen*
c. 离这儿远	3. 南邊兒	C. *ride a bike*
d. 南边儿	4. 黑筆	D. *the south*
e. 坐公共汽车	5. 大減價	E. *drive*
f. 骑自行车	6. 白紙	F. *the right-hand side*
g. 坐地铁	7. 中間	G. *white paper*
h. 开车	8. 坐地鐵	H. *ride the subway*
i. 半个钟头	9. 騎自行車	I. *ride the bus*
j. 一样慢	10. 左邊	J. *the left-hand side*
k. 左边	11. 坐公共汽車	K. *just as slow*
l. 右边	12. 半個鐘頭	L. *pay cash*
m. 中间	13. 開車	M. *a half hour*
n. 大减价	14. 右邊	N. *the middle*
o. 付现金	15. 離這兒遠	O. *a big sale*

▶ **Reading real-life texts**

10.45 *Look at the photo. Fill in the blanks.*

Yóu cǐ shàng lóu. = _____

_____ from here.

Where do you think this sign was posted? Check one.

a. ☐ in front of a flight of stairs

b. ☐ by an exit

10.46 *Look at the photo.* 特 tè *is an abbreviated form of* 特别 *tèbié, which means "special." What do you think this sign says?*

Write the English:

_____

10.47 *Look at the photo. What items of clothing do you think might be offered here, at ¥25 each? Check one.*

a. ☐ skirts

b. ☐ pants

c. ☐ shirts

10.48 *What is the price reduction on these shoes? Check one.*

a. ☐ 5% off

b. ☐ 50% off

c. ☐ 15% off

10.49 *Look at the sign. What do you think* 向前约50米／向前约50米 Xiàng qián yuē 50 mǐ *means? Take a guess; fill in the blank below.*

Answer: approximately _____

10.50 *Look at the sign. What is being offered for sale here?*

Answer: _____

▶ Learning to write characters

10.51 *For stroke order and other useful information about each of the following characters from this unit, go to the* Character Writing Workbook. *Choose either traditional or simplified characters and practice writing them until you can reproduce them on demand.*

到, 用, 心, 百, 貨／货, 商, 場／场, 店, 離／离, 遠／远, 近, 路, 左, 右, 南, 北, 面, 邊／边, 開／开, 車／车

▶ Writing a note

10.52 *Write a paragraph (perhaps as part of an e-mail message to a friend) about your shopping habits, such as where you like to shop for what. Mention a few things you have purchased recently.*

Cultural Bits 文化点滴

Shopping and finding specific items

View the video segment "Shopping and finding specific items" and then discuss the following questions with your classmates.

- What are some challenges you might face in asking for directions? How might you deal with these challenges?
- Think of three things you can tell someone about the 塤／埙 *xūn* (ocarina).
- List several cultural items you might be interested in shopping for in China.

Recap

▶ Grammar

Coverbs

Coverbs are transitive verbs that precede the main verb and provide an "environment" for the main verbal action.

Use *dào* to indicate "to" a place.

> Wǒ dào shāngchǎng qù mǎi dōngxi. *(I'm going to the mall to shop.)*

Use *cóng* to indicate "from" a place.

> Wǒ cóng xuéxiào lái jiàn nǐ. *(I'm coming from school to meet you.)*

Use *wǎng* to indicate "toward" a place.

> Wǎng zuǒ zǒu jiù dào le. *(Go left and you'll be right there.)*

Use *zài* to indicate "at" a place.

> Wǒ zài chāojí shìchǎng mǎi shuǐguǒ. *(I buy fruit at the supermarket.)*

Use *lí* to indicate "the distance from" a place.

> Wǒ jiā lí Xiǎo Wáng jiā sān lǐ lù. *(My house is three miles from Xiao Wang's.)*

Use *zuò* to indicate "taking a vehicle to" a place.

> Wǒ zuò diàntī shànglóu. *(I'm taking the elevator upstairs.)*

Use *dā* to indicate "riding a mode of public transport."

> Wǒ tiāntiān dā gōngchē shàngbān. *(I ride the bus to work every day.)*

Use *qí* to indicate "riding something astraddle."

> Wǒ qí zìxíngchē qù. *(I'll go by bicycle.)*

Measure words
(Starred items are for review.)

Every Chinese noun is "marked" by its appropriate measure word. This listing here reinforces the measure words you've encountered to date.

bǎ 把 things you grab in your fist (e.g., combs)

bàn* 半 halves (e.g., half an hour)

bāo 包 things that come in a packet (e.g., dental floss)

běn 本 things that come in volumes (e.g., books, notebooks)

céng 層／层 stories (in a building)

cì* 次 times, occurrences

dǐng 頂／顶 hats

fēn* 分 "cent" (spoken)

fēn* 分 minutes of clock time

ge* 個／个 (general use)

gēn 根 root-like things (e.g., a strand of dental floss)

hé 盒 things that come in a box (e.g., matches)

jiā 家 stores

jiàn 件 clothing (e.g., shirts, jackets, sweaters)

juǎn 卷 things that come in rolls (e.g., toilet paper)

kè* 刻 quarters of an hour

kuài* 塊／块 "dollar" (spoken)

kuài 塊／块 things that come in pieces (e.g., soap)

lǐ (lù) 里（路） "Chinese mile"

lóu 樓／楼 floors (in a building)

máo* 毛 "dime" (spoken)

píng 瓶 things that come in bottles (e.g., shampoo, conditioner)

shuāng 雙／双 things that come in pairs (e.g., shoes)

suì* 歲／岁 years of age

tái 台 electronic items put on a table (e.g., computers, TVs)

tiān* 天 days

tiáo 條／条 long, rope-like things (e.g., pants, skirts, towels)

wèi* 位 persons with standing (e.g., teachers, guests)

xiē* 些 small amount, several

zhāng 張／张 things that come in sheets (e.g., paper, postcards)

zhī 支 stick-like things (e.g., toothbrush, toothpaste)

▶ Vocabulary

Things to buy (with measure words)

diànnǎo (tái) 電腦／电脑 (台) computer

dōngxi (ge, xiē) 東西／东西 (個／个，些) thing(s), articles

jìniànpǐn (ge) 紀念品／纪念品 (個／个) souvenir

Clothing (with measure words)

kùzi (tiáo) 褲子／裤子 (條／条) pants, trousers

chènshān (jiàn) 襯衫／衬衫 (件) shirt

duǎnkù (tiáo) 短褲／短裤 (條／条) shorts

jiákè (jiàn) 夾克／夹克 (件) jacket

máoyī (jiàn) 毛衣 (件) sweater, jumper

qúnzi (tiáo) 裙子 (條／条) skirt

wàitào (jiàn) 外套 (件) overcoat

yīfu (jiàn) 衣服 (件) clothes, clothing

yùndòngfú (jiàn) 運動服／运动服 (件) athletic clothes

Shoes (with measure words)

gāogēnxié (shuāng) 高跟鞋 (雙／双) high-heeled shoes

liángxié (shuāng) 涼鞋／凉鞋 (雙／双) sandals

píxié (shuāng) 皮鞋 (雙／双) leather (dress) shoes

tuōxié (shuāng) 拖鞋 (雙／双) slippers

yùndòngxié (shuāng) 運動鞋／运动鞋 (雙／双) athletic shoes

Products for daily use (with measure words)

féizào (kuài) 肥皂 (塊／块) soap

hùfàsù (píng) 護髮素／护发素 (瓶) conditioner

máojīn (tiáo) 毛巾 (條／条) towel

shūzi (bǎ) 梳子 (把) comb

wèishēngzhǐ (juǎn) 衛生紙／卫生纸 (卷) toilet paper

xǐfàshuǐ (píng) 洗髮水／洗发水 (瓶) shampoo

yágāo (zhī) 牙膏 (支) toothpaste

yáshuā (zhī) 牙刷 (支) toothbrush

yáxiàn (hé, bāo, gēn) 牙線／牙线 (盒，包，根) floss

Stationery (with measure words)

bǐ (zhī) 筆／笔 (支) pen

bǐjìběn (ge) 筆記本／笔记本 (個／个) notebook

míngxìnpiàn (zhāng) 明信片 (張／张) postcard

wénjù (xiē) 文具 (些) stationery

zhǐ (zhāng) 紙／纸 (張／张) paper

Places to shop

bǎihuò shāngdiàn 百貨商店／百货商店 department store

gòuwù zhōngxīn 購物中心／购物中心 shopping center

shāngchǎng 商場／商场 shopping mall

shāngdiàn 商店 store

Locations and directions

běi(bian) 北(邊)／北(边) north (side/direction)

dōng(bian) 東(邊)／东(边) east (side/direction)

dōngběi 東北／东北 northeast

dōngnán 東南／东南 southeast

hòu(bian) 後(邊)／后(边) back, behind

lóushàng 樓上／楼上 upstairs

lóuxià 樓下／楼下 downstairs

nán(bian) 南(邊)／南(边) south (side/direction)

nǎr 哪兒／哪儿 where

nàr 那兒／那儿 there

qián(bian) 前(邊)／前(边) front, in front

shàng(mian) 上(面) top, above

xī(bian) 西(邊)／西(边) west (side/direction)

xià(mian) 下(面) bottom, below

xīběi 西北 northwest

xīnán 西南 southwest

yòu(bian) 右(邊)／右(边) right

zhèr 這兒／这儿 here

zhōng(jiān) 中間／中间 middle

zuǒ(bian) 左(邊)／左(边) left

Nouns

diàntī 電梯／电梯 elevator

dìtiě 地鐵／地铁 subway

dìtiězhàn 地鐵站／地铁站 subway stop/station

fúshǒu diàntī 扶手電梯／扶手电梯 escalator

gōnggòngqìchē (gōngchē) 公共汽車 (公車)／公共汽车 (公车) public bus

hónglǜdēng 紅綠燈／红绿灯 red (traffic) light

huǒchē 火車／火车 train

jiàoxuélóu 教學樓／教学楼 classroom building

jiàqian 價錢／价钱 price

lóu 樓／楼 a multistoried building

mótuōchē (liàng) 摩托車／摩托车（輛／辆） motorcycle, motorbike

rìyòngpǐn 日用品 articles of daily use

sùshè 宿舍 dormitory, dorm

xiànjīn 現金／现金 cash

xìnyòngkǎ 信用卡 credit card

zhàn 站 stop, station

zhōngtóu 鐘頭／钟头 hour

Coverbs

cóng 從／从 from

dā 搭 ride on/take (a form of public transportation)

dào 到 to

lí 離／离 from, away from

qí 騎／骑 ride (something astraddle)

wǎng 往 toward, to

zài 在 in, at, on

zuò 坐 ride on/take (a form of transportation)

Verbs and verbal expressions

chūmén 出門／出门 leave/go out of the house

dǎdī 打的 take a cab

dǎ diànhuà 打電話／打电话 make a phone call, phone

Dào le! 到了！ (We're) there!

dǎzhé 打折 give a discount

fùqián 付錢／付钱 pay (in money)

fù xiànjīn 付現金／付现金 pay cash

gàosu 告訴／告诉 tell, let know, inform

guǎi 拐 turn (in the direction of)

guò 過／过 pass by/over

jiǎnjià 減價／减价 be on sale

jiē 接 meet, pick up

juéde 覺得／觉得 feel, think

kāichē 開車／开车 drive a car

mǎi 買／买 buy, purchase

mài 賣／卖 sell

mǎi dōngxi 買東西／买东西 shop (literally, "buy things")

Nǐ kàn! 你看！ Take a look! Look!

qí 騎／骑 ride (a bike, horse)

qí zìxíngchē 騎自行車／骑自行车 ride a bicycle/go by bicycle

shàngkè 上課／上课 attend class, go to class, hold class

shuākǎ 刷卡 charge, swipe a credit card

yào 要 need, require (in time or effort)

yòng 用 use

yǒu 有 have

zhǎo 找 look for

zǒulù 走路 walk (on the road)

zuò dìtiě 坐地鐵／坐地铁 take the subway

zuò gōnggòngqìchē (gōngchē) 坐公共汽車(公車)／坐公共汽车(公车) go by bus

Stative Verbs

duō 多 more (in number), numerous

hǎo 好 better (in comparisons)

jìn 近 near

lèi 累 tired

piányi 便宜 cheap, inexpensive

yuǎn 遠／远 far

Adverbs

chángcháng 常常 often, frequently

dāngrán 當然／当然 certainly, of course, naturally

hǎo 好 very (precedes stative verbs)

hěn shǎo 很少 rarely

jiù 就 exactly, precisely; then, in that case

nàme 那麼／那么 then, in that case

tài 太 too, exceedingly

tōngcháng 通常 generally, in general, normally

zuìhǎo 最好 best

Conjunctions

háiyǒu 還有／还有 furthermore, in addition, what's more

hé 和 and (links nouns and nominal expressions, not clauses)

ránhòu 然後／然后 and then, after that

Other words and expressions

búdào 不到 less than (followed by a number expression)

duō 多 how/how much... (before a stative verb)

Ò 哦 Oh

qítā 其他 others, the rest

Wà 哇 Wow

▶ Checklist of "can do" statements

After completing this unit, you should be able to perform each of the following tasks.

Listening and speaking

☐ Find out where a certain item can be purchased.

☐ After making a comparison between items, express your preference for one.

☐ Handle ways to express prices and bargain appropriately.

☐ Tell a friend where you like to shop and give a reason why.

☐ Ask for and understand directions (including compass points) to a particular place.

☐ Ask about various modes of transportation.

☐ Find your way around a large store.

☐ Manage a sales transaction (i.e., ask about prices, discounts, methods of payment).

Reading and writing

☐ Interpret directional signs.

☐ Interpret key information on retail ads regarding prices and sales.

☐ Read and write simple sentences regarding purchases.

Cultural understanding

☐ Demonstrate an understanding of the different sources of goods and products available for sale in China, from roadside vendors to upscale shopping centers.

☐ Demonstrate an understanding of appropriate and inappropriate behavior in each of the above locations, and an ability to effectively conclude transactions based on need.

REFERENCE

Glossaries

The Chinese-English and English-Chinese glossaries list the words introduced in *Encounters* and additional words that are useful to the beginning learner. Look upon this section as a sort of mini-dictionary. In the glossaries, most nouns are accompanied by their appropriate measure word in square brackets. Traditional characters for each entry are given first, followed by simplified characters.

The following grammatical abbreviations are used throughout the glossaries:

A	adverb	PH	phrase
AV	auxiliary verb	PR	pronoun
C	conjunction	PREF	prefix
CV	coverb	PW	place word
EV	equative verb	QW	question word
I	interjection	S	suffix
IE	idiomatic expression	SP	specifier
M	measure word	SV	stative verb
N	noun	TW	time word
NP	noun phrase	V	verb
NU	number	VO	verb object
P	particle	VP	verbal phrase

Chinese-English Glossary

A

ǎi short (*height or stature*) 矮 SV

ài love; like 愛／爱 V

àiren spouse 愛人／爱人 N

āiyā Oh; Oh my goodness! 哎呀 I

Àodàlìyà Australia 澳大利亞／澳大利亚 PW

Àomén Macau 澳門／澳门 PW

Àomén yuán Macau pataca (*currency*) 澳門元／澳门元 N

Àoyuán Australian dollar 澳元 N

āyí aunt (*mother's sister*) 阿姨 N

B

ba (*particle of suggestion*) 吧 P

bā eight 八 NU

bàba dad; father 爸爸 N

bǎihuò shāngdiàn department store 百貨商店／百货商店 N

báisè white 白色 N

bāng help; assist 幫／帮 V

bàn ge zhōngtóu a half hour 半個鐘頭／半个钟头 TW

bāngzhù help; assist 幫助／帮助 V

bànyè midnight 半夜 TW

bǎo full; not hungry 飽／饱 SV

bào [fèn] newspaper 報 [份]／报 [份] N

bāshí eighty 八十 NU

bāshì bus 巴士 N

Bāyuè August 八月 N

(yì)bēi . . . a cup of; a glass of (一)杯…… N/M

běibian(r) north (*side, direction*) 北邊(兒)／北边(儿) PW

Běijīng Beijing 北京 PW

Běi Měizhōu North America 北美洲 PW

bēizi [ge] glass; cup 杯子 [個]／杯子 [个] N

bǐ than, compare; in comparison 比 CV

bǐ [zhī] pen 筆 [枝]／笔 [枝] N

bian(r) side (*left, right, north, etc.*) 邊(兒)／边(儿) PW

biǎo [kuài] watch; timepiece 錶 [塊]／表 [块] N

bié do not (*imperative*) 別 A

biéde another; different one 別的 SP

bié kèqi you're welcome; don't be so polite 別客氣／別客气 IE

biéren other people; others 別人 N

bǐjìběn [běn] notebook 筆記本 [本]／笔记本 [本] N

bìng sickness; illness 病 N

bìng le become ill/sick 病了 VP

bìxū must (*matter of obligation*) 必須／必须 AV

bóbo uncle (*father's older brother*) 伯伯 N

bómǔ aunt (*wife of father's older brother*) 伯母 N

bówùguǎn museum 博物館／博物馆 N

bù no; not 不 A

bùcháng seldom; not often 不常 A

búcuò not bad; pretty good 不錯／不错 SV

búdào . . . less than (*followed by number expression*) 不到…… VP

bú shì no; that's not the case 不是 EV

bù shūfu slightly sick; uncomfortable 不舒服 SV

bú yào don't; don't want 不要 V/AV

búyòng need not 不用 A

búyòng xiè you're welcome 不用謝／不用谢 IE

C

cái then; not until; until 才 A

cāicai kàn take a guess 猜猜看 VP

cāntīng cafeteria 餐廳／餐厅 N

cǎo grass 草 N

céng story (*in a building*) 層／层 M

cèsuǒ bathroom; toilet 廁所／厕所 N

chá check (*examine*) 查 V

chá [bēi] tea [cup of] 茶 [杯] N

chà lack(ing) ("*before the hour*") 差 V

cháng long 長／长 SV

chàng sing 唱 V

chángcháng often; frequently 常常 A

chànggē(r) sing a song 唱歌(兒)／唱歌(儿) VO

Cháng Jiāng Yangtze River 長江／长江 PW

chángkù [tiáo] pants; trousers 長褲 [條]／长裤 [条] N

chē vehicle; car 車／车 N

chènshān [jiàn] shirt; blouse 襯衫 [件]／衬衫 [件] N

chēzhàn bus stop 車站／车站 N

chī have a meal; eat a meal; eat 吃 V

chībǎo eat to fullness 吃飽／吃饱 V

chīfàn have a meal; eat a meal; eat 吃飯／吃饭 V／VO

chuān wear; dress; put on clothes 穿 V／VO

chuán [tiáo] boat; ship 船 [條]／船 [条] N

chuáng [zhāng] bed 床 [张]／床 [张] N

chuān yīfu wear; dress; put on clothes 穿衣服 V／VO

chūguó go abroad 出國／出国 VO

chūmén leave; go out of 出門／出门 VO

chūqu go out 出去 V

chūqu wánr go out for some fun 出去玩兒／出去玩儿 VP

chūshēngzài be born in 出生在 VP

chūzhōng junior high school 初中 N

chūzūqìchē [liàng] taxi 出租汽車 [輛]／出租汽车 [辆] N

cì times; occurrences 次 M

cóng from (a place, a time, etc.) 從／从 CV

cóng . . . lái come from . . . 從……來／从……来 VP

cónglái bù never 從來不／从来不 A

D

dà old (age); big; large 大 SV

dà (érzi, nǚér) eldest (son, daughter) 大(兒子, 女兒)／大(儿子, 女儿) N

dǎdī take a cab 打的 VO

dǎ diànhuà make a phone call; phone 打電話／打电话 VO

dǎgōng do part-time work; do odd jobs 打工 VO

dàhào large; big (size in clothing, etc.) 大號／大号 N

dài wear (hat, glasses, etc.) 戴 V

dāizai stay (at) 呆在 VP

dāizai jiāli remain at home; stay at home 呆在家裏／呆在家里 VP

dàizi [ge] bag 袋子 [個]／袋子 [个] N

dàjiā everyone 大家 N

dāng to be; act as; work as; serve as 當／当 V

dāngrán of course; naturally 當然／当然 A

dào to (a place or time) 到 CV

dàoguo been to (a place) 到過／到过 V

dào le to have arrived 到了 VP

dào . . . qù go to . . . (a place) 到……去 VP

dàxué university; college 大學／大学 N

dàxuéshēng college student 大學生／大学生 N

dǎzhé give a discount 打折 VO

Déguó Germany 德國／德国 PW

Déguóhuà German (language) 德國話／德国话 N

Déguórén German (person/people) 德國人／德国人 N

děi have to; must 得 AV

děng wait; wait for; await 等 V

děngyú equal(s) 等于 V

de shíhou when (at the time of) 的時候／的时候 TW

Déwén German (language) 德文 N

Déyǔ German (language) 德語／德语 N

dì (ordinal prefix) 第 PREF

diǎn (zhōng) o'clock; time on the clock 點(鐘)／点(钟) M

diànhuà [ge] telephone 電話 [個]／电话 [个] N

diànhuà hàomǎ telephone number 電話號碼／电话号码 N

diànnǎo [tái] computer 電腦 [台]／电脑 [台] N

diànshì [tái] television; TV 電視 [台]／电视 [台] N

diàntī elevator 電梯／电梯 N

diànxìn [fēng] e-mail message 電信 [封]／电信 [封] N

diànyǐng [bù] film; movie 電影 [部]／电影 [部] N

diànyǐngyuàn movie theater 電影院／电影院 N

diànyóu e-mail 電郵／电邮 N

diànzǐ yóuxì [ge] video game 電子遊戲 [個]／电子游戏 [个] N

dìbā (ge) eighth (one) 第八(個)／第八(个) N/NU

dìdi younger brother 弟弟 N

dìèr (ge) second (one) 第二(個)／第二(个) N/NU

dìfang [ge] place 地方 [個]／地方 [个] N

dìjiǔ (ge) ninth (one) 第九(個)／第九(个) N/NU

dìliù (ge) sixth (one) 第六(個)／第六(个) N/NU

dìqī (ge) seventh (one) 第七(個)／第七(个) N/NU

dìsān (ge) third (one) 第三(個)／第三(个) N/NU

dìshí (ge) tenth (one) 第十(個)／第十(个) N/NU

dìshí'èr (ge) twelfth (one) 第十二(個)／第十二(个) N/NU

dìshíyī (ge) eleventh (one) 第十一(個)／第十一(个) N/NU

dìsì (ge) fourth (one) 第四(個)／第四(个) N/NU

dìtiě subway 地鐵／地铁 N

dìtiězhàn subway stop/station 地鐵站／地铁站 N

dìtú [zhāng] map 地圖 [張]／地图 [张] N

dìwǔ (ge) fifth (one) 第五(個)／第五(个) N/NU

dìyī (ge) first (one) 第一(個)／第一(个) N/NU

dìzhǐ address; location; mailing address 地址 N

dǒng understand 懂 V

dōngběibian(r) northeast 東北邊(兒)／东北边(儿) PW

dōngbian(r) east (side, direction) 東邊(兒)／东边(儿) PW

dōngnán southeast 東南／东南 PW

dōngxi [ge] object; thing; stuff 東西 [個]／东西 [个] N

dōu both; all 都 A

dòufu tofu 豆腐 N

dú study 讀／读 V

duǎn short (length) 短 SV

duǎnkù [tiáo] shorts/short pants [pair of] 短褲 [條]／短裤 [条] N

duì right; correct 對／对 SV

duìbuqǐ I'm sorry; excuse me; sorry 對不起／对不起 IE

duì le yes; that's right 對了／对了 IE

duō how; to what extent 多 A

duō many; much; numerous 多 SV

duōshao how many (more than ten) 多少 QW

dúshēngnǚ only child (girl) 獨生女／独生女 N

dúshēngzǐ only child (boy) 獨生子／独生子 N

dúshū attend school 讀書／读书 VO

E

è hungry 餓／饿 SV
Éguó Russia 俄國／俄国 PW
Éguóhuà Russian (language) 俄國話／俄国话 N
Éguórén Russian (person/people) 俄國人／俄国人 N
èr two 二 NU
èrshí twenty 二十 NU
èrshíyī twenty-one 二十一 NU
Èryuè February 二月 N
érzi son 兒子／儿子 N
Éwén Russian (language) 俄文 N
Éyǔ Russian (language) 俄語／俄语 N

F

Fǎguó France 法國／法国 PW
Fǎguóhuà French (language) 法國話／法国话 N
Fǎguórén French (person/people) 法國人／法国人 N
fàn [wǎn] cooked rice [bowl of] 飯 [碗]／饭 [碗] N
fàngjià have or be on a holiday 放假 VO
fángjiān [ge] room 房間 [個]／房间 [个] N
fànguǎn(r) restaurant 飯館兒／饭馆儿 N
fāngxiàng way/direction 方向 N
fàngxué get out of school; dismiss school 放學／放学 VO
fángzi [dòng] house 房子 [棟／栋] N
fántǐzì traditional character 繁體字／繁体字 N
fāshāo have a fever 發燒／发烧 VO
Fǎwén French (language) 法文 N
Fǎyǔ French (language) 法語／法语 N
fēicháng extremely; very; rather; quite 非常 A
fēijī [jià] airplane 飛機 [架]／飞机 [架] N
féizào [kuài] soap [bar of] 肥皂 [塊]／肥皂 [块] N
Fēizhōu Africa 非洲 PW
Fēizhōurén African (person/people) 非洲人 N
fēn 1/100 of the primary monetary unit; "cent" 分 M
fēn minute (clock time) 分 M
fěnhóngsè pink 粉紅色／粉红色 N
fùmǔ parents 父母 N
fùqián pay money 付錢／付钱 VO
fùqin father; dad 父親／父亲 N
fúshǒu diàntī escalator 扶手電梯／扶手电梯 N
fúwùyuán waiter; waitress; service person; attendant; salesclerk 服務員／服务员 N
fù xiànjīn pay in cash 付現金／付现金 VO

G

gāng just; only a short time ago 剛／刚 A
Gǎngbì Hong Kong dollar 港幣／港币 N
gāngcái just now; just a moment ago 剛才／刚才 A
gāo tall; (also a surname) 高 SV
gāogēnxié [shuāng] high-heeled shoes [pair of] 高跟鞋 [雙]／高跟鞋 [双] N
gàosu tell; inform 告訴／告诉 V

gāoxìng happy; pleased 高興／高兴 SV
gāozhōng senior high school 高中 N
gēcǎo cut the grass; mow the lawn 割草 VO
gēge older brother 哥哥 N
gěi give 給／给 V
gēn with; and 跟 C
gèng still; even more (in comparisons) 更 A
gēxīng singing star 歌星 N
gōng (gòngqì) chē [liàng] public bus 公(共汽)車 [輛]／公(共汽)车 [辆] N
gōngchéngshī engineer 工程師／工程师 N
gōngkè homework; schoolwork; assignment 功課／功课 N
gōngrén laborer; worker 工人／工人 N
gōngyuán(r) public park 公園(兒)／公园(儿) N
gōngzuò job; work 工作 N/V
gǒu dog (Chinese zodiac) 狗 N
gòuwù zhōngxīn shopping center 購物中心／购物中心 N
guā húzi shave (one's) beard 刮鬍子／刮胡子 VO
guǎi turn (in the direction of) 拐 V
guàngjiē go shopping 逛街 VO
guàng shāngchǎng go to the mall 逛商場／逛商场 VO
Guǎngzhōu Canton (old name for Guangzhou) 廣州／广州 PW
gūgu aunt (father's sister) 姑姑 N
guì expensive; costly 貴／贵 SV
Guìlín Guilin (city in southwestern China) 桂林 PW
guìxìng what's your surname? 貴姓／贵姓 IE
guo (experiential verbal suffix) 過／过 S
guó country (suffix to names of countries) 國／国 N/S
guò exceed; past (the clock hour) 過／过 V
guò pass by (on the way) 過／过 V
guò yìhuǐr after a little while 過一會兒／过一会儿 VP

H

hái still; yet 還／还 A
hài Hi! 嗨 I
hái hǎo I'm OK; I'm fairly well 還好／还好 IE
hái méi not yet (in a negative sentence) 還沒／还没 A
hái shi still; yet 還是／还是 A
háishi or (when offering alternatives) 還是／还是 C
háiyǒu furthermore; in addition; what's more 還有／还有 C
háizi kid; child 孩子 N
háizimen children 孩子們／孩子们 N
hànbǎobāo [ge] hamburger 漢堡包 [個]／汉堡包 [个] N
Hánguó Korea 韓國／韩国 PW
Hánguóhuà Korean (language) 韓國話／韩国话 N
Hánguórén Korean (person/people) 韓國人／韩国人 N
Hánwén Korean (language) 韓文／韩文 N

Hányǔ Korean (*language*) 韓語／韩语 N

hǎo OK; good; fine; nice; well 好 SV

hào number (*in a series*) 號／号 M

hào day of the month 號／号 M

hào size (*small, medium, large, etc.*) 號／号 M

hǎochī delicious; good-tasting 好吃 SV

hǎokàn attractive; good-looking; pretty 好看 SV

hàomǎ number (*telephone number, etc.*) 號碼／号码 N

hē drink 喝 V

hé with (*in the company of*); and 和 C

hēisè black 黑色 N

hěn very (*usually light in sense*) 很 A

hěn gāoxìng rènshi nǐ/nín happy to meet you 很高興認識你(您)／很高兴认识你(您) IE

hěn shǎo rarely 很少 A

hóngdēng red light (*traffic*) 紅燈／红灯 N

hónglǜdēng traffic light 紅綠燈／红绿灯 N

hóngsè red 紅色／红色 N

hóu monkey (*Chinese zodiac*) 猴 N

hòubian(r) back; behind; in back of 後邊(兒)／后边(儿) PW

hòumian back; behind; in back of 後面／后面 PW

hòunián year after next 後年／后年 PW

hòutiān day after tomorrow 後天／后天 TW

hǔ tiger (*Chinese zodiac*) 虎 N

huā spend (*money*) 花 V

huà talk; speech; words 話／话 N

huàjiā painter; artist 畫家／画家 N

huàn exchange; change 換／换 V

Huáng Hé Yellow River 黃河 PW

huángsè yellow 黃色 N

huànqián exchange; change currency 換錢／换钱 VO

huāqián spend money 花錢／花钱 V/VO

huàzhuāng put on makeup 化妝／化妆 VO

huàzhuāngpǐn makeup 化妝品／化妆品 N

huàzhuāngshì bathroom 化妝室／化妆室 N

hùfàsù [píng] conditioner (*for hair*) [bottle of] 護髮素 [瓶]／护发素 [瓶] N

huí return (*to a place*) 回 V

huì likely to; will likely; sure to 會／会 AV

huì can, know (*how to*) 會／会 V

huíjiā go; return home 回家 VO

huílai come back to; return 回來／回来 V

huíqu return 回去 V

huīsè gray 灰色 N

huǒchē [liàng] train 火車 [輛]／火车 [辆] N

huòzhě or (*in statements*) 或者 C

hùshi nurse 護士／护士 N

húzi beard 鬍子／胡子 N

J

jī rooster; chicken (*Chinese zodiac*) 雞／鸡 N

jǐ (ge) how many (*less than ten*) 幾(個)／几(个) QW

jiā plus; add to 加 V

jiā home; family 家 N

jiādàhào size extra large 加大號／加大号 N

jiákè [jiàn] jacket 夾克 [件]／夹克 [件] N

jiālǐrén family members 家裏人／家里人 N

jiǎn subtract 減／减 V

jiàn see/meet up with (*someone*) 見／见 V

Jiānádà Canada 加拿大 PW

Jiānádàrén Canadian (*person/people*) 加拿大人 N

Jiānádà yuán Canadian dollar 加拿大元 N

jiǎngjià bargain (*for a better price*) 講價／讲价 VO

jiānglái future; in the future 將來／将来 TW/N

jiǎnjià be on sale 減價／减价 VO

jiǎntǐzì simplified character 簡體字／简体字 N

jiànzhùshī architect 建築師／建筑师 N

jiāo teach 教 V

jiǎo 1/10 of the primary monetary unit (*written*); "dime" 角 M

jiào tell (*someone to do something*) 叫 V

jiào called; be called (*by a given name*); be named 叫 EV

jiàoshòu [wèi] professor 教授 [位]／教授 [位] N

jiāoshū teach 教書／教书 VO

jiàoxuélóu classroom building 教學樓／教学楼 N

jiàqian price 價錢／价钱 N

jiāwù household chores/duties 家務／家务 N

jiāxiǎohào size extra small 加小號／加小号 N

Jiāzhōu California 加州 PW

jiē meet up with; pick up (*someone*) 接 V

jiē [tiáo] street 街 [條]／街 [条] N

jiějie elder sister 姐姐 N

jiěmèi sisters 姐妹 N

jìfù stepfather 繼父／继父 N

jíle (hǎojíle, kuàijíle . . .) extremely (good, fast, etc.) 極了(好極了, 快極了……)／极了(好极了,快极了……) S

jìmǔ stepmother 繼母／继母 N

jìn near 近 SV

jǐngchá police officer 警察 N

jīnglǐ manager (*of business, etc.*) 經理／经理 N

jìniànpǐn [ge] souvenir 紀念品 [個]／纪念品 [个] N

jīnnián this year 今年 TW

jìnqu go in 進去／进去 V

jīnsè gold (*color*) 金色 N

jīntiān today 今天 TW

jīntiān wǎnshang tonight; this evening 今天晚上 TW

jiǔ nine 九 NU

jiǔ wine; alcoholic beverage 酒 N

jiù only; exactly; precisely; then 就 A

jiùhuǒyuán firefighter 救火員／救火员 N

jiùjiu uncle (*mother's brother*) 舅舅 N

Jiǔyuè September 九月 N

juéde feel/think that 覺得／觉得 V

júhóngsè orange (*color*) 橘紅色 N

jūnrén soldier 軍人／军人 N

K

kāfēi [bēi] coffee [cup of] 咖啡 [杯] N
kāfēisè coffee-colored/brown 咖啡色 N
kāichē drive a car; go by car 開車／开车 VO
kāishǐ begin; start 開始／开始 V
kàn watch; look; see (*a movie, etc.*) 看 V
kàn read (*a book, etc.*) 看 V
kànbào read a newspaper 看報／看报 VO
kàn diànshì watch TV 看電視／看电视 VO
kàn diànyǐng see a movie 看電影／看电影 VO
kànjian see 看見／看见 V
kàn (yí) kàn look; take a look 看(一)看 VP
kànshū read; read a book; reading 看書／看书 VO/N
kǎoshì test; give or take a test 考試／考试 N/V
kě thirsty 渴 SV
kè lesson; class 课／课 N/M
kěn willing to 肯 AV
kěnéng probably; maybe 可能 A
kèqi polite 客氣／客气 SV
kěshì but; yet; however 可是 C
kěyǐ can; may (*permission to*) 可以 AV
kòng free time 空 N
kǒu mouth (*the radical*) 口 N
kuài quick; quickly; fast 快 SV
kuài primary monetary unit (*spoken*); denomination equivalent to a "dollar" 塊／块 M
kuàijìshī accountant 會計師／会计师 N
kuài yào + *verb* soon; about to; before long 快要 A
kuàizi [shuāng] chopsticks [pair of] 筷子 [雙]／筷子 [双] N
kùn sleepy 睏／困 SV
kùzi [tiáo] pants/trousers [pair of] 褲子 [條]／裤子 [条] N

L

lái come 來／来 V
lánsè blue 藍色／蓝色 N
lǎodà oldest child 老大 N
lǎo'èr second child (*in a family*) 老二 N
lǎogōng husband 老公 N
lǎolao maternal grandmother 姥姥 N
lǎopo wife 老婆 N
lǎoshī [wèi] teacher 老師 [位]／老师 [位] N
lǎoxiǎo youngest child 老小 N
lǎoyāo youngest child 老么／老幺 N
lǎoye maternal grandfather 姥爺／姥爷 N
lèi tired; weary 累 SV
lěng cold (*temperature*) 冷 SV
lí from (*distant from*) 離／离 CV
(yì) lǐ one mile (*Chinese mile*) (一)里 N/M
liǎng (ge) two; a couple of 兩(個)／两(个) NU
liángxié [shuāng] sandals [pair of] 涼鞋 [雙]／凉鞋 [双] N

liáotiān(r) chat 聊天兒／聊天儿 VO
lǐbianr in; inside 裏邊兒／里边儿 PW
líng zero 零 NU
línjū neighbor 鄰居／邻居 N
liù six 六 NU
liùshí sixty 六十 NU
Liùyuè June 六月
lóng dragon (*Chinese zodiac*) 龍／龙 N
lóu floor (*in a building*) 樓／楼 M
lóu [dòng] building (*multi-storied*) 樓 [棟]／楼 [栋] N
lóushàng upstairs 樓上／楼上 PW
lóuxià downstairs 樓下／楼下 PW
lù [tiáo] path; road 路 [條]／路 [条] N
Lúbǐ rupee (*India and Pakistan*) 盧比／卢比 N
Luòshānjī Los Angeles 洛杉磯／洛杉矶 PW
lùdēng green light (*traffic*) 綠燈／绿灯 N
lùsè green 绿色／绿色 N
lùshī lawyer 律師／律师 N
lǚxíng travel 旅行 V

M

ma (*question particle*) 嗎／吗 P
mā mom; mother 媽／妈 N
mǎ horse (*Chinese zodiac*) 馬／马 N
mǎi purchase; buy 買／买 V
mài sell 賣／卖 V
mǎi dōngxi shop (*buy things*) 買東西／买东西 VO
māma mom; mother 媽媽／妈妈 N
mǎma-hūhū fair to middling; so-so 馬馬虎虎／马马虎虎 IE
màn slow 慢 SV
máng busy; have something to do 忙 SV
máo 1/10 of the primary monetary unit (*spoken*); "dime" 毛 M
máobǐ [zhī] writing brush 毛筆 [枝]／毛笔 [枝] N
máojīn [tiáo] towel 毛巾 [條]／毛巾 [条] N
máoyī [jiàn] sweater 毛衣 [件] N
màozi [dǐng] hat; cap 帽子 [頂]／帽子 [顶] N
méi (*negator for* **yǒu**) 没 A
měi (ge) each 每(個)／每(个) PR
měi ge rén everyone 每個人／每个人 N
méi guānxi that's all right; no problem 没關係／没关系 IE
Měiguó America; U.S. 美國／美国 PW
Měiguórén American (*person/people*) 美國人／美国人 N
Měijīn U.S. money 美金 N
mèimei younger sister 妹妹 N
méi shì nothing's wrong; it doesn't matter; never mind 没事 IE
měitiān daily; every day 每天 TW

méi yìsi   uninteresting; dull   没意思   SV
méiyǒu   not have; be without   没有   V
míngnián   next year   明年   TW
míngtiān   tomorrow   明天   TW
míngxìnpiàn [zhāng]   postcard   明信片 [張]／明信片 [张]   N
míngzi [ge]   name; first name; given name   名字 [個]／名字 [个]   N
mǐsè   beige   米色   N
mìshu   secretary   秘書／秘书   N
mótuōchē [liàng]   motorcycle; motorbike   摩托車 [輛]／摩托车 [辆]   N
mù   tree; wood (*the radical*)   木   N
mǔqin   mother; mom   母親／母亲   N

N

nà   in that case; then   那   C
nà   that; that one   那   PR/SP
nǎinai   paternal grandmother   奶奶   N
nàli   there   那裏／那里   PW
nǎli, nǎli   (*polite rejection of a compliment*)   哪裡, 哪裡／哪里, 哪里   IE
nàme   then, in that case   那麼／那么   C
nán   difficult   難／难   SV
nánbian(r)   south (*side/direction*)   南邊(兒)／南边(儿)   PW
nánháir   boy   男孩兒／男孩儿   N
nánháizi   boy   男孩子   N
Nán Měizhōu   South America   南美洲   PW
nánpéngyou   boyfriend   男朋友   N
nǎr   where   哪兒／哪儿   QW
nàr   there   那兒／那儿   PW
ne   and what about X   呢   P
něi   which   哪   QW
nèi   that; that one   那   PR/SP
nèige   that, that one   那個／那个   PR/SP
néng   able to; can (*circumstances permitting*)   能   AV
nèr   there   那兒／那儿   PW
nǐ   you (*informal*)   你   PR
nián   year   年   N/M
niàn   study   念   V
niánjí   year (*in school*); grade   年級／年级   N
niànshū   attend school   念書／念书   VO
nǐ de   your(s)   你的   PR
Nǐ duō dà?   How old are you?   你多大   PH
nǐ hǎo   hello; how do you do?   你好   IE
Nǐ jǐ suì?   How old are you?   你幾歲／你几岁   PH
Nǐ kàn!   Take a look!   你看！   PH
nǐmen   you (*plural*)   你們／你们   PR
nǐmen zìjǐ   yourselves   你们自己   PR
nín   you (*formal*)   您   PR

nín guìxìng   what's your (honorable) name   您貴姓／您贵姓   IE
nín hǎo   hello; how do you do?   您好   IE
nín zǎo   good morning   您早   IE
niú   ox (*Chinese zodiac*)   牛   N
Niǔyuē   New York   紐約／纽约   PW
niúzǎikù [tiáo]   blue jeans; jeans   牛仔褲 [條]／牛仔裤 [条]   N
nǐ zǎo   good morning   你早   IE
nǐ zìjǐ   yourself   你自己   PR
nòng   make, cook   弄   V
nóngmín   farmer   農民／农民   N
nuǎnhuo   warm   暖和   SV
nǚ'ér   daughter   女兒／女儿   N
nǚháir   girl   女孩兒／女孩儿   N
nǚháizi   girl   女孩子／女孩子   N
nǚpéngyou   girlfriend   女朋友   N

O

Ò   oh (*sudden understanding*)   噢   I
Ōuyuán   Euro (*currency*)   歐元／欧元   N
Ōuzhōu   Europe   歐洲／欧洲   PW
Ōuzhōurén   European (*person/people*)   歐洲人／欧洲人   N

P

pá   climb; crawl   爬   V
pàng   fat   胖   SV
pǎo   run   跑   V
pǎobù   run; jog   跑步   VO
péngyou   friend   朋友   N
piányi   inexpensive; cheap   便宜   SV
píjiǔ [píng]   beer [bottle of]   啤酒 [瓶]   N
píng   bottle   瓶   N/M
píngcháng   generally   平常   A
píxié [shuāng]   leather shoes [pair of]   皮鞋 [雙]／皮鞋 [双]   N
Pǔtōnghuà   Standard Mandarin   普通話／普通话   N

Q

qī   seven   七   NU
qí   ride astride (a bike, horse, etc.)   騎／骑   V
qǐ   get up (*from bed*); rise   起   V
qián [kuài]   money   錢 [塊]／钱 [块]   N
qián(bian)   front; in front   前邊／前(边)   PW
qiánmian   front; in front   前面   PW
qiánnián   year before last   前年   TW
qiántiān   day before yesterday   前天   TW
qìchē [liàng]   car   汽車 [輛]／汽车 [辆]   N
qǐchuáng   get up from bed   起床   VO
qǐng   please (*used in polite requests*)   請／请   V

qǐng invite; treat somebody to a meal 請／请 V

qǐngwèn may I ask (*followed by inquiry*) 請問／请问 IE

qīnqi relative(s) 親戚／亲戚 N

qīshí seventy 七十 NU

qítā (de) others (*the rest, what remains*) 其他(的) PR

qiú [ge] ball 球 [個]／球 [个] N

Qīyuè July 七月 N

qīzi wife 妻子／妻子 N

qí zìxíngchē ride a bicycle 騎自行車／骑自行车 VO

qù go 去 V

qùguo gone to 去過／去过 VP

qù lǚxíng go on a journey 去旅行 VP

qù mǎi dōngxi go shopping 去買東西／去买东西 VP

qùnián last year 去年 TW

qúnzi [tiáo] skirt 裙子 [條]／裙子 [条] N

qù sànsanbù take a walk/stroll 去散散步 VP

qù wánr go have some fun 去玩兒／去玩儿 VP

R

ránhòu after(ward); and then; after that 然後／然后 TW

rè hot (*temperature*) 熱／热 SV

règǒu [ge] hot dog 熱狗 [個]／热狗 [个] N

rén [ge] person 人 [個]／人 [个] N

Rénmínbì [kuài] People's money (*PRC currency*) 人民幣 [塊]／人民币 [块] N

rènshi know a person 認識／认识 V

rènshi zì recognize/know Chinese characters; be literate 認識(字)／认识(字) V

rì sun; day (*the radical*) 日 N

Rìběn Japan 日本 PW

Rìběnhuà Japanese (*language*) 日本話／日本话 N

Rìběnrén Japanese (*person/people*) 日本人 N

Rìwén Japanese (*language*) 日文 N

rìyòngpǐn articles of everyday use 日用品 N

Rìyǔ Japanese (*language*) 日語／日语 N

Rìyuán Japanese yen 日元 N

róngyì easy 容易 SV

rúguǒ unless; if 如果 C

S

sān three 三 NU

sànbù take a walk/stroll 散步 VO

sānshí thirty 三十 NU

Sānyuè March 三月 N

shān [zuò] mountain 山 [座]／山 [座] N

shàng go to; attend (*school*) 上 V

shàngbān(r) go to work/the office 上班(兒)／上班(儿) VO

shàngbianr up; above 上邊兒／上边儿 PW

shàng cèsuǒ use the toilet 上廁所／上厕所 VO

shāngchǎng mall; market; bazaar; shopping mall 商場／商场 N

shāngdiàn [ge] store; shop 商店 [個]／商店 [个] N

shàng ge yuè 上個月／上个月 last month TW

Shànghǎi Shanghai 上海 PW

shàngkè attend class; start a class; go to class; hold class 上課／上课 VO

shàngmian top; above 上面 PW

shàngwǎng go on the web; go online; go on the Internet 上網／上网 VO

shàngwǔ morning (*from about 10 A.M. to noon*) 上午 PW

shàng xīngqī last week 上星期 TW

shàngxué go to school 上學／上学 VO

shǎo few (*in number*) 少 SV

shé snake (*Chinese zodiac*) 蛇 N

shéi who 誰／谁 QW

shēng be born; give birth to 生 V

shēng háizi give birth to a child 生孩子 VO

shēnghuó fāngshì lifestyle 生活方式 N

shēngfù birth father 生父 N

shēngmǔ birth mother 生母 N

shēngqì angry; upset; mad 生氣／生气 SV

shēngrì birthday 生日 N

shēngzài born in 生在 VP

shénme what 什麼／什么 QW

shénme shíhou when 什麼時候／什么时候 QW

shí ten 十 NU

shì to be 是 EV

shì room (*as in apartment unit*) 室 N

shì [jiàn] matter; affair 事 [件] N

shì de yes; that's right 是的 IE

shí'èr twelve 十二 NU

shí'èr shēngxiào the twelve animals of the Chinese zodiac 十二生肖 N

Shí'èryuè December 十二月 N

shīfu master craftsman; skilled worker 師傅／师傅 N

shíhou time; moment 時候／时候 N

shíjiān time 時間／时间 N

shìqing [jiàn] matter; affair 事情 [件] N

shíyī eleven 十一 NU

Shíyīyuè November 十一月 N

Shíyuè October 十月 N

shòu thin; slender 瘦 SV

shǒubiǎo [kuài] watch; wristwatch 手錶 [塊]／手表 [块] N

shòuhuòyuán sales clerk 售货员 N

shǒujī [ge] cell phone 手機 [個]／手机 [个] N

shǒujī hàomǎ cell phone number 手機號碼／手机号码 N

shū [běn] book 書 [本]／书 [本] N

shǔ to belong to one of 12 zodiac signs 屬／属 V

shǔ rat/mouse (*Chinese zodiac*) 鼠 N

shuākǎ charge; swipe a credit card 刷卡 VO

shuāng a pair of [something] 雙／双 M
shuāyá brush (one's) teeth 刷牙 VO
shūbāo [ge] bookbag 書包 [個]／书包 [个] N
shūdiàn bookstore 書店／书店 N
shūfu feel well; comfortable 舒服 SV
shuǐ [bēi/píng] water [glass/bottle of] 水 [杯／瓶] N
shuì sleep; go to sleep 睡 V/VO
shuìjiào sleep; go to sleep 睡覺／睡觉 V/VO
shuì lǎnjiào sleep in/late 睡懶覺／睡懒觉 VO
shuō talk; speak; say 説／说 V/VO
shuōhuà talk; speak; say 説話／说话 V/VO
shuō Zhōngguóhuà speak Chinese 説中國話／说中国话 VP
shūshu uncle (father's younger brother) 叔叔 N
shūtóufa comb (one's) hair 梳頭髮／梳头发 VO
shūzi [bǎ] comb 梳子 [把] N
sì four 四 NU
sījī driver; chauffeur 司機／司机 N
Sìyuè April 四月 N
suì age 歲／岁 M
suìshu age 歲數／岁数 N
suǒyǐ so; therefore 所以 C
sùshè dormitory 宿舍 N
Sūzhōu Suzhou (city in eastern China) 蘇州／苏州 PW

T

tā he 他 PR
tā she 她 PR
tā it (most often not translated) 它 PR
tài . . . (often takes **le**) too; exceedingly; extremely 太……(了) A
Táiběi Taipei 台北 PW
Táibì Taiwan dollar 台幣／台币 N
Tàiguó Thailand 泰國／泰国 PW
Tàiguórén Thai (person/people) 泰國人／泰国人 N
tàitai wife (formal) 太太 N
Táiwān Taiwan 台灣／台湾 PW
tāmen they; them 他們；她們；它們／他们；她们；它们 PR
táng [kuài] candy [piece of] 糖 [塊]／糖 [块] N
tiān day 天 N/M
tiān a good grief; my heavens 天啊 IE
tiānqì weather 天氣／天气 N
tiāntiān daily; every day 天天 TW
tīng listen to 聽／听 V
tǐng very; rather; quite 挺 A
tīng yīnyuè listen to music 聽音樂／听音乐 VO
tōngcháng usually 通常 A

(tóngfù) yìmǔ de xiōngdìjiěmèi half sibling (same father) (同父)異母的兄弟姐妹／(同父)异母的兄弟姐妹 N
(tóngmǔ) yìfù de xiōngdìjiěmèi half sibling (same mother) (同母)異父的兄弟姐妹／(同母)异父的兄弟姐妹 N
tóngshì colleague; fellow worker 同事 N
tóngshìmen colleagues; fellow workers 同事們／同事们 N
tóngxué schoolmate; classmate 同學／同学 N
tóngxuémen classmates; fellow students 同學們／同学们 N
tóufa hair (on human head) 頭髮／头发 N
tóuténg have a headache 頭疼／头疼 VO
tǔ soil; earth 土 N
tù rabbit (Chinese zodiac) 兔 N
tuōxié [shuāng] slippers [pair of] 拖鞋 [雙]／拖鞋 [双] N
túshūguǎn [ge] library 圖書館／图书馆 N
T-xù shān [jiàn] T-shirt T-恤衫 [件] N

W

wà wow 哇 I
wàigōng maternal grandfather 外公 N
wàiguó foreign country 外國／外国 N
wàiguóhuà foreign language 外國話／外国话 N
wàiguórén foreigner 外國人／外国人 N
wàipó maternal grandmother 外婆 N
wàitào [jiàn] jacket; coat; overcoat 外套 [件] N
wàiyǔ foreign language 外語／外语 N
wǎn late 晚 SV
wǎn bowl 碗 N
wǎncān supper; dinner 晚餐 N
wǎnfàn supper; dinner 晚飯／晚饭 N
wǎng toward(s) 往 CV
wǎng . . . guǎi turn (in direction of) 往……拐 VP
wàng le forgot 忘了 VP
wǎng qián zǒu go straight 往前走 VP
wán(r) play; have fun; amuse oneself 玩(兒)／玩(儿) V
wán(r) diànzǐ yóuxì play video games 玩(兒)電子遊戲／玩(儿)电子游戏 VP
wǎnshang night; evening (6 P.M. until midnight) 晚上 TW
wàzi [shuāng] socks [pair of] 襪子 [雙]／袜子 [双] N
wèi (polite measure word for people) 位 M
wèishēngzhǐ toilet paper 衛生紙／卫生纸 N
wèishénme why 爲什麼／为什么 QW
wèn ask; inquire 問／问 V
wénjù [xiē] stationery 文具 [些] N
wèntí [ge] question; problem 問題 [個]／问题 [个] N

wènwen ask; inquire 問問／问问 V

wǒ I; me 我 PR

wǒ de my; mine 我的 PR

Wǒ lǎo yàngzi. I'm the same as usual. 我老樣子／我老样子 PH

wǒmen we; us 我們／我们 PR

wǒmen de our(s) 我們的／我们的 PR

wǔ five 五 NU

wǔcān lunch 午餐 N

wǔfàn lunch 午飯／午饭 N

wǔjiào afternoon nap 午覺／午觉 N

wǔshuì afternoon nap; take a nap 午睡 N/V

Wǔyuè May 五月 N

X

xǐ wash 洗 V

xià(chē, huǒchē . . .) get off (a bus, train, etc.) 下(車,火車……)／下(车,火车……) V

xiàbān get off work 下班 VO

xiàcì next time 下次 N

xià (ge) next (in a series) 下 (個)／下 (个) SP

xià (ge) xīngqī next week 下(個)星期／下(个)星期 TW

xià ge yuè next month 下個月／下个月 TW

xiàkè get out of class 下課／下课 VO

xiàmian under; bottom; below; underneath 下面 PW

xiān first; in advance of 先 A

xiǎng think; want to; feel like; intend to 想 AV

Xiāng Gǎng Hong Kong 香港 PW

xiànjīn cash 現金／现金 N

xiānsheng husband; Mister, Mr. 先生 N

xiànzài now; at present; at this moment 現在／现在 TW

xiǎo small; little 小 SV

xiǎo háizi kid; child 小孩子 N

xiǎohào size small 小號／小号 N

xiǎojiě young lady; Miss 小姐 N

xiǎoxué elementary school 小學／小学 N

xiàozhǎng [wèi] principal 校長 [位]／校长 [位] N

xiàwǔ afternoon 下午 TW

xiàyǔ to rain 下雨 VO

Xībānyá Spain 西班牙 PW

Xībānyáhuà Spanish (language) 西班牙話／西班牙话 N

Xībānyárén Spanish (person/people) 西班牙人 N

Xībānyáwén Spanish (language) 西班牙文／西班牙文 N

Xībānyáyǔ Spanish (language) 西班牙語／西班牙语 N

xīběi northwest 西北 PW

xībian(r) west (side; direction) 西邊(兒)／西边(儿) PW

xiē (for a small amount) 些 M

xié [shuāng] shoes [pair of] 鞋 [雙]／鞋 [双] N

xiě write 寫／写 V

xiè thank; (also a surname) 謝／谢 V/N

Xièxie nǐ/nín thank you 謝謝你／您‖谢谢你／您 PH

xiězì write 寫字／写字 VO

xiě zuòyè do homework 寫作業／写作业 VO

xǐfàshuǐ [píng] shampoo [bottle of] 洗髮水 [瓶]／洗发水 [瓶] N

xīguā watermelon 西瓜 N

xǐhuan like; prefer 喜歡／喜欢 V

xǐliǎn wash one's face 洗臉／洗脸 VO

xīnán southwest 西南 PW

xíng be OK; all right 行 V

xìng surname 姓 N

xìng be surnamed 姓 V

xīngqī week 星期 TW

Xīngqī'èr Tuesday 星期二 TW

Xīngqīliù Saturday 星期六 TW

xīnqíng mood; state of mind 心情 N

Xīngqīrì Sunday 星期日 TW

Xīngqīsān Wednesday 星期三 TW

Xīngqīsì Thursday 星期四 TW

Xīngqītiān Sunday 星期天 TW

Xīngqīwǔ Friday 星期五 TW

Xīngqīyī Monday 星期一 TW

xìnyòngkǎ [zhāng] credit card 信用卡 [張]／信用卡 [张] N

xiōngdì brothers 兄弟 N

xiōngdìjiěmèi brothers and sisters 兄弟姐妹 N

xiūxi rest; take a rest; take it easy 休息 V

xǐ yīfu do the laundry 洗衣服 VO

xǐzǎo bathe; take a bath/shower 洗澡 VO

xué study; learn how to 學／学 V

xuésheng student 學生／学生 N

xuéxiào school 學校／学校 N

Y

yágāo [zhī] toothpaste [tube of] 牙膏 [支] N

yáng sheep/ram (Chinese zodiac) 羊 N

yàng kind; type; shape 樣／样 M

yǎngfù adoptive father 養父／养父 N

yǎngmǔ adoptive mother 養母／养母 N

Yángshuò Yangshuo (city in southern China) 陽朔／阳朔 PW

yánjiūshēngyuàn graduate school 研究生院 N

yánsè color 顏色／颜色 N

yǎnyuán actor 演員／演员 N

yào have a desire to; want to; going to; will 要 AV

yào medicine 藥／药 N

yàoshi if 要是 C

yáshuā [zhī] toothbrush 牙刷 [支] N

yáxiàn dental floss 牙線／牙线 N

yáyī dentist 牙醫／牙医 N

Yàzhōu Asia 亞洲／亚洲 PW

Yàzhōurén Asian (*person/people*) 亞洲人／亚洲人 N

yě too; also; as well 也 A

yèli at night; during the night; nighttime 夜裏／夜里 TW/N

yěxǔ perhaps; might; maybe 也许／也許 A

yéye paternal grandfather; Grandpa (*respectful form of address*) 爺爺／爷爷 N

yī one (*the number*) 一 NU

yībǎi, èrbǎi . . . one hundred, two hundred, etc. 一百, 二百...... NU

yìbān generally 一般 A

yìbān lái shuō generally speaking 一般來说／一般来说 VP

yícì once; one time 一次 NU/M

Yìdàlì Italy 意大利 PW

Yìdàlìhuà Italian (*language*) 意大利話／意大利话 N

Yìdàlìrén Italian (*person/people*) 意大利人 N

Yìdàlìwén Italian (*language*) 意大利文 N

Yìdàlìyǔ Italian (*language*) 意大利語 N

yìdiǎnr a bit; a little; some 一點兒／一点儿 NU/M

yídìng certainly; for sure 一定 A

yídìng děi certainly must 一定得 A/AV

yīfu [jiàn] clothing [article of] 衣服 [件] N

yí ge a; one of 一個／一个 NU/M

yígòng altogether; in all; in total 一共 A

yǐhòu later; afterwards 以後／以后 TW

yìhuǐr in a little while 一會兒／一会儿 TW

yìhuǐr jiàn see you in a little while 一會兒見／一会儿见 IE

yǐjing already 已經／已经 A

yí kèzhōng quarter of an hour 一刻鐘／一刻钟 N

yíkuàir together 一塊兒／一块儿 A

yīlóu first floor 一樓／一楼 N

Yìndù India 印度 PW

Yìndùhuà Hindi (*language*) 印度話／印度话 N

Yìndùrén Indian (*person/people*) 印度人 N

Yìndùwén Hindi (*language*) 印度文 N

Yìndùyǔ Hindi (*language*) 印度語 N

Yīngbàng British pound 英鎊／英镑 N

yīnggāi should; ought to 應該／应该 AV

Yīngguó Britain; England 英國／英国 PW

Yīngguórén British (*person/people*) 英國人／英国人 N

Yīngwén English (*language*) 英文 N

Yīngyǔ English (*language*) 英语 N

yínháng bank 銀行／银行 N

yínsè silver (*color*) 銀色／银色 N

yīnwéi because; because of 因爲／因为 C

yīnyuè music 音樂／音乐 N

yīnyuèjiā musician 音樂家／音乐家 N

yìqǐ together 一起 A

yǐqián ago; before; previously 以前 TW

yīshēng physician; doctor 醫生／医生 N

yìshùjiā artist 藝術家／艺术家 N

yì tiān liǎng cì twice a day 一天兩次／一天两次 TW

yìxiē a few; several; some 一些 NU/M

yíyàng same; identical; alike 一樣／一样 SV

Yīyuè January 一月 N

yìzhí all along (*in time or place*) 一直 A

yìzhí zǒu go straight ahead 一直走 VP

yì zhōu jǐ cì several times a week 一周幾次／一周几次 TW

yòng use; utilize; make use of 用 V

yǒu there is/are; have; possess 有 V

yòu . . . yòu both . . . and 又......又 C

yòubian(r) right side 右邊(兒)／右边(儿) PW

yǒude shíhou sometimes 有的時候／有的时候 TW

yǒukòng be free, have free time 有空 VO

yǒushì busy; have something to do 有事 VO

yǒu yìsi interesting; fun 有意思 SV

yǒuyòng useful 有用 SV

yú [tiáo] fish 魚 [條]／鱼 [条] N

yǔ rain 雨 N

yuán primary monetary unit (*written*); "dollar" 元 M

yuǎn far 遠／远 SV

yuè month (*in words designating the months*) 月 N

yújiā yoga 瑜珈 N

yùndòngfú [jiàn] athletic clothes 運動服／运动服 [件] N

yùndòngxié [shuāng] sneakers/athletic shoes [pair of] 運動鞋 [雙]／运动鞋 [双] N

yùndòngyuán athlete 運動員／运动员 N

Z

zài on; at; in; be located at 在 V

zài . . . de shíhou during 在......的時候／在......的时候 TW

zàijiàn good-bye; see you again 再見／再见 IE

zài shuō yícì repeat what was said 再说一次／再说一次 VP

zài wàibian outside 在外邊／在外边 VP/PW

zǎo early 早 SV

zǎo morning (*as a greeting*) 早 IE

zǎocān breakfast 早餐 N

zǎocāo morning calisthenics 早操 N

zǎodiǎn breakfast 早點／早点 N

zǎofàn breakfast 早飯／早饭 N

zǎoshang morning (*until about 9–10 A.M.*) 早上 TW

zǎoshang hǎo good morning 早上好 IE

zěnme how; how come 怎麼／怎么 QW

zěnme le what's the matter 怎麼了／怎么了 VP

zěnmeyàng how does that sound to you (*after a suggestion*) 怎麼樣／怎么样 QW

zěnmeyàng how's it going 怎麼樣／怎么样 IE

zhàn [ge]   station/stop (*of a bus, train, etc.*)   站 [個]／站 [个]   N

zhǎngdà   grow up   長大／长大   V

zhàngfu   husband   丈夫   N

zhǎo   look for   找   V

zháojí   worried; nervous; anxious   著急／着急   V

zhǎoqián   make change; give in change   找錢／找钱   VO

zhàoyàng   as usual; as before   照樣／照样   A

zhè   this; this one   這／这   PR/SP

zhège   this one   這個／这个   PR/SP

zhèi   this; this one   這／这   PR/SP

zhèige   this one   這個／这个   PR/SP

zhèlǐ   here   這裏／这里   PW

zhème   (to) this extent; such; so   這麼／这么   A

zhēn   really; truly; indeed   真   A

zhēn de ma   really; is that true?   真的嗎／真的吗   IE

zhèr   here   這兒／这儿   PW

zhèxiē   these   這些／这些   PR

zhèyàng   so; like this   這樣／这样   A

zhǐ   only   只   A

zhǐ [zhāng]   paper [sheet of]   紙 [張]／纸 [张]   N

zhīdao   know (*have knowledge of*)   知道   V

zhōngfàn   lunch   中飯／中饭   N

Zhōngguó   China   中國／中国   PW

Zhōngguóhuà   Chinese (*language*)   中國話／中国话   N

Zhōngguórén   Chinese (*person/people*)   中國人／中国人   N

zhōnghào   size medium   中號／中号   N

zhōngjiānr   between; center; middle   中間兒／中间儿   PW

zhōngtóu [ge]   hour   鐘頭 [個]／钟头 [个]   N

Zhōngwén   Chinese (*language*)   中文   N

zhōngwǔ   noon; midday   中午   TW

zhōngxué   middle school; secondary school   中學／中学   N

zhōumò   weekend   週末／周末   N

Zhōurì   Sunday   週日／周日   TW

zhū   pig/boar (*Chinese zodiac*)   豬／猪   N

zhù   stay at; reside; live   住   V

zhuǎn   turn in direction of   轉／转   V

zhuànqián   earn money   賺錢／赚钱   VO

zhuōzi [zhāng]   table   桌子 [張]／桌子 [张]   N

zhùzai   reside (at); live (at)   住在   VP

zì [ge]   character; word   字 [個]／字 [个]   N

zìdiǎn [běn]   dictionary   字典 [本]   N

zìjǐ   myself; by myself; oneself   自己   PR

zǐsè   purple   紫色   N

zìxíngchē [liàng]   bicycle   自行車 [輛]／自行车 [辆]   N

zǒu   go by way of; walk   走   V

zǒu   leave (*depart from a place*)   走   V

zǒulù   walk; walk on the road   走路   VO

zuì   most; exceedingly (*superlative prefix*)   最   A/PREF

zuìhǎo   best   最好   SV

zuìhòu   finally; at the end   最後／最后   A

zuìjìn   recently   最近   TW

zuò   ride on; take; go by (*a bus, train, etc.*)   坐   V/CV

zuò   make; cook; do; engage in   做   V

zuǒbian(r)   left side   左邊(兒)／左边(儿)   PW

zuò dìtiě   take the subway   坐地鐵／坐地铁   VO

zuòfàn   do the cooking; cook food; prepare a meal   做飯／做饭   VO

zuò gōngchē qù   go by bus   坐公車去／坐公车去   VP

zuò gōngkè   do homework   做功課／做功课   VO

zuòjiā   writer   作家   N

zuò jiāwù   do housework   做家務／做家务   VO

zuótiān   yesterday   昨天   TW

zuò wǎnfàn   cook dinner   做晚飯／做晚饭   VO

zuòyè   homework   作業／作业   N

zuò yújiā   do yoga   做瑜伽   VO

zuò zǎocāo   work out in the morning   做早操   VO

zuò zǎofàn   cook breakfast   做早飯／做早饭   VO

zuò zhōngfàn   cook lunch   做中飯／做中饭   VO

English-Chinese Glossary

A

a (one of) yí ge 一個／一个 NU

a bit yìdiǎnr 一點兒／一点儿 NU/M

a couple of liǎng ge 兩個／两个 NU

a little yìdiǎnr 一點兒／一点儿 NU/M

able to néng; huì 能; 會／能; 会 AV

above shàngbian; shàngmian 上邊; 上面／上边; 上面 PW

accountant kuàijìshī 會計師／会计师 N

actor yǎnyuán 演員／演员 N

add to jiā 加 V

address dìzhǐ 地址 N

adoptive father yǎngfù 養父／养父 N

adoptive mother yǎngmǔ 養母／养母 N

affair (business) shì(qing) [jiàn] 事(情) [件] N

Africa Fēizhōu 非洲 PW

African (person/people) Fēizhōurén 非洲人 N

after yǐhòu 以後／以后 TW

after(ward/s) ránhòu 然後／然后 TW

afternoon xiàwǔ 下午 TW

afternoon nap wǔshuì 午睡 N

age suì; suìshu 歲; 歲數／岁; 岁数 M/N

ago yǐqián 以前 TW

ah āi yā 哎呀 INT

airplane fēijī [jià] 飛機 [架]／飞机 [架] N

alcoholic beverage jiǔ 酒 N

alike yíyàng 一樣／一样 SV

all dōu 都 A

all along (in time or place) yìzhí 一直 A

all right hǎo; xíng 好; 行 SV

already yǐjing 已經／已经 A

also yě 也 A

altogether (in total) yígòng 一共 A

A.M. shàngwǔ 上午 TW

America Měiguó 美國／美国 PW

American (person/people) Měiguórén 美國人／美国人 N

American dollar Měijīn; Měiyuán 美金; 美元 N

and gēn; hé 跟; 和 C

and then ránhòu 然後／然后 TW

and what about ... ... ne ......呢 P

angry shēngqì 生氣／生气 SV

another (a different one) biéde 別的 SP

anxious zháojí 著急／着急 SV

April Sìyuè 四月 N

architect jiànzhùshī 建築師／建筑师 N

arrived, to have dào le 到了 VP

articles of daily use rìyòngpǐn 日用品 N

artist yìshùjiā 藝術家／艺术家 N

as before zhàoyàng 照樣／照样 A

as usual zhàoyàng 照樣／照样 A

Asia Yàzhōu 亞洲／亚洲 PW

Asian (person/people) Yàzhōurén 亞洲人／亚洲人 N

ask wèn; wènwen 問; 問問／问; 问问 V

assignment (school) gōngkè 功課／功课 N

assist bāng; bāngzhù 幫; 幫助／帮; 帮助 V

at (the location of) zài 在 V

at night yèli; wǎnshang 夜裏; 晚上／夜里; 晚上 TW

at the time of/when ...de shíhou ......的時候／......的时候 TW

athlete yùndòngyuán 運動員／运动员 N

athletic clothes yùndòngfú [jiàn] 運動服／运动服 [件] N

athletic shoes yùndòngxié 運動鞋／运动鞋 N

attend (school, class) shàng 上 V

attend class shàngkè 上課／上课 VO

attend school dúshū; niànshū 讀書; 念書／读书; 念书 VO

attractive hǎokàn 好看 SV

August Bāyuè 八月 N

aunt (father's sister) gūgu 姑姑 N

aunt (mother's sister) āyí 阿姨 N

aunt (wife of father's older brother) bómǔ 伯母 N

aunt (wife of father's younger brother) shěnshen 嬸嬸 N

aunt (wife of mother's brother) jiùmā 舅媽／舅妈 N

Australia Àodàlìyà 澳大利亞／澳大利亚 PW

Australian dollar Àoyuán 澳元 N

automobile qìchē [liàng] 汽車 [輛]／汽车 [辆] N

await děng 等 V

B

back hòumian; hòubian(r) 後面; 後邊(兒)／后面; 后边(儿) PW

bag dàizi [ge] 袋子 [個]／袋子 [个] N

ball qiú [ge] 球 [個]／球 [个] N

bank yínháng 銀行／银行 N

bargain (for a better price) jiǎngjià 講價／讲价 VO

bathe xǐzǎo 洗澡 VO

bathroom cèsuǒ 廁所／厕所 N

bazaar shāngchǎng 商場／商场 N

be shì 是 EV

beard húzi 鬍子／胡子 N

because yīnwèi 因爲／因为 C

become ill/sick bìng le 病了 VP

bed chuáng [zhāng] 床 [張] ／床 [张] N

been to (*a place*) dàoguo; qùguo 到過; 去過 ／到过; 去过 VP

beer [bottle of] píjiǔ [píng] 啤酒 [瓶] N

before (*in advance of*) xiān 先 A

before (*in the past*) yǐqián 以前 TW

before noon shàngwǔ 上午 TW

begin kāishǐ 開始 ／开始 V

behind hòumian; hòubian(r) 後面; 後邊(兒) ／后面; 后边(儿) PW

beige mǐsè 米色 N

Beijing Běijīng 北京 PW

belong to (*one of 12 zodiac signs*) shǔ 屬 ／属 V

below xiàmian 下面 PW

best zuìhǎo 最好 SV

better hǎo yìdiǎnr 好一點兒 ／好一点儿 SV

between zhōngjiānr 中間兒 ／中间儿 PW

bicycle zìxíngchē [liàng] 自行車 [輛] ／自行车 [辆] N

big dà 大 SV

big (*size in clothing, etc.*) dàhào 大號 ／大号 N

birth father shēngfù 生父 N

birth mother shēngmǔ 生母 N

birthday shēngrì 生日 N

bit (yì)diǎn(r) (一)點(兒) ／(一)点(儿) N/M

black hēisè 黑色 N

blouse chènshān [jiàn] 襯衫 [件] ／衬衫 [件] N

blue lánsè 藍色 ／蓝色 N

blue jeans [pair of] niúzǎikù [tiáo] 牛仔褲 [條] ／牛仔裤 [条] N

boar (*Chinese zodiac*) zhū 豬 ／猪 N

boat chuán [tiáo] 船 [條] ／船 [条] N

book shū [běn] 書 [本] ／书 [本] N

bookbag shūbāo [ge] 書包 [個] ／书包 [个] N

bookstore shūdiàn 書店 ／书店 N

born, be shēng 生 V

born in shēng zài 生在 VP

both dōu 都 A

both . . . and yòu . . . yòu 又⋯⋯又 C

bottle of (*something*) yì píng . . . 一瓶⋯⋯ N/M

bottom xiàmian 下面 PW

bowl wǎn 碗 N/M

bowl of (*something*) yì wǎn . . . 一碗⋯⋯ N/M

boy nánháir; nánháizi 男孩兒; 男孩子 ／男孩儿; 男孩子 N

boyfriend nánpéngyou 男朋友 N

breakfast zǎofàn; zǎocān; zǎodiǎn 早飯; 早餐; 早點 ／早饭; 早餐; 早点 N

Britain Yīngguó 英國 ／英国 PW

British (*person/people*) Yīngguórén 英國人 ／英国人 N

British pound Yīngbàng 英鎊 ／英镑 N

brother (*older*) gēge 哥哥 N

brother (*younger*) dìdi 弟弟 N

brothers xiōngdì 兄弟 N

brothers and sisters xiōngdìjiěmèi 兄弟姐妹 N

brown (*coffee-colored*) kāfēisè 咖啡色 N

brush (one's) teeth shuāyá 刷牙 VO

building (*multistoried*) lóu [dòng] 樓 [棟] ／楼 [栋] N

bus gōng (gòng qì) chē; bāshì 公(共汽)車; 巴士 ／公(共汽)车; 巴士 N

bus stop chēzhàn 車站 ／车站 N

business matter shì(qing) [jiàn] 事(情) [件] N

busy yǒushì; máng 有事; 忙 VP/SV

but kěshì 可是 C

buy mǎi 買 ／买 V

by myself zìjǐ 自己 P

C

cafeteria cāntīng 餐廳 ／餐厅 N

California Jiāzhōu 加州 PW

called (*by a given name*) jiào 叫 EV

can (*know how to*) huì 會 ／会 AV

can (*may*) kěyǐ 可以 AV

can (*be capable of*) néng 能 AV

Canada Jiānádà 加拿大 PW

Canadian (*person/people*) Jiānádàrén 加拿大人 N

Canadian dollar Jiānádà yuán 加拿大元 N

candy [piece of] táng [kuài] 糖 [塊] ／糖 [块] N

Canton (*old name for Guangzhou*) Guǎngzhōu 廣州 ／广州 PW

cap màozi [dǐng] 帽子 [頂] ／帽子 [顶] N

car qìchē [liàng] 汽車 [輛] ／汽车 [辆] N

cash xiànjīn 現金 ／现金 N

cell phone shǒujī [ge] 手機 [個] ／手机 [个] N

cell phone number shǒujī hàomǎ 手機號碼 ／手机号码 N

cent (yì) fēn (qián) (一)分(錢) ／(一)分(钱) N

center zhōngjiānr 中間兒 ／中间儿 PW

certainly yídìng 一定 A

change huàn 換 ／换 V

change currency huànqián 換錢 ／换钱 VO

character (*Chinese word*) zì [ge] 字 [個] ／字 [个] N

charge (*on a credit card*) shuākǎ 刷卡 VO

chat liáotiān(r) 聊天(兒) ／聊天(儿) VO

chauffeur sījī 司機 ／司机 N

cheap piányi 便宜 SV

check (*examine*) chá 查 V

chicken (*Chinese zodiac*) jī 雞 ／鸡 N

child háizi [ge] 孩子 [個] ／孩子 [个] N

children háizimen 孩子們 ／孩子们 N

China Zhōngguó 中國 ／中国 PW

Chinese (*language*) Zhōngguóhuà; Zhōngwén 中國話; 中文 ／中国话; 中文 N

Chinese (*person/people*) Zhōngguórén 中國人 ／中国人 N

chopsticks [pair of] kuàizi [shuāng] 筷子 [雙] ／筷子 [双] N

class (*in school*) kè 課／课 N
classmate tóngxué 同學／同学 N
classroom building jiàoxuélóu 教學樓／教学楼 N
climb (*stairs, etc.*) pá 爬 V
clothes, put on chuān yīfu 穿衣服 V/VO
clothing [*article of*] yīfu [jiàn] 衣服 [件] N
coat wàitào [jiàn]; jiákè [jiàn] 外套 [件]；夹克 [件]／夹克 [件] N
coffee [*cup of*] kāfēi [bēi] 咖啡 [杯] N
coffee-colored kāfēisè 咖啡色 N
cold (*temperature*) lěng 冷 SV
colleague tóngshì 同事 N
college dàxué 大學／大学 N
college student dàxuéshēng 大學生／大学生 N
color yánsè 顏色／颜色 N
comb shūzi [bǎ] 梳子 [把] N
comb (*one's*) **hair** shūtóufa 梳頭髮／梳头发 VO
come lái 來／来 V
come back huílai 回來／回来 V
come from . . . cóng . . . lái 從……來／从……来 VP
comfortable shūfu 舒服 SV
compare bǐ 比 CV
computer diànnǎo [tái] 電腦 [台]／电脑 [台] N
conditioner [*bottle of*] (*for hair*) hùfàsù [píng] 護髮素 [瓶]／护发素 [瓶] N
cook breakfast zuò zǎofàn 做早飯／做早饭 VO
cook dinner zuò wǎnfàn 做晚飯／做晚饭 VO
cook food zuòfàn 做飯／做饭 VO
cook lunch zuò zhōngfàn 做中飯／做中饭 VO
correct duì 對／对 SV
costly guì 貴／贵 SV
country (*suffix for names of countries*) guó 國／国 N/S
crawl pá 爬 V
credit card xìnyòngkǎ [zhāng] 信用卡 [張]／信用卡 [张] N
cup bēizi [ge] 杯子 [個]／杯子 [个] N
cup of (*something*) yì bēi . . . 一杯…… N/M
cut the grass/lawn gēcǎo 割草 VO

D

dad bàba 爸爸 N
daily měitiān; tiāntiān 每天；天天 TW
daily-use articles rìyòngpǐn 日用品 N
daughter nǚ'ér 女兒／女儿 N
day tiān 天 N/M
day after tomorrow hòutiān 後天／后天 TW
day before yesterday qiántiān 前天 TW
day of the month hào 號／号 M
December Shí'èryuè 十二月 N
delicious hǎochī 好吃 SV
delighted gāoxìng 高興／高兴 SV

dentist yáyī 牙醫／牙医 N
depart zǒu 走 V
department store bǎihuò shāngdiàn 百貨商店／百货商店 N
dictionary zìdiǎn [běn] 字典 [本] N
different one biéde 別的 SP
difficult nán 難／难 SV
dime (*spoken*) (yì) máo (qián) （一)毛(錢)／（一)毛(钱) N
dime (*written*) jiǎo 角 N
dinner wǎnfàn; wǎncān 晚飯；晚餐／晚饭；晚餐 N
direction fāngxiàng 方向 N
disembark (*from a train, car, bus, etc.*) xiàchē 下車／下车 VO
dislike bù xǐhuan 不喜歡／不喜欢 VP
dismiss school fàngxué 放學／放学 VO
do zuò 做 V
do homework zuò gōngkè ‖ xiě zuòyè 做功課／做功课 ‖ 寫作業／写作业 VO
do housework zuò jiāwù 做家務／做家务 VO
do morning calisthenics zuò zǎocāo 做早操 VO
do not (*imperative*) bié; bú yào 別；不要 V/AV
do odd jobs dǎgōng 打工 VO
do part-time work dǎgōng 打工 VO
do the cooking zuòfàn 做飯／做饭 VO
do the laundry xǐ yīfu 洗衣服 VO
doctor yīshēng 醫生／医生 N
dog (*Chinese zodiac*) gǒu 狗 N
dollar, American Měijīn; Měiyuán 美金；美元 N
dollar (*spoken*) (yí) kuài (qián) （一)塊(錢)／（一)块(钱) N
dollar (*written*) yuán 元 N
don't (*imperative*) bié; bú yào 別；不要 V/AV
don't be so polite bié kèqi 別客氣／别客气 IE
don't know bù zhīdao 不知道 VP
don't want to bú yào 不要 V/AV
downstairs lóuxià 樓下／楼下 PW
dragon (*Chinese zodiac*) lóng 龍／龙 N
dress chuān; chuān yīfu 穿；穿衣服 V/VO
drink hē 喝 V
drive a car kāichē 開車／开车 VO
driver sījī 司機／司机 N
dull méiyìsi 没意思 SV
during . . . zài . . . de shíhou 在……的時候／在……的时候 VP
during the night yèli; wǎnshang 夜裏；晚上／夜里；晚上 TW

E

each měi (ge) 每(個)／每(个) SP
early zǎo 早 SV
earn money zhuànqián 賺錢／赚钱 VO
earth (*the radical*) tǔ 土 N

east (*side, direction*) dōngbian(r) 東邊(兒)／东边(儿) PW

easy róngyì 容易 SV

eat chī 吃 V

eat a meal chī fàn 吃飯／吃饭 VO

eat to fullness chībǎo 吃飽／吃饱 V

eight bā 八 NU

eighth (one) dìbā (ge) 第八(個)／第八(个) N/NU

eighty bāshí 八十 NU

eldest (*son, daughter, etc.*) dà (érzi, nǚ'ér . . .) 大(兒子, 女兒……)／大(儿子, 女儿……) N

elementary school xiǎoxué 小學／小学 N

elevator diàntī 電梯／电梯 N

eleven shíyī 十一 NU

eleventh (one) dìshíyī (ge) 第十一(個)／第十一(个) N/NU

e-mail diànyóu 電郵／电邮 N

e-mail address diànyóu dìzhǐ 電郵地址／电邮地址 N

e-mail message diànxìn [fēng] 電信 [封]／电信 [封] N

engineer gōngchéngshī 工程師／工程师 N

England Yīngguó 英國／英国 PW

English (*language*) Yīngwén; Yīngyǔ 英文; 英語／英文; 英语 N

English (*person/people*) Yīngguórén 英國人／英国人 N

enter jìnqu 進去／进去 V

equal(s) děngyú 等於／等于 V

escalator fúshǒu diàntī 扶手電梯／扶手电梯 N

Euro (*currency*) Ōuyuán 歐元／欧元 N

Europe Ōuzhōu 歐洲／欧洲 PW

European (*person/people*) Ōuzhōurén 歐洲人／欧洲人 N

even more (*in comparisons*) gèng 更 A

evening (*6 P.M. until midnight*) wǎnshang 晚上 TW

eventually zuìhòu 最後／最后 A

ever (*"have you ever" [verbal suffix] . . .?*) guò 過／过 S

every (*day, week, year, etc.*) měi 每 SP

every day měitiān; tiāntiān 每天; 天天 TW

everyone měi ge rén; dàjiā 每個人; 大家／每个人; 大家 N

exam, take an kǎoshì 考試／考试 V

examination (*school*) kǎoshì 考試／考试 N

exceed (*the clock hour*) guò 過／过 V

exceedingly tài . . . (le) 太……(了) A

exchange huàn 換／换 V

exchange currency huànqián 換錢／换钱 VO

excuse me duìbuqǐ 對不起／对不起 IE

expensive guì 貴／贵 SV

extent, to what duō 多 A

extra large (*size in clothing, etc.*) jiādàhào 加大號／加大号 N

extra small (*size in clothing, etc.*) jiāxiǎohào 加小號／加小号 N

extremely (good, fast, etc.) jíle (hǎojíle, kuàijíle . . .) 極了(好極了, 快極了……)／极了(好极了, 快极了……) S

extremely fēicháng 非常 A

F

family jiā 家 N

family members jiālǐrén 家裏人／家里人 N

family jiā 家 N

far yuǎn 遠／远 SV

farmer nóngmín 農民／农民 N

fast kuài 快 SV

fat pàng 胖 SV

father fùqīn; bàba 父親; 爸爸／父亲; 爸爸 N

February Èryuè 二月 N

feel juéde 覺得／觉得 V

feel (*like doing something*) xiǎng 想 AV

feel well shūfu 舒服 SV

fellow student tóngxué 同學／同学 N

fellow worker tóngshì 同事 N

few (*in number*) shǎo 少 SV

few yìxiē 一些 SP

fifteen minutes yí kèzhōng 一刻鐘／一刻钟 NP

fifth (one) dìwǔ (ge) 第五(個)／第五(个) N/NU

film (*movie*) diànyǐng [bù] 電影 [部]／电影 [部] N

finally zuìhòu 最後／最后 A

fine hǎo 好 SV

firefighter jiùhuǒyuán 救火員／救火员 N

first (*before, earlier*) xiān 先 A

first (one) dìyī (ge) 第一(個)／第一(个) N/NU

first floor yīlóu 一樓／一楼 N

first name míngzi 名字 N

fish yú [tiáo] 魚 [條]／鱼 [条] N

five wǔ 五 NU

floor (*in a building*) lóu 樓／楼 M

floss (*dental*) yáxiàn 牙線／牙线 N

for sure yídìng 一定 A

foreign country wàiguó 外國／外国 N

foreign language wàiyǔ; wàiguóhuà 外語; 外國話／外语; 外国话 N

foreigner wàiguórén 外國人／外国人 N

forgot wàng le 忘了 VP

four sì 四 NU

fourth (one) dìsì (ge) 第四(個)／第四(个) N/NU

France Fǎguó 法國／法国 PW

free, to be (*to have free time*) yǒukòng 有空 VO

free time kòng 空 N

French (*language*) Fǎguóhuà; Fǎyǔ; Fǎwén 法國話; 法語; 法文／法国话; 法语; 法文 N

French (*person/people*) Fǎguórén 法國人／法国人 N

frequently chángcháng 常常 A

Friday Xīngqīwǔ 星期五 TW

friend péngyou 朋友 N

from (*a place, a time, etc.*) cóng 從／从 CV

from (*distant from*) lí 離／离 CV
front qiánmian; qiánbian 前面; 前邊／前面; 前边 PW
full (*no longer hungry*) bǎo le 飽了／饱了 VP
fun yǒu yìsi 有意思 SV
furthermore háiyǒu 還有／还有 C
future jiānglái 將來／将来 TW/N

G

generally yìbān; píngcháng 一般; 平常 A
generally speaking yìbān lái shuō 一般來說／一般来说 A
German (*language*) Déguóhuà; Déyǔ; Déwén 德國話; 德語; 德文／德国话; 德语; 德文 N
German (*person/people*) Déguórén 德國人／德国人 N
Germany Déguó 德國／德国 PW
get off (*bus, train, etc.*) xià(chē, huǒchē . . .) 下(車,火車⋯⋯)／下(车,火车⋯⋯) VO
get off work xiàbān 下班 VO
get out of class xiàkè 下課／下课 VO
get out of school fàngxué 放學／放学 VO
get up (*from bed*) qǐchuáng 起床 VO
girl nǚháizi; nǚháir 女孩子; 女孩兒／女孩子; 女孩儿 N
girlfriend nǚpéngyou 女朋友 N
give gěi 給／给 V
give a discount dǎzhé 打折 VO
give birth shēng 生 V
give birth (*to a child*) shēng háizi 生孩子 VO
given name míngzi 名字 N
glass (*container*) bēizi [ge] 杯子 [個]／杯子 [个] N
glass of (*something*) yì bēi . . . 一杯⋯⋯ N/M
go qù 去 V
go abroad chūguó 出國／出国 VO
go back huíqu 回去 VO
go by bus zuò gōngchē qù 坐公車去／坐公车去 VP
go by car kāichē qù 開車去／开车去 VP
go have some fun qù wánr 去玩兒／去玩儿 VP
go home huíjiā 回家 V
go in jìnqu 進去／进去 V
go online shàngwǎng 上網／上网 VO
go out chūqu 出去 V
go out for some fun chūqu wánr 出去玩兒／出去玩儿 VP
go shopping qù mǎi dōngxi; guàngjiē 去買東西; 逛街／去买东西; 逛街 VP
go to (*a place*) dào . . . qù; qù . . . 到⋯⋯去; 去⋯⋯ VP
go to class shàngkè 上課／上课 VO
go to school shàngxué 上學／上学 VO
go to sleep shuìjiào 睡覺／睡觉 VO
go to the mall guàng shāngchǎng 逛商場／逛商场 VO
go to work/the office shàngbān 上班 VO

going to yào; huì 要; 會／要; 会 AV
gold (*color*) jīnsè 金色 N
gone to (*a place*) qùguo 去過／去过 VP
good hǎo 好 SV
good-bye zàijiàn 再見／再见 IE
good grief tiān a 天啊 IE
good-looking hǎokàn 好看 SV
good morning nín/nǐ zǎo; zǎoshang hǎo 您／你早; 早上好 IE
good-tasting hǎochī 好吃 SV
grade (*in school*) niánjí 年級／年级 N
grade school xiǎoxué 小學／小学 N
graduate school yánjiūshēngyuàn 研究生院 N
grandfather (*maternal*) lǎoye; wàigōng 姥爺; 外公／姥爷; 外公 N
grandfather (*paternal*) yéye 爺爺／爷爷 N
grandmother (*maternal*) lǎolao; wàipó 姥姥; 外婆 N
grandmother (*paternal*) nǎinai 奶奶 N
Grandpa (*respectful form of address*) yéye 爺爺／爷爷 N
grass cǎo; cǎodì 草; 草地 N
gray huīsè 灰色 N
green lǜsè 綠色／绿色 N
green light (*traffic*) lǜdēng 綠燈／绿灯 N
grow up zhǎngdà 長大／长大 V
guess, take a cāicai kàn 猜猜看 VP
Guilin (*city in southern China*) Guìlín 桂林 PW

H

haggle (*for a better price*) jiǎngjià 講價／讲价 VO
hair (*on human head*) tóufa 頭髮／头发 N
half an hour bàn ge zhōngtóu 半個鐘頭／半个钟头 N
half sibling (*same father*) (tóngfù) yìmǔ de xiōngdìjiěmèi (同父)異母的兄弟姐妹／(同父)异母的兄弟姐妹 N
half sibling (*same mother*) (tóngmǔ) yìfù de xiōngdìjiěmèi (同母)異父的兄弟姐妹／(同母)异父的兄弟姐妹 N
hamburger hànbǎobāo [ge] 漢堡包 [個]／汉堡包 [个] N
happy gāoxìng 高興／高兴 SV
happy to meet you hěn gāoxìng rènshi nǐ (nín) 很高興認識你(您)／很高兴认识你(您) IE
hat màozi [dǐng] 帽子 [頂]／帽子 [顶] N
have yǒu 有 V
have a desire to yào 要 V
have a fever fāshāo 發燒／发烧 VO
have a headache tóuténg 頭疼／头疼 VO
have a meal chīfàn 吃飯／吃饭 VO
have fun wánr 玩兒／玩儿 V
have something to do yǒushì; máng 有事; 忙 VO/SV
have to děi 得 AV
he tā 他 PR
headache, have a tóuténg 頭疼／头疼 VO

hello   nín/nǐ hǎo   您／你好   IE
help   bāng; bāngzhù   幫；幫助／帮；帮助   V
here   zhèr; zhèlǐ   這兒；這裏／这儿；这里   PW
hi   hāi   嗨   I
high-heeled shoes [pair of]   gāogēnxié [shuāng]   高跟鞋 [雙]／高跟鞋 [双]   N
high school (*senior, grades 10–12*)   gāozhōng   高中   N
Hindi (*language*)   Yìndùhuà; Yìndùwén; Yìndùyǔ   印度話；印度文；印度語／印度话；印度文；印度语   N
hold class   shàngkè   上課／上课   VO
holiday, be on a   fàngjià   放假   VO
home   jiā   家   N
homework   gōngkè ‖ zuòyè   功課／功课 ‖ 作業／作业   N
Hong Kong   Xiāng Gǎng   香港   PW
Hong Kong dollar   Gǎngbì   港幣／港币   N
honorable surname, what's your   Nín guìxìng?   您貴姓／您贵姓?   IE
horse (*Chinese zodiac*)   mǎ   馬／马   N
hot (*temperature*)   rè   熱／热   SV
hot dog   règǒu [ge]   熱狗 [個]／热狗 [个]   N
hour   zhōngtóu [ge]   鐘頭 [個]／钟头 [个]   N
house   fángzi [dòng]   房子 [棟／栋]   N
household chores/duties   jiāwù   家務／家务   N
how (*to what extent*)   duō   多   QW
how (*what*)   zěnme   怎麼／怎么   QW
how come   zěnme   怎麼／怎么   QW
how many (*less than ten*)   jǐ (ge)   幾(個)／几(个)   QW
how many (*more than ten*)   duōshao (*usually without measure word*)   多少   QW
How old are you?   Nǐ duō dà?; Nǐ jǐ suì?   你多大; 你幾歲／你几岁   PH
How's it going?   zěnmeyàng   怎麼樣／怎么样   IE
however   kěshì   可是   C
hundred (*one, two hundred, etc.*)   (yì)bǎi, (èr)bǎi . . .   (一)百, (二)百……   NU
hungry   è   餓／饿   SV
husband   lǎogōng; xiānsheng; zhàngfu   老公; 先生; 丈夫   N

I

I   wǒ   我   PR
I'm OK   hái hǎo   還好／还好   IE
I'm sorry   duìbuqǐ   對不起／对不起   IE
identical   yíyàng   一樣／一样   SV
if   yàoshi   要是   A
ill/become ill   bìng le   病了   VP
illness   bìng   病   N
in   lǐbianr   裏邊兒／里边儿   PW
in/at/on   zài   在   V
in a little while   guò yìhuǐr   過一會兒／过一会儿   PH
in addition   háiyǒu   還有／还有   C
in advance of   xiān   先   A

in all (*total*)   yígòng   一共   A
in back of   hòumian; hòubian(r)   後面; 後邊(兒)／后面; 后边(儿)   PW
in comparison   bǐ   比   CV
in front   qiánmian; qiánbian   前面; 前邊／前面; 前边   PW
in that case   nà; nàme   那; 那麼／那么   C
in the future   jiānglái   將來／将来   TW
in the position of, be   dāng   當／当   V
in the same way   zhàoyàng   照樣／照样   A
in total   yígòng   一共   A
indeed   zhēn   真   A
India   Yìndù   印度   PW
Indian (*person/people*)   Yìndùrén   印度人   N
inexpensive   piányi   便宜   SV
inquire   wèn; wènwen   問; 問問／问; 问问   V
inside   lǐbianr   裏邊兒／里边儿   PW
intend   xiǎng   想   AV
interesting   yǒu yìsi   有意思   SV
Internet, go on the   shàngwǎng   上網／上网   VO
introduce   jièshào   介紹／介绍   V
introduction   jièshào   介紹／介绍   N
invite   qǐng   請／请   V
it (*most often not translated*)   tā   它   P
Italian (*language*)   Yìdàlìhuà; Yìdàlìwén; Yìdàlìyǔ   意大利話; 意大利文; 意大利語／意大利话; 意大利文; 意大利语   N
Italian (*person/people*)   Yìdàlìrén   意大利人   N
Italy   Yìdàlì   意大利   PW

J

jacket   jiákè; wàitào [jiàn]   夾克／夹克; 外套 [件]   N
January   Yīyuè   一月   N
Japan   Rìběn   日本   PW
Japanese (*language*)   Rìběnhuà; Rìyǔ; Rìwén   日本話; 日语; 日文／日本话; 日语; 日文   N
Japanese (*person/people*)   Rìběnrén   日本人   N
Japanese yen   Rìyuán   日元   N
jeans [pair of]   niúzǎikù [tiáo]   牛仔褲 [條]／牛仔裤 [条]   N
job   gōngzuò   工作   V/N
jog   pǎobù   跑步   VO
journey, go on a   qù lǚxíng   去旅行   VP
July   Qīyuè   七月   N
June   Liùyuè   六月   N
junior high school   chūzhōng   初中   N
just (*only a short time ago*)   gāng   剛／刚   A
just now   gāngcái   剛才／刚才   A

K

kid   háizi   孩子   N
kind (*type; shape*)   yàng   樣／样   M

know (*be acquainted with*) rènshi 認識／认识 V
know (*have knowledge of*) zhīdao 知道 V
know (*how to*) huì 會／会 AV
know Chinese characters rènshi zì 認識字／认识字 V
Korea Hánguó 韓國／韩国 PW
Korean (*language*) Hánwén; Hányǔ; Hánguóhuà 韓文；韓語；韓國話／韩文；韩语；韩国话 N
Korean (*person/people*) Hánguórén 韓國人／韩国人 N

L

laborer gōngrén 工人 N
large dà 大 SV
large (*size in clothing, etc.*) dàhào 大號／大号 N
last month shàng ge yuè 上個月／上个月 TW
last week shàng xīngqī 上星期 TW
last year qùnián 去年 TW
late wǎn 晚 SV
later yǐhòu 以後／以后 TW
lawn cǎo; cǎodì 草；草地 N
lawyer lǜshī 律師／律师 N
learn how to xué 學／学 V
leather shoes [pair of] píxié [shuāng] 皮鞋 [雙]／皮鞋 [双] N
leave (*depart from a place*) zǒu 走 V
leave (*go out*) chūmén 出門／出门 VO
left side zuǒbian(r) 左邊（兒）／左边（儿） PW
left turn wǎng zuǒ guǎi 往左拐 VP
less than (*followed by number expression*) búdào 不到 VP
lesson/class kè 課／课 N
library túshūguǎn [ge] 圖書館／图书馆 N
lifestyle shēnghuó fāngshì 生活方式 N
like/prefer xǐhuan 喜歡／喜欢 V
like this zhèyàng 這樣／这样 PR
likely to huì 會／会 AV
listen to tīng 聽／听 V
listen to music tīng yīnyuè 聽音樂／听音乐 VO
literate, be rènshi zì 認識字／认识字 V
little xiǎo 小 SV
little (*size in clothing, etc.*) xiǎohào 小號／小号 N
little while, in a yìhuǐr 一會兒／一会儿 TW
live (*at*) zhùzai 住在 VP
located at, be zài 在 V
location/address dìzhǐ 地址 N
long cháng 長／长 SV
look/watch kàn 看 V
look for zhǎo 找 V
look, take a kàn (yí) kàn 看(一)看 VP
Los Angeles Luòshānjī 洛杉磯／洛杉矶 PW
love ài 愛／爱 V
lunch wǔfàn; wǔcān; zhōngfàn 午飯；午餐；中飯／午饭；午餐；中饭 N

M

Macau Àomén 澳門／澳门 PW
Macau pataca (*currency*) Àoményuán 澳門元／澳门元 N
mad/angry shēngqì 生氣／生气 SV
mailing address dìzhǐ 地址 N
make (*cook*) zuò‖nòng 做‖弄 V
make a phone call dǎ diànhuà 打電話／打电话 VO
make change zhǎoqián 找錢／找钱 VO
make up (*with powder, rouge, etc.*) huàzhuāng 化妝／化妆 VO
makeup (*cosmetics*) huàzhuāngpǐn 化妝品／化妆品 N
mall shāngchǎng 商場／商场 N
mall, go to the guàng shāngchǎng 逛商場／逛商场 VO
manager (*of business, etc.*) jīnglǐ 經理／经理 N
Mandarin (*Standard*) pǔtōnghuà 普通話／普通话 N
many duō 多 SV
map dìtú [zhāng] 地圖 [張]／地图 [张] N
March Sānyuè 三月 N
market shāngchǎng 商場／商场 N
master craftsman shīfu 師傅／师傅 N
matter, what's the zěnme le 怎麼了／怎么了 VP
May Wǔyuè 五月 N
may (*permission to*) kěyǐ 可以 AV
May I ask . . . Qǐngwèn . . . 請問……／请问…… VP
maybe yěxǔ; kěnéng 也許／也许；可能 A
me wǒ 我 PR
meal (*cooked rice*) fàn 飯／饭 N
meal, eat a chīfàn 吃飯／吃饭 VO
medicine yào 藥／药 N
medium (*size in clothing, etc.*) zhōnghào 中號／中号 N
meet (*with someone*) jiàn 見／见 V
meet up with (*someone*) jiē 接 V
midday zhōngwǔ 中午 TW
middle zhōngjiānr 中間兒／中间儿 PW
middle school zhōngxué 中學／中学 N
midnight bànyè 半夜 TW
might (*maybe*) yěxǔ 也許／也许 A
mile (*Chinese mile*) lǐ 里 N/M
mine (*my own*) wǒ de 我的 PR
minute, (one) (*unit of time*) yì fēnzhōng 一分鐘／一分钟 N
Miss Xiǎojie 小姐 N
Mister Xiānsheng 先生 N
mom mā; māma 媽；媽媽／妈；妈妈 N
moment, at the (*now, at present*) xiànzài 現在／现在 TW
moment (*point in time; duration*) shíhou 時候／时候 N
Monday Xīngqīyī 星期一 TW
money qián 錢／钱 N
monkey (*Chinese zodiac*) hóu 猴 N

month yuè [ge] 月 [個]／月 [个] TW
mood (*state of mind*) xīnqíng 心情 N
more (*in number*) duō 多 SV
morning (*until about 9–10 A.M.*) zǎoshang 早上 TW
morning (*from about 10 A.M. to noon*) shàngwǔ 上午 TW
morning (*as a greeting*) zǎo 早 IE
morning calisthenics zǎocāo 早操 N
most (*superlative prefix*) zuì 最 A/PREF
mother mǔqin 母親／母亲 N
motorbike mótuōchē [liàng] 摩托車 [輛]／摩托车 [辆] N
motorcycle mótuōchē [liàng] 摩托車 [輛]／摩托车 [辆] N
mountain shān [zuò] 山 [座]／山 [座] N
mouse (*Chinese zodiac*) shǔ 鼠 N
mouth (*the radical*) kǒu 口 N
movie diànyǐng [bù] 電影 [部]／电影 [部] N
movie theater diànyǐngyuàn 電影院／电影院 N
mow the lawn gēcǎo 割草 VO
Mr. Xiānsheng 先生 N
much duō 多 SV
museum bówùguǎn 博物館／博物馆 N
music yīnyuè 音樂／音乐 N
musician yīnyuèjiā 音樂家／音乐家 N
must (*matter of obligation*) bìxū 必須／必须 AV
my wǒ de 我的 N
my heavens tiān a 天啊 IE
myself zìjǐ 自己 P

N

name míngzi [ge] 名字 [個]／名字 [个] N
named jiào 叫 EV
nap, take a (*afternoon*) wǔshuì 午睡 V
naturally dāngrán 當然／当然 A
near jìn 近 SV
need (*in time or effort*) yào 要 AV
need not búyòng; búbì 不用；不必 AV
neighbor línjū 鄰居／邻居 N
nervous zháojí 著急／着急 SV
never cónglái bù; cónglái méi 從來不；從來没／从来不；从来没 A
never mind/doesn't matter/nothing's wrong méi shì 没事 IE
New Taiwan dollar Táibì 台幣／台币 N
New York Niǔyuē 紐約／纽约 PW
newspaper bào [fèn] 報 [份]／报 [份] N
next (*in a series*) xià (ge) 下 (個)／下 (个) SP
next month xià ge yuè 下個月／下个月 TW
next time xiàcì 下次 TW
next week xià (ge) xīngqī 下(個)星期／下(个)星期 TW
next year míngnián 明年 TW

nice/good/fine hǎo 好 SV
nighttime yèli; wǎnshang 夜裏；晚上／夜里；晚上 TW
nine jiǔ 九 NU
ninth (**one**) dìjiǔ (ge) 第九(個)／第九(个) N/NU
no bù; bú shì 不；不是 A
noon zhōngwǔ 中午 TW
no problem/it doesn't matter méi guānxi 没關係／没关系 IE
north (*side, direction*) běibian(r) 北邊(兒)／北边(儿) PW
North America Běi Měizhōu 北美洲 PW
northeast dōngběi 東北／东北 PW
northwest xīběi 西北 PW
not bù; bú shì 不；不是 A
not able to bùnéng 不能 V
not bad búcuò 不錯／不错 SV
not have méiyǒu 没有 V
not often bù cháng 不常 SV
not until cái 才 A
notebook bǐjìběn [běn] 筆記本 [本]／笔记本 [本] N
nothing's wrong/never mind méi shì 没事 IE
November Shíyīyuè 十一月 N
now xiànzài 現在／现在 TW
number (*in a series*) hào 號／号 N
number (*telephone number, etc.*) hàomǎ 號碼／号码 N
numerous duō 多 SV
nurse hùshi 護士／护士 N

O

object dōngxi [ge] 東西 [個]／东西 [个] N
o'clock . . . diǎn (zhōng) ......點(鍾)／......点(钟) PH
occurrences/times cì 次 M
October Shíyuè 十月 N
of course dāngrán 當然／当然 A
office, go to the/go to work shàngbān 上班 VO
often chángcháng 常常 A
oh (*sudden understanding*) ō 噢 I
OK hǎo; xíng 好；行 SV
old (*in age*) dà 大 SV
older brother gēge 哥哥 N
older sister jiějie 姐姐 N
oldest child lǎodà 老大 N
on zài . . . shang 在......上 VP
on a holiday, be fàngjià 放假 VO
on sale, be jiǎnjià 減價／减价 VO
once (*one time*) yícì 一次 NU/M
one (*the number*) yī 一 NU
oneself zìjǐ 自己 P
only (*just*) jiù 就 A
only (*merely*) zhǐ 只 A
only child (*boy*) dúshēngzǐ 獨生子／独生子 N
only child (*girl*) dúshēngnǚ [ge] 獨生女／独生女 N
or (*in statements*) huòzhě 或者 C
or (*when offering alternatives*) háishi 還是／还是 C

orange (*color*) júhóngsè 橘红色 N
ordinary yìbān; píngcháng 一般; 平常 SV
other people biéren 别人 P
others (*the rest, what remains*) qítā (de) 其他(的) N
ought to yīnggāi 應該／应该 A
our(s) wǒmen de 我們的／我们的 PR
outside zài wàibian 在外邊／在外边 VP/PW
overcoat wàitào [jiàn] 外套 [件] N
ox (*Chinese zodiac*) niú 牛 N

P

painter huàjiā 畫家／画家 N
pair of (*something*) (yì) shuāng . . . (一)雙……／(一)双…… NU/M
pants [pair of] kùzi; chángkù [tiáo] 褲子; 長褲 [條]／裤子; 长裤 [条] N
paper [sheet of] zhǐ [zhāng] 紙 [張]／纸 [张] N
parents fùmǔ 父母 N
park (*public*) gōngyuán(r) 公園兒／公园儿 N
part-time, work dǎgōng 打工 VO
pass by (*on the way*) guò 過／过 V
past (*the clock hour*) guò 過／过 V
path lù [tiáo] 路 [條]／路 [条] N
pay in cash fù xiànjīn 付現金／付现金 VO
pay money fùqián 付錢／付钱 VO
pen bǐ [zhī] 筆 [枝]／笔 [枝] N
penny, a yì fēn (qián) 一分(錢)／一分(钱) N
people rén [ge] 人 [個]／人 [个] N
People's money (*PRC currency*) Rénmínbì 人民幣／人民币 N
perhaps yěxǔ 也許／也许 A
person rén [ge] 人 [個]／人 [个] N
phone diànhuà 電話／电话 N
phone, to dǎ diànhuà 打電話／打电话 VO
physician yīshēng 醫生／医生 N
pick up (*someone*) jiē 接 V
pig (*Chinese zodiac*) zhū 豬／猪 N
pink fěnhóngsè 粉红色／粉红色 N
place dìfang [ge] 地方 [個]／地方 [个] N
plan (*to do something*) xiǎng 想 AV
play wánr 玩兒／玩儿 V
play video games wánr diànzǐ yóuxì 玩兒電子遊戲／玩儿电子游戏 VP
please (*used in polite requests*) qǐng 請／请 V
pleased/happy gāoxìng 高興／高兴 SV
plus/add to jiā 加 V
police officer jǐngchá 警察／警察 N
polite kèqi 客氣／客气 SV
possess yǒu 有 V
postcard míngxìnpiàn [zhāng] 明信片 [張]／明信片 [张] N
prefer/like xǐhuan 喜歡／喜欢 V
prepare a meal zuòfàn 做饭／做饭 VO

present (*right now*) xiànzài 現在／现在 TW
pretty hǎokàn 好看 SV
pretty good búcuò 不錯／不错 SV
previously yǐqián 以前 TW
price jiàqian 價錢／价钱 N
principal xiàozhǎng [wèi] 校长 [位]／校长 [位] N
probably kěnéng 可能 A
problem wèntí [ge] 問題 [個]／问题 [个] N
professor jiàoshòu [wèi] 教授 [位]／教授 [位] N
public bus gōng (gòngqì) chē [liàng] 公(共汽)車 [輛]／公(共汽)车 [辆] N
purchase mǎi 買／买 V
purple zǐsè 紫色／紫色 N
put on chuān 穿 V
put on clothes chuān yīfu 穿衣服 VO
put on makeup huàzhuāng 化妝／化妆 VO

Q

quarter of an hour yí kèzhōng 一刻鐘／一刻钟 N
question wèntí [ge] 問題 [個]／问题 [个] N
quick kuài 快 SV
quite/rather tǐng 挺 A

R

rabbit (*Chinese zodiac*) tù 兔 N
rain yǔ 雨 N
rain xiàyǔ 下雨 VO
ram (*Chinese zodiac*) yáng 羊 N
rarely hěn shǎo 很少 A
rat (*Chinese zodiac*) shǔ 鼠 N
rather tǐng 挺 A
read kàn 看 V
read a book kànshū 看書／看书 VO
read a newspaper kànbào 看報／看报 VO
really zhēn 真 A
Really? (*Is that true?*) zhēn de ma 真的嗎／真的吗 IE
recently zuìjìn 最近 A
recognize rènshi 認識／认识 V
recognize Chinese characters rènshi zì 認識字／认识字 V
red hóngsè 紅色／红色 N
red light (*traffic*) hóngdēng [ge] 紅燈／红灯 N
reduce price jiǎnjià 減價／减价 VO
relative(s) qīnqi 親戚／亲戚 N
remain at home dāizài jiālǐ 呆在家裏／呆在家里 PH
repeat (*what was said*) zài shuō yícì 再说一次／再说一次 PH
require (*in time or effort*) yào 要 AV
reside (*at*) zhùzai 住在 VP
rest xiūxi 休息 V
restaurant fànguǎn(r) 飯館兒／饭馆儿 N

return (*to a place*) huí 回 V
return (*come back*) huílai 回來／回来 V
return home huíjiā 回家 VO
rice [bowl of] fàn [wǎn] 飯 [碗]／饭 [碗] N
ride (*a bike, horse, astride*) qí 騎／骑 V
ride a bicycle qí zìxíngchē 騎自行車／骑自行车 VO
ride on (*a bus, train, etc.*) zuò 坐 V
right (*correct*) duì 對／对 SV
right (*side*) yòubian(r) 右邊(兒)／右边(儿) PW
right after jiù 就 A
rise up qǐ 起 V
road lù [tiáo] 路 [條]／路 [条] N
room fángjiān [ge] 房間 [個]／房间 [个] N
room (*as in apartment unit*) shì 室 N
rooster (*Chinese zodiac*) jī 雞／鸡 N
run pǎo; pǎobù 跑; 跑步 V/VO
rupee (*India and Pakistan*) Lúbǐ 盧比／卢比 N
Russia Éguó 俄國／俄国 PW
Russian (*language*) Éwén; Éyǔ; Éguóhuà 俄文; 俄語; 俄國話／俄文; 俄语; 俄国话 N
Russian (*person/people*) Éguórén 俄國人／俄国人 N

S

sad bù gāoxìng 不高興／不高兴 SV
sale, be on jiǎnjià 減價／减价 VO
sales clerk fúwùyuán; shòuhuòyuán 服務員; 售貨員／服务员; 售货员 N
same yíyàng 一樣／一样 SV
sandals [pair of] liángxié [shuāng] 涼鞋 [雙]／凉鞋 [双] N
Saturday Xīngqīliù 星期六 TW
say shuō; shuōhuà 說; 說話／说; 说话 V/VO
school xuéxiào [ge] 學校 [個]／学校 [个] N
schoolmate tóngxué 同學／同学 N
schoolwork gōngkè 功課／功课 N
second (one) dìèr (ge) 第二(個)／第二(个) N/NU
second child (*in a family*) lǎo'èr 老二 N
secondary school zhōngxué 中學／中学 N
secretary mìshu 秘書／秘书 N
see (*catch sight of*) kànjian 看見／看见 V
see (*to watch, as a movie, etc.*) kàn 看 V
see (*meet with someone*) jiàn 見／见 V
see a movie kàn diànyǐng 看電影／看电影 VO
see you again/good-bye zàijiàn 再見／再见 IE
see you in a little while yìhuǐr jiàn 一會兒見／一会儿见 IE
seldom bù cháng 不常 SV
sell mài 賣／卖 V
senior high school gāozhōng 高中 N
September Jiǔyuè 九月 N
serve (*in a position*) dāng 當／当 V
service person fúwùyuán 服務員／服务员 N
seven qī 七 NU

seventeen shíqī 十七 NU
seventh (one) dìqī (ge) 第七(個)／第七(个) N/NU
seventy qīshí 七十 NU
several yìxiē 一些 NU/M
several times a week yì zhōu jǐ cì 一周幾次／一周几次 TW
shampoo [a bottle of] xǐfàshuǐ [píng] 洗髮水 [瓶]／洗发水 [瓶] N
Shanghai Shànghǎi 上海 PW
shape yàngzi 樣子／样子 N
shave (one's) beard guā húzi 刮鬍子／刮胡子 VO
she tā 她 PR
sheep (*Chinese zodiac*) yáng 羊 N
sheet (*of paper*) zhǐ [zhāng] 紙 [張]／纸 [张] N
ship chuán [tiáo] 船 [條]／船 [条] N
shirt chènshān [jiàn] 襯衫 [件]／衬衫 [件] N
shoes [pair of] xié [shuāng] 鞋 [雙]／鞋 [双] N
shop (*buy things*) mǎi dōngxi 買東西／买东西 VO
shop shāngdiàn 商店／商店 N
shop assistant fúwùyuán; shòuhuòyuán 服務員; 售貨員／服务员; 售货员 N
shopping center gòuwù zhōngxīn 購物中心／购物中心 N
shopping mall shāngchǎng 商場／商场 N
short (*in height or stature*) ǎi 矮 SV
short (*in length*) duǎn 短 SV
shorts [pair of] duǎnkù [tiáo] 短褲 [條]／短裤 [条] N
should yīnggāi 應該／应该 A
sick bìng le 病了 VP/SV
sick (*slightly*) bù shūfu 不舒服 SV
sickness bìng 病 N
side (*left, right, north, etc.*) bian(r) 邊(兒)／边(儿) PW
silver (*color*) yínsè 銀色／银色 N
simplified character jiǎntǐzì 簡體字／简体字 N
sing chàng 唱 V
sing a song chànggē(r) 唱歌(兒)／唱歌(儿) VO
singing star gēxīng 歌星／歌星 N
sister (*older*) jiějie [ge] 姐姐 [個]／姐姐 [个] N
sister (*younger*) mèimei [ge] 妹妹 [個]／妹妹 [个] N
sisters jiěmèi 姐妹 N
sit zuò 坐 V
six liù 六 NU
sixteen shíliù 十六 NU
sixth (one) dìliù (ge) 第六(個)／第六(个) N/NU
sixty liùshí 六十 NU
size (*small, medium, large, etc.*) hào 號／号 M
skilled worker shīfu 師傅／师傅 N
skirt qúnzi [tiáo] 裙子 [條]／裙子 [条] N
sleep shuì; shuìjiào 睡; 睡覺／睡; 睡觉 V/VO
sleep in shuì lǎnjiào 睡懶覺／睡懒觉 VP
sleepy kùn 睏／困 SV
slender shòu 瘦 SV
slippers [pair of] tuōxié [shuāng] 拖鞋 [雙]／拖鞋 [双] N
slow màn 慢 SV

small (*size in clothing, etc.*) xiǎohào 小號／小号 N
small xiǎo 小 SV
snake (*Chinese zodiac*) shé 蛇 N
sneakers [pair of] yùndòngxié [shuāng] 運動鞋 [雙]／运动鞋 [双] N
so zhème; zhèyàng 這麼; 這樣／这么; 这样 A/PR
so (*therefore*) suǒyǐ 所以 A
soap [bar of] féizào [kuài] 肥皂 [塊]／肥皂 [块] N
socks [pair of] wà zi [shuāng] 襪子 [雙]／袜子 [双] N
soil tǔ 土 N
soldier jūnrén 軍人／军人 N
some yìxiē 一些 NU/M
sometimes yǒude shíhou 有的時候／有的时候 TW
son érzi [ge] 兒子／儿子 N
sorry, I'm duìbuqǐ 對不起／对不起 IE
so-so mǎma-hūhū 馬馬虎虎／马马虎虎 IE
south (*side, direction*) nánbian(r) 南邊(兒)／南边 (儿) PW
South America Nán Měizhōu 南美洲 PW
southeast dōngnán 東南／东南 PW
southwest xīnán 西南 PW
souvenir jìniànpǐn [ge] 紀念品 [個]／纪念品 [个] N
Spain Xībānyá 西班牙 PW
Spanish (*language*) Xībānyáhuà; Xībānyáwén; Xībānyáyǔ 西班牙話; 西班牙文; 西班牙語／西班牙话; 西班牙文; 西班牙语 N
Spanish (*person/people*) Xībānyárén 西班牙人 N
speak shuō; shuōhuà 説;説話／说;说话 V/VO
speak Chinese shuō Zhōngguóhuà 説中國話／说中国话 VP
speech/talk huà 話／话 N
spend (*money*) huā; huāqián 花; 花錢／花; 花钱 V/VO
spouse àiren 愛人／爱人 N
start kāishǐ 開始／开始 V
start/hold a class shàngkè 上課／上课 VO
state of mind xīnqíng 心情 N
station (*of bus, train, etc.*) zhàn [ge] 站 [個]／站 [个] N
stationery wénjù [xiē] 文具 [些] N
stay at zhù; dāizai 住; 呆在 V/VP
stay at home dāizài jiālǐ 呆在家裏／呆在家里 VP
stepfather jìfù 繼父／继父 N
stepmother jìmǔ 繼母／继母 N
still (*even more*) gèng 更 A
still (*yet*) hái; hái shi 還; 還是／还; 还是 A
stop (*of bus, train, etc.*) zhàn 站 N
store/shop shāngdiàn 商店／商店 N
story (*in a building*) céng 層／层 M
straight, go yìzhí zǒu; wǎng qián zǒu 一直走; 往前走 VP
street jiē [tiáo] 街 [條]／街 [条] N
student xuésheng 學生／学生 N
study niàn; xué 念;學／念;学 V
study niànshū 念書／念书 VO
stuff dōngxi 東西／东西 N

subtract jiǎn 減／减 V
subway dìtiě 地鐵／地铁 N
subway stop/station dìtiězhàn [ge] 地鐵站 [個]／地铁站 [个] N
such zhème 這麼／这么 A
sun (*the radical*) rì 日 N
Sunday Xīngqīrì; Xīngqītiān; Zhōurì 星期日; 星期天; 週日／星期日; 星期天; 周日 TW
supper wǎnfàn; wǎncān 晚飯; 晚餐／晚饭; 晚餐 N
sure to huì 會／会 A
surname xìng 姓 N
surname, what's your guìxìng 貴姓／贵姓 IE
surnamed, be xìng 姓 V
Suzhou (*a city in eastern China*) Sūzhōu 蘇州／苏州 PW
sweater máoyī [jiàn] 毛衣 [件] N
swipe a credit card shuākǎ 刷卡 VO

T

table zhuōzi [zhāng] 桌子 [張]／桌子 [张] N
Taipei Táiběi 台北 PW
Taiwan Táiwān 台灣／台湾 PW
take (*a bus, train, etc.*) zuò; dā 坐; 搭 V
take a bath xǐzǎo 洗澡 VO
take a cab dǎdī 打的 VO
take a rest xiūxi 休息 V
take a shower xǐzǎo 洗澡 VO
take a walk/stroll qù sànsanbù 去散散步 VP
take it easy/take a rest xiūxi 休息 V
talk shuō; shuōhuà 説; 説話／说; 说话 V/VO
talk/speech huà 話／话 N
talk on the telephone dǎ diànhuà 打電話／打电话 VO
tall gāo 高 SV
taxi chūzūqìchē [liàng] 出租汽車 [輛]／出租汽车 [辆] N
tea [cup of] chá [bēi] 茶 [杯] N
teach jiāo; jiāoshū 教; 教書／教; 教书 V/VO
teacher lǎoshī [wèi] 老師 [位]／老师 [位] N
telephone diànhuà [ge] 電話 [個]／电话 [个] N
telephone, to dǎ diànhuà 打電話／打电话 VO
telephone number diànhuà hàomǎ 電話號碼／电话号码 N
television diànshì [tái] 電視 [台]／电视 [台] N
tell (*inform*) gàosu 告訴／告诉 V
tell (*someone to do something*) jiào 叫 V
ten shí 十 NU
tenth (one) dìshí (ge) 第十(個)／第十(个) N/NU
test kǎoshì 考試／考试 N/V
Thai (*person/people*) Tàiguórén 泰國人／泰国人 N
Thailand Tàiguó 泰國／泰国 PW
than (*in comparisons*) bǐ 比 CV

thank xièxie 謝謝／谢谢 V

thank you xièxie (nǐ/nín) 謝謝(你／您)／谢谢(你／您) IE

that nà/nèi 那 PR/SP

that one nàge/nèige 那個／那个 PR/SP

theirs tāmen de 他們的／他们的 PR

them tāmen 他們／他们 PR

then (*afterward*) ránhòu 然後／然后 C

then (*in that case*) nà; nàme 那；那麼／那；那么 C

there nàr; nàli 那兒；那裏／那儿；那里 PW

there is/are yǒu 有 V

thereafter ránhòu 然後／然后 C

therefore suǒyǐ 所以 C

these zhèxiē 這些／这些 PR

they tāmen 他們／他们 PR

thin shòu 瘦 SV

things dōngxi 東西／东西 N

think (*feel*) juéde 覺得／觉得 V

think (*would like to, feel like*) xiǎng 想 AV

third (one) dìsān (ge) 第三(個)／第三(个) N/NU

thirsty kě 渴 SV

thirteen shísān 十三 NU

thirty sānshí 三十 NU

this zhè; zhèi 這／这 PR/SP

this evening jīntiān wǎnshang 今天晚上 TW

this extent, to zhème 這麼／这么 A

this one zhège; zhèige 這個／这个 PR/SP

this way zhèyàng 這樣／这样 PR

this year jīnnián 今年 TW

three sān 三 NU

Thursday Xīngqīsì 星期四 TW

tiger (*Chinese zodiac*) hǔ 虎 N

time (*period*) shíjiān 時間／时间 N

time (*point in time; duration*) shíhou 時候／时候 N

time on the clock . . . diǎn (zhōng) ……點(鐘)／……点(钟) PH

times/occurrences cì 次 M

tired lèi 累 SV

tissue (*toilet paper*) wèishēngzhǐ 衛生紙／卫生纸 N

to (*a place or time*) dào 到 CV

to what extent duō 多 A

today jīntiān 今天 TW

tofu dòufu 豆腐 N

together (*in the company of*) yíkuàir; yìqǐ 一塊兒；一起／一块儿；一起 A

together (*in total*) yígòng 一共 A

toilet cèsuǒ 廁所／厕所 N

toilet, use the shàng cèsuǒ 上廁所／上厕所 VO

toilet paper wèishēngzhǐ 衛生紙／卫生纸 N

tomorrow míngtiān 明天 TW

tonight jīntiān wǎnshang 今天晚上 TW

too (*much*) tài . . . (le) 太……(了) A

too (*also*) yě 也 A

toothbrush yáshuā [zhī] 牙刷 [枝] N

toothpaste [tube of] yágāo [guǎn] 牙膏 [管] N

top shàngmian; shàngbian 上面；上邊／上面；上边 PW

toward(s) (*a certain direction*) wǎng 往 CV

towel máojīn [tiáo] 毛巾 [條]／毛巾 [条] N

traditional character fántǐzì 繁體字／繁体字 N

traffic light hónglǜdēng 紅綠燈／红绿灯 N

train huǒchē 火車／火车 N

travel lǚxíng 旅行 V

travel by (*train, bus, etc.*) zuò; dā 坐；搭 CV

treat (*somebody to a meal, etc.*) qǐng 請／请 V

trousers [pair of] kùzi; chángkù [tiáo] 褲子;長褲 [條]／裤子;长裤 [条] N

truly zhēn 真 A

T-shirt T-xù shān [jiàn] T-恤衫 [件] N

Tuesday Xīngqī'èr 星期二 TW

turn (*in direction of*) wǎng . . . guǎi 往……拐 VP

TV diànshì [tái] 電視 [台]／电视 [台]

twelfth (one) dìshí'èr (ge) 第十二(個)／第十二(个) N/NU

twelve shí'èr 十二 NU

twelve animals of the zodiac shí'èr (ge) shēngxiào 十二(個)生肖／十二(个)生肖 N

twenty èrshí 二十 NU

twenty-one èrshíyī 二十一 NU

twice a day yì tiān liǎng cì 一天兩次／一天两次 TW

two èr 二 NU

two/a couple of liǎng (ge) 兩(個)／两(个) NU

type (*kind*) yàng; zhǒng 樣；種／样；种 M

U

uncle (*father's older brother*) bóbo 伯伯 N

uncle (*father's younger brother*) shūshu 叔叔 N

uncle (*mother's older or younger brother*) jiùjiu 舅舅 N

uncomfortable (*physical feeling*) bù shūfu 不舒服 SV

under xiàmian 下面 PW

underneath xiàmian 下面 PW

understand dǒng 懂 V

unhappy bù gāoxìng 不高興／不高兴 SV

uninteresting méi yìsi 沒意思／没意思 SV

United States Měiguó 美國／美国 PW

university dàxué 大學／大学 N

unless chúfēi 除非 C

unnecessary búyòng 不用 A

until cái 才 A

unusually fēicháng 非常 A

up shàngbian 上邊／上边 PW

upset shēngqì 生氣／生气 SV

upstairs lóushàng 樓上／楼上 PW

us wǒmen 我們／我们 PR

U.S. dollar/money Měijīn; Měiyuán 美金；美元 N

use yòng 用 V

useful yǒuyòng 有用 SV

usually tōngcháng 通常 A

V

vehicle chē [liàng] 車 [輛]／车[辆] N
very fēicháng 非常 A
very tǐng 挺 A
very (*usually light in sense*) hěn 很 A
video game diànzǐ yóuxì [ge] 電子遊戲 [個]／电子游戏 [个] N

W

wait (for) děng 等 V
waiter fúwùyuán 服務員／服务员 N
waitress fúwùyuán 服務員／服务员 N
walk zǒu; zǒulù 走；走路 V/VO
want to yào; xiǎng 要；想 AV
warm nuǎnhuo 暖和 SV
wash xǐ 洗 V
wash (one's) face xǐliǎn 洗臉／洗脸 VO
watch kàn 看 V
watch (*timepiece*) biǎo [kuài] 錶 [塊]／表 [块] N
watch TV kàn diànshì 看電視／看电视 VO
water [glass/bottle of] shuǐ [bēi/píng] 水 [杯／瓶] N
watermelon xīguā 西瓜 N
way (*direction*) fāngxiàng 方向 N
we wǒmen 我們／我们 PR
wear (*hat, glasses, etc.*) dài 戴 V
wear (*clothes*) chuān; chuān yīfu 穿；穿衣服 V/VO
weary lèi 累 SV
weather tiānqi 天氣／天气 N
Wednesday Xīngqīsān 星期三 TW
week xīngqī 星期 N
weekend zhōumò 周末 N
welcome, you're bié kèqi; búyòng xiè 別客氣；不用謝／别客气；不用谢 IE
well/good/fine hǎo 好 SV
west (*side, direction*) xībian(r) 西邊（兒）／西边（儿） PW
what shénme 什麼／什么 QW
when (*at the time of*) . . . de shíhou ……的時候／……的时候 TW
when (*at what time*) shénme shíhou 什麼時候／什么时候 QW
where nǎr; nǎli 哪兒；哪裏／哪儿；哪里 QW
which nǎ(ge); něi(ge) 哪(個)／哪(个) QW
while (*in the time that*) . . . de shíhou ……的時候／……的时候 TW
white báisè 白色 N
who shéi 誰／谁 QW
why wèishénme 爲什麼／为什么 QW
wife qīzi; lǎopo; tàitai 妻子；老婆；太太 N
will (*intend*) huì; yào 會；要；／会；要 AV
willing to kěn 肯 A
wine jiǔ 酒 N
with (*in the company of*) hé; gēn 和；跟 C

without méiyǒu 没有 V
wood (*the radical*) mù 木 N
word zì 字／字 N
words (*speech*) huà 話／话 N
work gōngzuò 工作 N/V
work as dāng 當／当 V
work part time dǎgōng 打工 VO
worker gōngrén 工人 N
worried zháojí 著急／着急 SV
would like to xiǎng 想 AV
wow wā 哇 I
wristwatch shǒubiǎo [kuài] 手錶 [塊]／手表 [块] N
write xiě; xiězì 寫；寫字／写；写字 V/VO
writer zuòjiā 作家 N
writing brush máobǐ [zhī] 毛筆[枝]／毛笔[枝] N
wrong bú duì 不對／不对 SV

Y

Yangshuo (*city in southern China*) Yángshuò 陽朔／阳朔 PW
Yangtze River Cháng Jiāng 長江／长江 PW
year nián 年 N/M
year (*in school*) niánjí 年级 N
year after next hòunián 後年／后年 TW
year before last qiánnián 前年 TW
yellow huángsè 黄色 N
Yellow River Huáng Hé 黄河 PW
yes shì; shì de; duì 是；是的；對／是；是的；对 IE
yesterday zuótiān 昨天 TW
yet (*however*) kěshì 可是 C
yet (*still*) hái; hái shi 還；還是／还；还是 A
yet (*in a negative sentence*) hái méi 還沒／还没 A
yoga yújiā 瑜伽 N
yoga, do zuò yújiā 做瑜伽 VO
you (*informal*) nǐ 你 PR
you (*formal*) nín 您 PR
you (*plural*) nǐmen 你們／你们 PR
you're welcome bié kèqi; búyòng xiè 別客氣；不用謝／别客气；不用谢 IE
young lady xiǎojie 小姐 N
younger brother dìdi 弟弟 N
younger sister mèimei 妹妹 N
younger than bǐ . . . xiǎo 比……小 PH
youngest child lǎoxiǎo; lǎoyāo 老小；老么 ／老幺 N
your(s) nǐ de 你的 PR
yourself nǐ zìjǐ 你自己 P
yourselves nǐmen zìjǐ 你们自己 P

Z

zero líng 零 NU

Index

This index includes grammatical terms and concepts, cultural information that appears in "FYI" boxes, and language functions, as well as occasional notes in the text.